Domestic Violence

SOURCEBOOK

Sixth Edition

Health Reference Series

Sixth Edition

Domestic Violence SOURCEBOOK

Basic Consumer Health Information about Intimate Partner Abuse, Stalking, Sexual Harassment, and Human Trafficking, Including Facts about Risk Factors, Warning Signs, and Forms of Physical, Sexual, Mental, Emotional, and Financial Abuse in Women, Men, Adolescents, Immigrants, Elders, and Other Specific Populations

Along with Facts about Digital Dating Abuse and Cyberbullying, Victims and Abusers, Strategies for Preventing and Intervening in Abusive Situations, Interventions through Workplaces and Faith Communities, Tips Regarding Legal Protections, a Glossary of Related Terms, and a Directory of Resources for Further Information

OMNIGRAPHICS

615 Griswold, Ste. 901, Detroit, MI 48226

Bibliographic Note

Because this page cannot legibly accommodate all the copyright notices, the Bibliographic Note portion of the Preface constitutes an extension of the copyright notice.

* * *

OMNIGRAPHICS

Angela L. Williams, *Managing Editor*

* * *

Copyright © 2019 Omnigraphics

ISBN 978-0-7808-1654-1

E-ISBN 978-0-7808-1655-8

Domestic Violence Sourcebook

Library of Congress Cataloging in Publication Control Number: 2018046367 (print)

Table of Contents

Part IV: Preventing and Intervening in Domestic Violence

Part V: Emergency Management, Moving Out, and Moving On

Part VI: Additional Help and Information

Preface

About This Book

Domestic violence, also known as intimate partner violence, is a form of violence that occurs within a domestic relationship. Its scope in our society is staggering. The victims include women and men and people of every age, race, ethnicity, religion, sexual orientation, and economic level. According to the National Intimate Partner and Sexual Violence Survey (NISVS), nearly one in four among women, and one in seven among men have experienced severe physical violence by an intimate partner during their lifetime. U.S. Congress has recognized it as an important social problem and has passed a number of Acts related to violence against women to stem this tide.

Domestic Violence Sourcebook, Sixth Edition offers information to victims of domestic violence and to those who care about them. It defines domestic abuse, describes the risk factors for abuse, and offers tips for recognizing abuse. It describes the different types of abuse, including rape, physical violence, emotional and verbal abuse, stalking, and human trafficking. Information about abuse in specific populations—including the lesbian, gay, bisexual, and transgender (LGBT) communities, immigrant communities, teen and elder populations, and within the military—is also provided. In addition, the book discusses tips for building healthy relationships and intervening in abusive situations. It also offers detailed guidelines for managing emergency situations, protecting oneself before, during, and after a separation from an abuser, navigating the legal system, and preventing workplace violence. The book concludes with a glossary of related terms and directories of resources for additional help and information.

How to Use This Book

This book is divided into parts and chapters. Parts focus on broad areas of interest. Chapters are devoted to single topics within a part.

Part I: Facts about Domestic Violence, Stalking, and Sexual Harassment provides basic information about what domestic violence is, which characteristics and situations place victims at risk, and how victims, abusers, and those wanting to help can identify abuse. It also explains what stalking and sexual harassment are and what victims can do to increase their safety and end the abuse.

Part II: Intimate Partner Abuse describes the different types of intimate partner abuse and their physical, emotional, and socioeconomic effects. It also describes the effect domestic violence has on children exposed to it and discusses the co-occurrence of child abuse and intimate partner abuse.

Part III: Abuse in Specific Populations provides information about child abuse, teen dating violence, abuse of men, elder abuse, and abuse in the lesbian, gay, bisexual, and transgender (LGBT) population. It also describes the special issues involved when the abuse occurs within the military, or when the abuse occurs within the immigrant community. The part concludes with a discussion of human trafficking and the types of assistance available to its victims.

Part IV: Preventing and Intervening in Domestic Violence explains how to recognize and build healthy relationships. It also discusses how parents, caretakers, friends, coworkers, healthcare providers, and others can intervene in cases of abuse, and it describes measures employers can take to prevent violence in the workplace.

Part V: Emergency Management, Moving Out, and Moving On discusses why victims stay with their abusers and details what victims will need to know if they decide to leave. It explains the steps involved in calling the police, preserving and collecting evidence, and documenting abuse. It describes the sources of help available to victims of domestic abuse and offers suggestions for safety planning, safeguarding children, and protecting pets. It also provides detailed information about Internet safety and identity protection and describes how to navigate the legal system.

Part VI: Additional Help and Information includes a glossary of terms related to domestic violence and directories of resources offering additional help and support, including domestic violence hotlines, child abuse reporting numbers, and programs offering shelter for pets of domestic violence victims.

Bibliographic Note

This volume contains documents and excerpts from publications issued by the following U.S. government agencies: Administration for Children and Families (ACF); Administration for Community Living (ACL); Administration on Aging (AOA); Agency for Healthcare Research and Quality (AHRQ); Centers for Disease Control and Prevention (CDC); Child Welfare Information Gateway; Community Oriented Policing Services (COPS); Federal Bureau of Investigation (FBI); Federal Trade Commission (FTC); Food and Nutrition Service (FNS); National Center for Posttraumatic Stress Disorder (NCPTSD); National Criminal Justice Reference Service (NCJRS); National Institute on Aging (NIA); National Institute of Justice (NIJ); National Institutes of Health (NIH); National Responsible Fatherhood Clearinghouse (NRFC); Office of Adolescent Health (OAH); Office of Disease Prevention and Health Promotion (ODPHP); Office of Equity, Diversity, and Inclusion (EDI); Office on Women's Health (OWH); U.S. Agency for International Development (USAID); U.S. Citizenship and Immigration Services (USCIS); U.S. Department of Agriculture (USDA); U.S. Department of Health and Human Services (HHS); U.S. Department of Homeland Security (DHS); U.S. Department of Justice (DOJ); U.S. Department of Labor (DOL); U.S. Department of Veterans Affairs (VA); and Youth.gov.

It may also contain original material produced by Omnigraphics and reviewed by medical consultants.

About the Health Reference Series

The *Health Reference Series* is designed to provide basic medical information for patients, families, caregivers, and the general public. Each volume takes a particular topic and provides comprehensive coverage. This is especially important for people who may be dealing with a newly diagnosed disease or a chronic disorder in themselves or in a family member. People looking for preventive guidance, information about disease warning signs, medical statistics, and risk factors for health problems will also find answers to their questions in the *Health*

Reference Series. The *Series*, however, is not intended to serve as a tool for diagnosing illness, in prescribing treatments, or as a substitute for the physician/patient relationship. All people concerned about medical symptoms or the possibility of disease are encouraged to seek professional care from an appropriate healthcare provider.

A Note about Spelling and Style

Health Reference Series editors use *Stedman's Medical Dictionary* as an authority for questions related to the spelling of medical terms and the *Chicago Manual of Style* for questions related to grammatical structures, punctuation, and other editorial concerns. Consistent adherence is not always possible, however, because the individual volumes within the *Series* include many documents from a wide variety of different producers, and the editor's primary goal is to present material from each source as accurately as is possible. This sometimes means that information in different chapters or sections may follow other guidelines and alternate spelling authorities. For example, occasionally a copyright holder may require that eponymous terms be shown in possessive forms (Crohn's disease vs. Crohn disease) or that British spelling norms be retained (leukaemia vs. leukemia).

Medical Review

Omnigraphics contracts with a team of qualified, senior medical professionals who serve as medical consultants for the *Health Reference Series*. As necessary, medical consultants review reprinted and originally written material for currency and accuracy. Citations including the phrase "Reviewed (month, year)" indicate material reviewed by this team. Medical consultation services are provided to the *Health Reference Series* editors by:

Dr. Vijayalakshmi, MBBS, DGO, MD
Dr. Senthil Selvan, MBBS, DCH, MD
Dr. K. Sivanandham, MBBS, DCH, MS (Research), PhD

Our Advisory Board

We would like to thank the following board members for providing initial guidance on the development of this series:

- Dr. Lynda Baker, Associate Professor of Library and Information Science, Wayne State University, Detroit, MI

- Nancy Bulgarelli, William Beaumont Hospital Library, Royal Oak, MI

- Karen Imarisio, Bloomfield Township Public Library, Bloomfield Township, MI

- Karen Morgan, Mardigian Library, University of Michigan-Dearborn, Dearborn, MI

- Rosemary Orlando, St. Clair Shores Public Library, St. Clair Shores, MI

Health Reference Series *Update Policy*

The inaugural book in the *Health Reference Series* was the first edition of *Cancer Sourcebook* published in 1989. Since then, the *Series* has been enthusiastically received by librarians and in the medical community. In order to maintain the standard of providing high-quality health information for the layperson the editorial staff at Omnigraphics felt it was necessary to implement a policy of updating volumes when warranted.

Medical researchers have been making tremendous strides, and it is the purpose of the *Health Reference Series* to stay current with the most recent advances. Each decision to update a volume is made on an individual basis. Some of the considerations include how much new information is available and the feedback we receive from people who use the books. If there is a topic you would like to see added to the update list, or an area of medical concern you feel has not been adequately addressed, please write to:

Managing Editor
Health Reference Series
Omnigraphics
615 Griswold, Ste. 901
Detroit, MI 48226

Part One

Facts about Domestic Violence, Stalking, and Sexual Harassment

Chapter 1

What Is Domestic Violence?

Chapter Contents

Section 1.1

Introduction to Domestic Violence

This section contains text excerpted from the following sources: Text in this section begins with excerpts from "Domestic Violence," MedlinePlus, National Institutes of Health (NIH), December 21, 2016; Text beginning with the heading "Terms Associated with Domestic Violence" is excerpted from "Domestic and Intimate Partner Violence," Centers for Disease Control and Prevention (CDC), September 15, 2017.

Domestic violence, also known as intimate partner violence (IPV), is a type of abuse. It usually involves a spouse or partner, but it can also be a child, elderly relative, or another family member.

Domestic violence may include:

- Physical violence that can lead to injuries such as bruises or broken bones

- Sexual violence

- Threats of physical or sexual violence

- Emotional abuse that may lead to depression, anxiety, or social isolation

- Economic abuse, which involves controlling access to money

- Stalking, which causes fear for your own safety

Terms Associated with Domestic Violence

Common terms used to describe domestic violence are intimate partner violence, domestic abuse, spousal abuse, dating violence, battering, marital rape, and date rape.

What Makes Intimate Partner Violence a Social Problem

Intimate partner violence (IPV) is a substantial public health problem that affects millions of Americans. IPV has serious consequences and costs for individuals, families, communities, and society.

The term "intimate partner violence" includes threatened physical or sexual violence when the threat is used to control a person's actions.

- **Sexual violence** is forcing a partner to take part in a sex act when the partner does not consent, including rape, being made to penetrate someone else, sexual coercion, unwanted sexual contact, and noncontact unwanted sexual experiences

- **Physical violence** is when a person hurts or tries to hurt a partner by hitting, kicking, or using another type of physical force.

- **Stalking** victimization involves a pattern of harassing or threatening tactics used by a perpetrator that is both unwanted and causes fear or safety concerns in the victim.

- **Psychological/emotional aggression** includes threatening a partner or his or her possessions or loved ones, harming a partner's sense of self-worth, and monitoring and controlling a partner. Examples are name calling, insulting or humiliating an intimate partner, intimidation, or not letting a partner see friends and family.

- **Control of reproductive or sexual health** includes the refusal by an intimate partner to use a condom or attempting to impregnate or conceive a child with a partner who does not want to conceive.

IPV exists along a continuum from a single episode of violence to ongoing battering. Incidents of IPV can vary in frequency and severity. Often, IPV starts with emotional abuse and can progress to physical or sexual assault. Several types of IPV may occur together.

IPV can affect health in many ways. The longer the violence goes on, the more serious the effects. Victims can suffer physical injuries that can be minor (cuts, scratches, bruises, and welts) and very serious (broken bones, internal bleeding, head trauma, death). IPV can also cause emotional difficulties, trauma symptoms, and suicide. Victims may try to cope with their trauma in unhealthy ways, including smoking, drinking, and taking drugs.

Who's at Risk of Intimate Partner Violence?

Both men and women are victims of IPV though women are more frequently the victims. Based on data from the National Intimate Partner and Sexual Violence Survey (NISVS):

- On average, 24 people per minute are victims of rape, physical violence, or stalking by an intimate partner in the United

States—more than 12 million women and men over the course of a year.

- About one in four women (24.3%) and one in seven men (13.8%) have experienced severe physical violence by an intimate partner (e.g., hit with a fist or something hard, beaten, slammed against something) at some point in their lifetime.

- Nearly one in ten women (9.4%) has been raped by an intimate partner in her lifetime, and an estimated 16.9 percent of women and 8 percent of men have experienced sexual violence other than rape by an intimate partner at some point in their lifetime.

- Among adult victims of rape, physical violence, and/or stalking by an intimate partner, 22.4 percent of women and 15 percent of men first experienced some form of partner violence between 11–17 years of age.

Teen dating violence is a form of IPV. Unhealthy relationships during adolescence are a risk factor for violence into future relationships. Approximately nine percent of high school students report being hit, slapped, or physically hurt on purpose by a boyfriend or girlfriend in the 12 months before surveyed.

Can Intimate Partner Violence Be Prevented?

Like all forms of violence, IPV can be prevented, though the solution is just as complex as the problem. Stopping IPV includes services for victims and perpetrators of IPV and their children in order to interrupt the violence and to support healing and safety. Because the goal is to prevent IPV before it starts, primary prevention activities are essential. Primary prevention efforts promote healthy, respectful, nonviolent relationship skills, and behaviors. These efforts could include programs that teach young people healthy problem-solving and communication skills and change social norms about the acceptability of violence in order to prevent teen dating violence and future IPV during adulthood. Communities can help by coordinating violence prevention initiatives that strengthen safety networks and the implementation of prevention strategies for individuals and families. Research is inconclusive regarding the effectiveness of police arrest policies as a deterrent to IPV. Nonetheless, increased public awareness can inform the development of policies and interventions directed toward preventing IPV.

Section 1.2

Myths and Truths about Domestic Violence

This section includes text excerpted from "Myths and Facts about Domestic Violence," Food and Nutrition Service (FNS), U.S. Department of Agriculture (USDA), November 17, 2005. Reviewed October 2018.

Myth: Domestic violence is a private family matter.

Fact: Domestic violence is everyone's business. Keeping domestic violence secret helps no one, has been shown to harm children, incurs substantial costs to society, and serves to perpetuate abuse through learned patterns of behavior.

Myth: Most of the time, domestic violence is not really that serious.

Fact: Domestic violence is an illegal act in the United States and is considered a crime with serious repercussions. Although there are aspects of domestic violence (e.g., emotional, psychological, spiritual abuse) that may not be considered criminal in a legal sense, serious and long-lasting physical, emotional, and spiritual harm can and often does, occur. Each and every act of domestic violence needs to be taken seriously.

Myth: Victims provoke their partners' violence.

Fact: Whatever problems exist in a relationship, the use of violence is never justifiable or acceptable. There is NO EXCUSE for domestic violence.

Myth: Domestic violence is an impulse control or anger management problem.

Fact: Abusers act deliberately and with forethought. Abusers choose whom to abuse. For example, an abuser will selectively batter his wife but not his boss.

Myth: No one would beat his pregnant wife or girlfriend.

Fact: Domestic violence may begin or escalate during pregnancy. Homicide is the single most frequent cause of maternal death during pregnancy and in the first year after giving birth.

Myth: Women are just as violent as men in relationships.

Fact: Some women report striking their male partners during the course of the conflict, often in self-defense. Women, however, rarely commit deliberate acts that result in fear, injury, rape, or death.

Myth: Domestic violence is bad, but it happens elsewhere. It doesn't happen in my community, my neighborhood, my culture, my religion, or my congregation.

Fact: Domestic violence happens to people of every educational and socioeconomic level. Domestic violence happens in all races, religions, and age groups. Domestic violence occurs in both heterosexual and same-sex relationships.

Myth: It is easy for a victim to leave her abuser, so if she doesn't leave, it means she likes the abuse or is exaggerating how bad it is.

Fact: Fear, lack of safe options, and an inability to survive economically prevent many women from leaving abusive relationships. Threats of harm, including death to the victim and/or children, keep many battered women trapped in abusive situations. The most dangerous time for a battered woman is when she attempts to leave the relationship, or when the abuser discovers that she has made plans to leave.

Myth: Children are generally neither aware of, nor affected by, their mother's abuse.

Fact: Nearly 90 percent of children who live in homes in which there is domestic violence will see or hear the abuse. Children as young as toddlers can suffer from the effects of exposure to abuse. Children exposed to violence and other forms of trauma may have permanent alterations in brain structure, chemistry, and function.

Myth: Domestic violence can occur in older women, but it is quite rare.

Fact: Approximately half of all elder abuse in women is thought to be domestic violence "grown old." Older battered women are less likely to seek and receive help.

Myth: Anger-management programs are briefer, more cost effective than, and just as successful as certified batterer intervention programs.

Fact: Although briefer and less expensive than certified batterer intervention programs, anger-management programs are not effective to address the deep-rooted issues of batterers.

Myth: Since domestic violence is a problem in the relationship, marriage, or couple-focused pastoral counseling is key to restoring tranquility in the family or relationship.

Fact: This type of counseling often increases the risk of violence to the victim. Faith and religious community representatives can promote safety and restore personal integrity and self-esteem to the victim, and can suggest batterer intervention services for the abuser, but should not engage in couples counseling unless the long-term safety of the survivor, and of staff, can be assured.

Myth: Services for victims are staffed by people angry at the traditional society who want to break up the family unit.

Fact: Programs that help battered women and their children, and counselors who provide assistance, are concerned first and foremost with the safety of the survivor and her dependent children. The goal of counseling and other survivor services is not to break up the family unit, but to preserve the safety of all its members. Achieving this goal, unfortunately, may mean that some relationships may need to end.

Myth: Since our religion doesn't condone divorce, an abusive man should speak with the religious leader to mend his ways.

Fact: Although some religions do frown on divorce, no religion advocates abuse. Some abusers misinterpret or intentionally misuse religious writing to justice violence against their partners and children or to prevent marriage—even one wracked by violence and abuse—from dissolving. Helpful conversations with a batterer, even if conducted carefully by a religious leader, may bring short-term relief, but cannot take the place of qualified batterer intervention services, and may even pose a safety risk for the victim and her children.

Section 1.3

Signs of Domestic Violence or Abuse

This section includes text excerpted from "Signs of Domestic Violence or Abuse," Office on Women's Health (OWH), U.S. Department of Health and Human Services (HHS), September 17, 2018.

How Do You Know Whether You Are Being Abused?

You may be experiencing domestic violence if your partner:

- Controls what you're doing
- Checks your phone, email, or social networks without your permission
- Forces you to have sex when you don't want to
- Controls your birth control or insists that you get pregnant
- Decides what you wear or eat or how you spend money
- Prevents or discourages you from going to work or school or seeing your family or friends
- Humiliates you on purpose in front of others
- Unfairly accuses you of being unfaithful
- Destroys your things
- Threatens to hurt you, your children, other loved ones, or your pets
- Hurts you physically (e.g., hitting, beating, punching, pushing, kicking), including with a weapon
- Blames you for his or her violent outbursts
- Threatens to hurt herself or himself because of being upset with you
- Threatens to report you to the authorities for imagined crimes
- Says things like, "If I can't have you, then no one can"

What Are Signs of Domestic Violence or Abuse in Same-Sex Relationships?

If you are in a same-sex relationship, many signs of domestic violence are the same as other people in an abusive relationship. Your partner may hit you, try to control you, or force you to have sex. But you may also experience additional signs of abuse, including:

- Threatening to "out you" to your family, friends, employer, or community
- Telling you that you have to be legally married to be considered a victim of domestic violence and to get help
- Saying women aren't or can't be violent
- Telling you the authorities won't help a lesbian, bisexual, transgender, or another nonconforming person
- Forcing you to "prove" your sexuality by performing sex acts that you do not consent to

Regardless of your gender identity or sexual orientation, no one has the right to physically hurt you or threaten your safety.

What Can You Do If You Are Being Abused?

Your safety is the most important concern. If you are in immediate danger, call 911.

If you are not in immediate danger, consider these options:

- **Get medical care.** If you have been injured or sexually assaulted, go to a local hospital emergency room or urgent care center. You need medical care and may need medicines after being injured or raped.
- **Call a helpline for free, anonymous help.** Call the National Domestic Violence Hotline (NDVH) at 800-799-SAFE (800-799-7233) or 800-787-3224 (TDD). The hotline offers help 24 hours a day, seven days a week, in many languages. Hotline staff can give you numbers for other resources, such as local domestic violence shelters. If you are deaf or hard of hearing, there are resources available for you. The National Coalition of Anti-Violence Programs (NCAVP) has a hotline to help lesbian, gay, bisexual, transgender, questioning, queer (LGBTQ) victims of violence. Call 212-714-1141 for 24-hour support in English or Spanish.
- **Make a safety plan to leave.** Domestic violence usually does not get better. Think about a safe place for you to go and other things you will need. Staff at the NDVH can help you plan.

- **Save the evidence.** Keep evidence of abuse, such as pictures of your injuries or threatening emails or texts, in a safe place the abuser cannot get to.

- **Find out where to get help in your community.** Look up local resources for a list of local places to get help.

- **Talk to someone.** Reach out to someone you trust. This might be a family member, a friend, a coworker, or a spiritual leader. Look for ways to get emotional help, like a support group or mental-health professional.

- **Look into a restraining order.** Consider getting a protection order.

If you are the victim of domestic violence, know that you are not alone. There are people who want to help you and who are trained to respond.

Chapter 2

Prevalence of Domestic Abuse

How Common Is Domestic Violence against Women?

Domestic or intimate partner violence (IPV) is a very common type of violence against women:

- Domestic or IPV happens in all types of relationships, including dating couples, married couples, same-sex couples, former or ex-couples, and couples who live together but are not married.

- IPV happens more often among younger couples.

- Almost half of American Indian and Alaskan Native (AI/AN) women, more than four in ten African-American women, and more than one in three white and Hispanic women have experienced sexual or physical violence or stalking by their intimate partner.

This chapter contains text excerpted from the following sources: Text under the heading "How Common Is Domestic Violence against Women?" is excerpted from "Signs of Domestic Violence or Abuse," Office on Women's Health (OWH), U.S. Department of Health and Human Services (HHS), September 17, 2018; Text under the heading "Domestic Violence—Crime Trends" is excerpted from "Intimate Partner Violence," National Criminal Justice Reference Service (NCJRS), April 10, 2018.

• Nearly 23 million women in the United States have been raped or experienced attempted rape in their lifetimes.

• More than 33 million women—including one in three African-American and white women and one in four Hispanic women—have experienced unwanted sexual contact, other than rape, by an intimate partner.

• Women who identify as lesbian experience as much or more physical and sexual violence as heterosexual women by an intimate partner. Women who identify as bisexual experience IPV more often than heterosexual women.

Domestic Violence—Crime Trends

In the 20 years from 1995–2015, the estimated rates of violent intimate partner victimization among women and men decreased from 15.5 and 2.8, respectively, to 5.4 per 1,000 women and 0.5 per 1,000 men. Because the personal nature of these victimizations often influences a victim's decision to report the crime, victimizations by intimate partners are highly underreported. In 2015, 67 percent of violent victimizations were committed by a relative, 54 percent by an intimate partner, 43 percent by an acquaintance (either well-known or casual), and 42 percent by strangers.

According to the National Intimate Partner and Sexual Violence Survey (NISVS), an estimated 47 percent of men and women will be victims of psychological aggression by an intimate partner in their lifetime. In addition, 32 percent of women will be victims of physical violence, and 16 percent of contact sexual violence, by an intimate partner. About seven percent of men will be victims of contact sexual violence by an intimate partner.

All races and ethnicities experience IPV. However, women of multiple ethnicities and (AI/AN) women experience the highest percentage of intimate partner victimization, respectively, compared to other races/ethnicities and sexes.

People who self-identify as lesbian, gay, or bisexual are at an increased risk of rape, physical violence, and stalking by an intimate partner, and victimization of bisexual men and women is most prevalent. Compared to an estimated 35 percent of heterosexual women, a greater percentage (61%) of bisexual women will be a victim of intimate partner violence in their lifetime. Compared to an estimated 29 percent of heterosexual men, 37 percent of bisexual men will be victims of intimate partner violence in their lifetime.

In more than 80 percent of intimate partner violent victimizations in 2015, the victim did not receive assistance from victim service agencies.

Households earning between $15,000 and $24,999 reported slightly more intimate partner victimizations in 2015 than other households. However, IPV is not isolated to any particular income bracket.

1 in 4 women and **1 in 9 men** have experienced contact sexual violence*, physical violence, or stalking by an intimate partner with a negative impact (e.g., injury, fear, concern for safety, or needing services).

Among high school students who dated in the past year,

20% of females and **10% of males** reported either physical violence, sexual violence, or both from a dating partner.

Figure 2.1. *Statistics on Intimate Partner Violence* (Source: "Intimate Partner Violence," Centers for Disease Control and Prevention (CDC).)

* Contact sexual violence includes rape, being made to penetrate, sexual coercion, and/or unwanted sexual contact.

Chapter 3

Risk Factors for Domestic Violence

Chapter Contents

Section 3.1

Why Does Intimate Partner Violence Occur?

This section includes text excerpted from "Practical Implications of
Current Intimate Partner Violence Research for Victim Advocates
and Service Providers," National Criminal Justice Reference Service
(NCJRS), January 9, 2013. Reviewed October 2018.

Early in the domestic violence (DV) movement, four competing theories about the causality of intimate partner violence (IPV) gained the
most traction among scholars and activists: psychological impairment,
anger-management problems, conflict-resolution deficits, and male
dominance over women based in patriarchy and misogyny.

Over the ensuing decades, more than 20 theories emerged attempting to explain the reasons for IPV, usually referred to as DV. Most
envisioned offenders, especially repeat offenders, as antisocial, mal-
adaptive, or otherwise psychopathic, a view continued to be implied
in much media coverage of DV murders and the like.

However, subsequent research has been unable to find empirical
evidence sufficient to support these explanations. For example, a
15-month follow-up analysis of 580 convicted offenders in four cities
found that only "11 percent of repeat assaulters exhibited primary
psychopathic disorders," and more than half did not show indications
of secondary psychopathic disorders, a much broader classification.
The researchers note that almost two-thirds (60%) of the batterers
had "subclinical or low levels of personality dysfunction" and pos-
sessed a multitude of personality types, with re-assaulters no more
likely to have a psychopathic disorder than others. Other Researchers
have determined that only about 10 percent of IPV is due to mental
disorders.

If psychological theories cannot explain 90 percent of intimate partner abuse, then there must be alternative causal explanations. The
National Violence Against Women Survey (NVAWS) attempted to
develop predictive models of abusive behavior using logistic regression.
The strongest models found significant positive associations between
abuse and unmarried, cohabitating couples and abuse of the victim
as a child. A negative associated with IPV was found if the victim was
white. This model also found significant relationships between abuse
and abuser jealousy, abuser isolation of the victim, and verbal abuse
of the victim by the partner. The researchers suggest that these relationships offer empirical support to what another researcher refers to

a "patriarchal terrorism." In their view, IPV is often "violence perpetrated against women by male partners as part of a systemic pattern of dominance and control."

Some posit that males operate in abuse-supporting peer groups that reinforce social norms allowing males to abuse females. These social supports do not operate in a social vacuum, but rather are bolstered by dominant social patriarchal patterns and coalesce with traditional perceptions of masculinity, privacy, sexual objectification of women, and heavy alcohol use.

As social science data becomes more accurate, researchers are better able to empirically verify (or reject) various theoretical causal assumptions. Evolving research, for example, questions the initial correlation between race and domestic violence by suggesting that social disorganization variables, not race, are associated with increased intimate partner violence. While previous indicators pointed to a higher incidence of intimate partner abusive behavior among African-Americans, researchers did not consider community contextual factors, i.e., limited informal and formal social controls that influence the collective efficacy of an area. Researchers suggest that "area racial composition and violent crime rates can be explained by other structural correlates of race," including high unemployment, poverty, family fragmentation, economic hardship, and isolation from conventional society; all features that potentially reduce legitimate opportunity structures and weaken informal ties and social control, which are said to foster increased crime and violence. Using data from the National Survey of Families and Households (NSFH) and the 1990 U.S. Census, these researchers suggest that neighborhood disadvantage is responsible for much of the correlation between race and domestic violence, explaining that "the rate of intimate violence is highest in the most disadvantaged communities and lowest in the least disadvantaged communities."

Research utilizing results of California's massive health survey links neighborhood bar concentration with increased IPV emergency room visits. Researchers suggest that bars, likely frequented by men with and without their partners, may encourage heavy drinking linked to increased aggression. Like other such studies, this research goes beyond individual risk factors for IPV and looks at neighborhood and environmental risk factors. The researchers note that using emergency room visits as their measure of IPV means they were finding much more serious IPV than that found in studies measuring IPV reported in police incident reports or arrests.

Research, thus, sheds important empirical light upon the race-IPV connection by suggesting that varying ecological factors are more powerful predictors.

It is important to note that "correlation" is not the same thing as "causation."

Implications: While further testing of theories of causality will enable enhanced victim services and advocacy, as well as, improved strategies for perpetrator intervention and accountability, Victim Advocates and Service Providers can now draw on ample evidence-based research to support IPV causality based on perpetrator behavior to control, isolate, and dominate intimate partners, as well as, to retaliate, humiliate, and punish victims for resistance to IPV.

Section 3.2

Individual, Relational, Community, and Societal Risk Factors

This section includes text excerpted from "Intimate Partner Violence: Risk and Protective Factors," Centers for Disease Control and Prevention (CDC), August 22, 2017.

Risk Factors for Intimate Partner Violence
Individual Risk Factors

- Low self-esteem

- Low income

- Low academic achievement

- Young age

- Aggressive or delinquent behavior as a youth

- Heavy alcohol and drug use

- Depression

- Anger and hostility

- Antisocial personality traits
- Borderline personality traits
- Prior history of being physically abusive
- Having few friends and being isolated from other people
- Unemployment
- Emotional dependence and insecurity
- Belief in strict gender roles (e.g., male dominance and aggression in relationships)
- The desire for power and control in relationships
- Perpetrating psychological aggression
- Being a victim of physical or psychological abuse (consistently one of the strongest predictors of perpetration)
- History of experiencing poor parenting as a child
- History of experiencing physical discipline as a child

Relationship Factors

- Marital conflict-fights, tension, and other struggles
- Marital instability—divorces or separations
- Dominance and control of the relationship by one partner over the other
- Economic stress
- Unhealthy family relationships and interactions

Community Factors

- Poverty and associated factors (e.g., overcrowding)
- Low social capital—lack of institutions, relationships, and norms that shape a community's social interactions
- Weak community sanctions against IPV (e.g., the unwillingness of neighbors to intervene in situations where they witness violence)

Section 3.3

Theories of Violence

This section contains text excerpted from the following sources: Text in this section begins with excerpts from "Interventions for Domestic Violence Offenders: Duluth Model," National Institute of Justice (NIJ), September 13, 2013. Reviewed October 2018; Text under the heading "Theory of Power and Control/Coercion and Control" is excerpted from "Way Off Base: An Argument Against Intimate Partner Violence Cases in Veterans Treatment Courts," Child Welfare Information Gateway (CWIG), U.S. Department of Veterans Affairs (VA), 2012. Reviewed October 2018.

The World Health Organization (WHO) defines IPV as, ".... any behavior within an intimate relationship that causes physical, psychological, or sexual harm to those in that relationship. It includes acts of physical aggression (slapping, hitting, kicking or beating), psychological abuse (intimidation, constant belittling or humiliation), forced sexual intercourse, or any other controlling behavior (isolating a person from family and friends, monitoring their movements and restricting access to information or assistance)." Intimate partner violence, as defined by the Centers for Disease Control and Prevention (CDC), describes physical, sexual, or psychological harm by a current or former partner or spouse. This type of violence can occur among heterosexual or same-sex couples and does not require sexual intimacy. Often the term "domestic violence" is used interchangeably with intimate partner violence.

The Duluth Model

The following figure depicts multiple forms of abuse and violence that allow a perpetrator to establish and maintain power and control by creating an intimidating, threatening environment. The Power and Control Wheel in Dating Relationships, developed by the Kansas Coalition Against Sexual and Domestic Violence and adapted from the Power and Control Wheel developed by the Domestic Abuse Intervention Programs, Duluth, MN, illustrates how many different actions fit into a larger system of abuse and violence.

Practice Goals of The Duluth Model

There are a number of interventions that are common in the treatment of domestic violence offenders. One prominent clinical intervention

Figure 3.1. *The Duluth Model* (Source: "Violence and Safety Programs in Women's Prisons and Jails: Addressing Prevention, Intervention and Treatment," U.S. Department of Justice (DOJ).)

employs a feminist psychoeducational approach and is widely known as the Duluth Model. Originating in 1981 from the Duluth Domestic Abuse Intervention Project in Duluth, Minnesota, this intervention proposes that the principal cause of domestic violence is a social and cultural patriarchal ideology that historically has allowed men to control women through power and violence. Violence perpetrated on women and children originates from their relative positions of weakness and vulnerability socially, politically, economically, and culturally. As such, the model does not assume that domestic violence is caused by mental or behavioral health problems, substance use, anger, stress, or dysfunctional relationships. The program concentrates on providing group-facilitated exercises that challenge a male's perception of entitlement to control and dominate his partner. The Duluth Model is considered less of a therapy and more of a psychoeducational program for domestic violence perpetrators. This treatment technique focuses on providing an improved and broadened understanding of the causes and effects of the underlying problems experienced by the offender.

Practice Components

The Duluth Model makes use of the "Power and Control Wheel" as a tool to understand patterns of abusive behavior, including acts and threats of physical and sexual violence. These behaviors are used by the abuser to control domestic violence victims.

The wheel includes eight items:

1. Intimidation
2. Emotional abuse
3. Isolation
4. Economic abuse
5. Male privilege
6. Coercion and threats
7. Using children
8. Minimizing, denying, and blaming

The wheel is designed so abusers recognize the patterns of domestic violence rather than viewing domestic violence as isolated or cyclical acts. The aim of the intervention is to convince men to use nonviolent strategies outlined in the "Equality Wheel."

The eight items making up this wheel are:

1. Negotiation and fairness
2. Economic partnership
3. Shared responsibility
4. Responsible parenting
5. Honesty and accountability
6. Trust and support
7. Respect
8. Nonthreatening behavior

These are seen as the foundations for a strong and egalitarian relationship.

Theory of Power and Control/Coercion and Control

Violent intimate relationships are characterized by the dynamic of power and control where an abuser employs a set of tactics designed to enforce his will upon the victim. While there are often misconceptions that victims of domestic violence experience constant physical violence at the hands of their abusers, the reality is that physical assaults are only one facet of the experience of being a battered individual. Most often, the physical violence punctuates other methods of abuse such as restricted access to money and property, constant insults and humiliation, and threats of harm to children or other family members. Additionally, victims of domestic violence experience extremely high rates of sexual assault, which is estimated at a range of thirty-three to sixty percent of battered women.

Intimate partner violence is often characterized by abusers' assertion of control over the daily activities of their victims. Victims are often isolated from family and other support systems and abusers frequently prevent access to basic necessities such as food, money, healthcare, transportation, telephones, and personal property. Sometimes an abuser's rules are explicit and even result in written documents detailing specific conditions ranging from the direction of the vacuum marks on the carpets to specific sexual acts the victim must perform. In other instances, the batterer controls his partner with no formal expression of rules and victims become adept at understanding nonverbal cues from the abuser related to acceptable and unacceptable behavior. In either case, physical violence is often the consequence for violating the rules. In this way, physical violence is always a looming threat and the victim's fear of future attacks allow the abuser to control her behavior. Most importantly, "it's vital to understand that battering is not a series of isolated blow-ups. It is a process of deliberate intimidation intended to coerce the victim to do the will of the victimizer." Evan Stark describes this concept as "coercive control":

> Coercion entails the use of force or threats to compel or dispel a particular response. In addition to causing immediate pain, injury, fear, or death, coercion can have long-term physical, behavioral, or psychological consequences. . . . Control is comprised of structural forms of deprivation, exploitation, and command that compel obedience indirectly by monopolizing vital resources, dictating preferred choices, microregulating a partner's behavior, limiting her options, and depriving her of supports needed to exercise independent judgment. . . . Control may be implemented through specific acts of prohibition or coercion, as when a victim is kept home from work, denied access to a car or phone, or forced to turn over her paycheck. . . . The result when coercion and control are combined is the condition . . . victims experience as entrapment.

Abusers will also cut their victims off from friends and family, prevent them from working outside the home, and become jealous of people and activities external to the relationship.

Cycle of Violence

In 1979, Lenore Walker developed the Cycle of Violence Theory through her work and research with victims of intimate partner violence to explain a pattern of violence that "intensifies in degree and frequency over time and holds the people involved in an established pattern of behavior." The cycle generally consists of three repeating phases: tension-building, acute battering, and honeymoon or loving contrition. Throughout the tension-building phase, the abuser may perpetrate less severe physical assaults including slapping, pushing, and so on, as well as the destruction of property and verbal threats and insults. Eventually an acute battering incident occurs and the victim is seriously and brutally assaulted, although she may not seek medical or police intervention for several days or weeks, if at all. Immediately following a serious assault, an abuser's behavior and attitude often change abruptly, as noted by Walker:

> When the acute battering incident ends, the final phase in the Cycle of Violence begins. In this phase, usually all tension and violence are gone . . . . This is a tranquil period, during which the batterer may exhibit warm, nurturing, loving behavior . . . . He knows he's been "bad," and tries to atone; he promises never to do it again; he begs for forgiveness. . . . During the third phase, the battered woman may join with the batterer in sustaining this illusion of bliss. She convinces herself, too, that it will never happen again; her lover can change, she tells herself. This "good" man, who is gentle and sensitive and nurturing towards her now, this is the "real" man, the man she married, the man she loves. Many battered women believe that they are the sole support of the batterer's emotional stability and sanity, the one link their men have to the normal world. Sensing the batterer's isolation and despair, they feel responsible for his well-being. . . . It is in this phase of loving contrition that the battered woman is most thoroughly victimized psychologically.

The honeymoon or loving contrition phase, as described by Walker, is arguably the most significant aspect of a battered woman's experience. "Here she receives discernable reinforcement of her identity as the good wife and her importance to her partner. . . . Here she remembers that abuse is not the only significant aspect of her relationship. . . . She cares about how he feels, his health, his survival if she leaves, his reputation, and so forth." This ever-changing pattern of violence and nonviolence has tangible psychological, cognitive, and behavioral consequences, which has been described as a form of "intermittent reinforcement.

Behavioral psychologists have found that behavior that has been intermittently reinforced is the most difficult behavior to stop. Finally, the honeymoon phase also reinforces the victim's belief and hope that the abuser will change, bolstered by his promises to stop the violence or to seek treatment, which is often cited as the most powerful reason abuse victims remain in the violent relationship.

Section 3.4

Economic Stress and Intimate Partner Violence

"Economic Stress and Domestic Violence,"
© 2016 Omnigraphics. Reviewed October 2018.

Economic stress and domestic violence are intricately linked. Studies have found that the rate of domestic violence is three times higher among couples who report severe financial strain than among couples who report little or no financial strain. Stress related to economic factors can contribute to domestic violence in many ways. People who experience severe financial hardships are likely to feel anger, frustration, and a sense of inadequacy. Sometimes these feelings translate into aggression, control, and violence toward family members living in the household.

Although nothing excuses abusive behavior, in some cases it is related to a psychological need to exert dominance or control. Since cultural norms of masculinity define men as patriarchs, providers, and heads of the family unit, financial hardships and unemployment can undermine their sense of self-worth. Some men may respond to their perceived failure to measure up to cultural expectations by becoming violent and exerting power over their intimate partners or children. Research has shown that the risk of perpetrating domestic violence increased from 4.7 percent among couples where the male partner was consistently employed to 12.3 percent among couples where the male partner experienced multiple periods of unemployment.

The relationship between economic stress and domestic violence works both ways, however, as abuse can also create financial problems for families. Although abuse certainly occurs in middle-class and affluent families, studies have shown that the likelihood of domestic violence decreases as financial security increases. One study found that domestic violence rates were five times higher in American households with the lowest annual incomes than in those with the highest annual incomes. People who experience domestic violence are more likely to miss work and perform poorly on the job, which increases their risk of unemployment and economic insecurity. These financial hardships, in turn, can force domestic violence victims to remain in an abusive relationship.

Domestic Violence and Employment

One of the ways domestic violence impacts financial security is by affecting women's employment. Although women who are victims of domestic violence report the same desire to work as other women, their abusers may try to prevent them from obtaining paid employment. Some abusive partners—especially men who are unemployed—may view a female partner's decision to seek employment as a threat to their power or status. One study found that a woman's likelihood of being abused increased as her income rose relative to that of her partner.

Economic abuse is a form of domestic violence in which an abuser deliberately sabotages their intimate partner's efforts to find or keep a job. The tactics used in economic abuse may include destroying work clothes, damaging computers or other job-related equipment, interfering with child care arrangements, inflicting visible injuries, or stalking in the workplace. As a result of such efforts, women who experience domestic violence tend to have higher absenteeism and lower productivity rates than other female workers. These issues may result in job loss, which reduces the financial resources available for women to leave abusive relationships.

Poverty and Domestic Violence

The connection between economic stress and domestic violence can create a downward spiral that traps people in both abusive

28

relationships and poverty. This cycle often perpetuates itself, as children who are raised in low-income households with domestic violence are much more likely to abuse others. Many families who live in impoverished circumstances only associate with others in their community who face similar economic situations, which reinforces the pattern by making domestic violence seem commonplace and socially accepted.

Domestic violence victims who live in poverty, therefore, often cannot count on family and friends to help them. Although many women who leave abusive relationships end up staying with family or friends, this resource may not be available to low-income women because their friends and family members may also face economic insecurity. As a result, an estimated one-third of domestic violence survivors end up homeless as a result of ending an abusive relationship.

Obtaining financial assistance from state and federal agencies can be difficult or even dangerous for survivors of domestic abuse. Many aid programs require applicants with children to help child support agencies locate and collect payments from the other parent. These requirements can put domestic violence survivors at risk by revealing their whereabouts to abusers. Although waivers are available in some cases, only a small fraction of eligible welfare applicants disclose the fact that they have experienced domestic violence. Some battered women do not report this information because they worry that child protective services agencies may remove the children from their custody.

Some steps that may help end the cycle of poverty and domestic violence include:

- Dismantling cultural norms that define masculinity as dominant and controlling;

- Promoting education and employment to help women be independent and resist economic abuse;

- Providing jobs and reliable forms of government assistance to reduce economic stress on poor and unemployed couples;

- Offering unemployment insurance to help domestic violence survivors who have to quit their jobs;

- Increasing the minimum wage to provide low-income women with resources to leave abusive relationships; and

- Supporting paid leave initiatives, which would allow survivors of domestic violence to take time off from work to seek medical care, find shelter, or obtain legal protection.

References

1. "Domestic Violence and Poverty," Get Domestic Violence Help, n.d.

2. Doyle, Sady. "The Poverty of Domestic Violence," In These Times, May 7, 2012.

3. Renzetti, Claire M., and Vivian M. Larkin. "Economic Stress and Domestic Violence," National Resource Center on Domestic Violence (NRCDV), 2011.

Section 3.5

Are Separated or Divorced Persons at Increased Risk for Intimate Partner Violence?

This section includes text excerpted from "Practical Implications of Current Intimate Partner Violence Research for Victim Advocates and Service Providers," National Criminal Justice Reference Service (NCJRS), January 9, 2013. Reviewed October 2018.

Rates of intimate partner violence (IPV) for persons separated from intimate partners are higher than for divorced, married, or never married persons. National Crime Victimization Survey (NCVS) data reveal that approximately 0.042 percent of separated women and 0.013 percent of separated men were victims of IPV compared to 0.011 percent for divorced women and 0.003 percent of divorced men, 0.006 percent of women never married and 0.002 percent of men never married and 0.002 percent of married women and 0.001 percent of married men.

Similarly, an international review of IPV research found that divorced women are nine times more likely than married women to be physically assaulted by intimate partners, and separated women are at 30 times the risk.

Further, women victims of IPV may be at greater risk of sexual violence and rape after separation. In an exploratory rural study of battered women separated from their male partners, the rate of sexual assaults of women upon telling abusers of their intent to leave was 74 percent. At the time of trying to leave, it was 49 percent, and after leaving, it was 33 percent. Formerly married battered women were subjected to sexual assaults at a higher rate than formerly cohabiting battered women.

Although stalking often begins while the IPV perpetrator and victim are living together, not surprisingly, victims appear to be at elevated risk of stalking after separation and/or divorce.

A study in Canada reported that separated and divorced women are at a very high risk for serious forms of violence, including death. Other studies find women victims may be at greater risk of death trying to leave, immediately after leaving, or when their abusive partners are attempting to reconcile with them after separation.

Not all victims are at equal risk after they separate from or divorce their intimate abuser. One study found that in the two-year period after separation, a third of abusers assaulted their victims, mostly often severely. The perpetrators most likely to assault their victims were those who had frequently threatened their partners with violence after separation, who were "sexually suspicious," and who had lived with their victims long before they first assaulted them. Yet, the same study found that, for most women, separation proved protective against ongoing abuse. The relocation of the abuser to another city was a significant protective factor. Other research has found that separation may prevent or reduce the likelihood of physical and emotional abuse against women IPV victims.

While some argue that this research proves that marriage is the safest place for women to be, the comparatively lower rate of victimization for married couples may be a function of the fact that married couples tend to have less risk factors for IPV, including being older. In fact, research comparing women IPV victims under and over sixty years of age has found that, for the older victims, marriage is the most unsafe marital status. These victims continue to suffer abuse well beyond age sixty.

Implications: Victim advocates and service providers should advise victims that IPV perpetrators may continue or escalate violence and stalking when they believe their intimate partners are thinking of separation and immediately after separation. However, many victims are not targeted for violence or stalking after separation. For this reason, it is important to assist victims in assessing the risk of "separation violence" and to devise safety strategies accordingly. It is also important to advise aging married victims that abuse will not necessary end when they become elderly.

Section 3.6

Domestic Violence in the Wake of Disasters

This section includes text excerpted from "Disasters and Domestic Violence," National Center for Posttraumatic Stress Disorder (NCPTSD), U.S. Department of Veterans Affairs (VA), February 23, 2016.

Prevalence and Impact of Domestic Violence in the Wake of Disasters

Two questions require attention when considering the implications of domestic violence for postdisaster recovery.

The first question is whether domestic violence increases in prevalence after disasters. There are only minimal data that are relevant to this question. Mechanic et al. undertook the most comprehensive examination of intimate violence in the aftermath of a disaster after the 1993 Midwestern flood. A representative sample of 205 women who were either married or cohabitating with men and who were highly exposed to this disaster acknowledged considerable levels of domestic violence and abuse. Over the nine-month period after flood onset, 14 percent reported at least one act of physical aggression from their partners, 26 percent reported emotional abuse, 70 percent reported verbal abuse, and 86 percent reported partner anger. Whether these rates of physical aggression are greater than normal is not known because studies of domestic violence from previous years and under normal conditions have shown the existence of rates of violence as low as one percent and as high as 12 percent.

A few studies have produced evidence that supports the above. Police reports of domestic violence increased by 46 percent following the eruption of the Mt. St. Helens volcano. One year after Hurricane Hugo, marital stress was more prevalent among individuals who had been severely exposed to the hurricane (e.g., life threat, injury) than among individuals who had been less severely exposed or not exposed at all. Within six months after Hurricane Andrew, 22 percent of adult residents of the stricken area acknowledged having a new conflict with someone in their household. In a study of people directly exposed to the bombing of the Murrah Federal Building in Oklahoma City, 17 percent of noninjured persons and 42 percent of persons whose injuries required hospitalization reported troubled interpersonal relationships.

The second question is whether domestic violence, regardless of the reasons how or why it occurs, influences women's postdisaster recovery. An important finding from Mechanic et al.'s (2001) study was that the presence of domestic violence strongly influenced women's postdisaster mental health. Thirty-nine percent of women who experienced postflood partner abuse developed postflood posttraumatic stress disorder (PTSD) compared to 17 percent of women who did not experience postflood abuse. Fifty-seven percent of women who experienced postflood partner abuse developed postflood major depression compared to 28 percent of nonabused women. Similarly, Norris and Uhl found that as marital stress increased, so too did psychological symptoms such as depression and anxiety. Likewise, Norris et al. found that 6 and 30 months after Hurricane Andrew, new conflicts and other socially disruptive events were among the strongest predictors of psychological symptoms.

These findings take on additional significance when it is remembered that not only are women generally at greater risk than men for developing postdisaster psychological problems, but women who are married or cohabitating with men also may be at even greater risk than single women. In contrast, married status is often a protective factor for men. It also has been found that the severity of married women's symptoms increases with the severity of their husbands' distress, even after similarities in their exposure have been taken into account.

In summary, although the research regarding the interplay of disaster and domestic violence is not extensive and little of it has been derived from studies of incidents of mass violence, the available evidence does suggest that services related to domestic violence should be integrated into other mental-health services for disaster-stricken families. Screening for women's safety may be especially important. Helping men find appropriate ways to manage/direct their anger will benefit them and their wives. It will also help their children, as children are highly sensitive to postdisaster conflict and irritability in the family.

Summary of Empirical Findings

- Although there is little conclusive evidence that domestic violence increases after major disasters, research suggests that its postdisaster prevalence may be substantial.

- In the most relevant study, 14 percent of women experienced at least one act of postflood physical aggression and 26 percent reported postflood emotional abuse over a nine-month period.

- One study reported a 46 percent increase in police reports of domestic violence after a disaster.

- Other studies show that substantial percentages of disaster victims experience marital stress, new conflicts, and troubled interpersonal relationships.

- There is more-conclusive evidence that domestic violence harms women's abilities to recover from disasters.

- In the most relevant study, 39 percent of abused women developed postdisaster PTSD compared to 17 percent of other women, and 57 percent of abused women developed postdisaster depression, compared to 28 percent of other women.

- Marital stress and conflicts are highly predictive of postdisaster symptoms.

- In light of the fact that, in general, married women are a high-risk group for developing postdisaster psychological problems, it seems advisable to integrate violence-related screenings and services into programs for women, men, and families.

Section 3.7

When Are Abusers Likely to Reabuse?

This section includes text excerpted from "Practical Implications of Current Intimate Partner Violence Research for Victim Advocates and Service Providers," National Criminal Justice Reference Service (NCJRS), January 9, 2013. Reviewed October 2018.

Studies agree that for those abusers who reoffend, a majority do so relatively quickly. In states where no-contact orders are automatically imposed after an arrest for domestic violence, arrests for order violations begin to occur immediately upon the defendant's release from the police station or court. For example, in both a Massachusetts misdemeanor arrest study and a Brooklyn, NY, felony arrest study, the majority of defendants rearrested for new abuse were arrested while their initial abuse cases were still pending in court. The arrest rate for violation of no-contact orders was 16 percent with a 14 percent arrest rate for new felony offenses.

Similarly, a little more than one-third of the domestic violence probationers in Rhode Island who were arrested for domestic violence were rearrested within two months of being placed under probation supervision. More than half (60%) were arrested within six months. A multistate study of abusers referred to batterer programs found that almost half of the men (44%) who reassaulted their partners did so within three months of batterer-program intake, and two-thirds within six months. The men who reassaulted within the first three months were more likely to repeatedly assault their partners than the men who committed the first reassault after the first three months. In the Bronx, similarly, reoffending happened early among those convicted for misdemeanor or domestic violence violations. Of those rearrested for domestic violence, approximately two-thirds reoffended within the first six months.

Implications: Victim advocates and service providers should advise victims that they may be particularly subject to reabuse after criminal justice intervention. Advocates should encourage criminal justice officials to take appropriate countermeasures in this heightened period of victim risk.

Chapter 4

Detecting Abuse

Chapter Contents

Section 4.1

Comparing Healthy and Abusive Relationships

This section includes text excerpted from "Characteristics of Healthy and Unhealthy Relationships," Youth.gov, February 7, 2012. Reviewed October 2018.

Respect for both oneself and others is a key characteristic of healthy relationships. In contrast, in unhealthy relationships, one partner tries to exert control and power over the other physically, sexually, and/or emotionally.

Healthy Relationships

Healthy relationships share certain characteristics that include:

- **Mutual respect.** Respect means that each person values who the other is and understands the other person's boundaries.

- **Trust.** Partners should place trust in each other and give each other the benefit of the doubt.

- **Honesty.** Honesty builds trust and strengthens the relationship.

- **Compromise.** In a dating relationship, each partner does not always get his or her way Each should acknowledge different points of view and be willing to give and take.

- **Individuality.** Neither partner should have to compromise who she/he is, and his/her identity should not be based on a partner's. Each should continue seeing his or her friends and doing the things she/he loves. Each should be supportive of his/her partner wanting to pursue new hobbies or make new friends.

- **Good communication.** Each partner should speak honestly and openly to avoid miscommunication. If one person needs to sort out his or her feelings first, the other partner should respect those wishes and wait until she or he is ready to talk.

- **Anger control.** We all get angry, but how we express it can affect our relationships with others. Anger can be handled in healthy ways such as taking a deep breath, counting to ten, or talking it out.

- **Fighting fair.** Everyone argues at some point, but those who are fair, stick to the subject and avoid insults are more likely to come up with a possible solution. Partners should take a short break away from each other if the discussion gets too heated.

- **Problem-solving.** Dating partners can learn to solve problems and identify new solutions by breaking a problem into small parts or by talking through the situation.

- **Understanding.** Each partner should take time to understand what the other might be feeling.

- **Self-confidence.** When dating partners have confidence in themselves, it can help their relationships with others. It shows that they are calm and comfortable enough to allow others to express their opinions without forcing their own opinions on them.

- **Being a role model.** By embodying what respect means, partners can inspire each other, friends, and family to also behave in a respectful way.

- **Healthy sexual relationship.** Dating partners engage in a sexual relationship that both are comfortable with, and neither partner feels pressured or forced to engage in sexual activity that is outside his or her comfort zone or without consent.

Unhealthy Relationships

Unhealthy relationships are marked by characteristics such as disrespect and control. It is important to be able to recognize signs of unhealthy relationships before they escalate. Some characteristics of unhealthy relationships include:

- **Control.** One dating partner makes all the decisions and tells the other what to do, what to wear, or who to spend time with. She or he is unreasonably jealous, and/or tries to isolate the other partner from his or her friends and family.

- **Hostility.** One dating partner picks a fight with or antagonizes the other dating partner. This may lead to one dating partner changing his or her behavior in order to avoid upsetting the other.

- **Dishonesty.** One dating partner lies to or keeps information from the other. One dating partner steals from the other.

- **Disrespect.** One dating partner makes fun of the opinions and interests of the other partner or destroys something that belongs to the partner.

- **Dependence.** One dating partner feels that she or he "cannot live without" the other. She or he may threaten to do something drastic if the relationship ends.

- **Intimidation.** One dating partner tries to control aspects of the other's life by making the other partner fearful or timid. One dating partner may attempt to keep his or her partner from friends and family or threaten violence or a break-up.

- **Physical violence.** One partner uses force to get his or her way (such as hitting, slapping, grabbing, or shoving).

- **Sexual violence.** One dating partner pressures or forces the other into sexual activity against his or her will or without consent.

It is important that partners in a relationship know about the value of respect and the characteristics of healthy and unhealthy relationships before they start to date. One may not be equipped with the necessary skills to develop and maintain a healthy relationship, and may not know how to break up in an appropriate way when necessary. Maintaining open lines of communication may help to form healthy relationships and allow people in a relationship to recognize the signs of unhealthy relationships, thus preventing the violence before it starts.

Section 4.2

Indicators of Domestic Violence

This section includes text excerpted from "5 Signs That You May Be in an Abusive Relationship," National Responsible Fatherhood Clearinghouse (NRFC), U.S. Department of Health and Human Services (HHS), November 5, 2015. Reviewed October 2018.

Domestic violence is a violation of people at the core of their being. It betrays love, destroys trust, inflicts irrevocable damage, and often leaves a jaded perception of love in its wake. Many individuals that have been harmed by an intimate partner feel afraid and embarrassed, blame themselves, and believe that they are unable to reveal their pain to family members, friends, or others—even when they are in dire need of assistance.

Contrary to the myth, domestic violence is not is not limited to male perpetrators attacking female victims. According to the National Coalition Against Domestic Violence (NCADV), one in four men has been the victim of some form of physical violence by an intimate partner. Due to society's general apathetic response when it comes to the abuse of men (despite the severity), domestic violence is often dismissed when men seek assistance from law enforcement and social services agencies. Men are threatened physically, emotionally, verbally; psychologically abused; and in many instances seriously injured by the person who bears their last name and with whom they share children.

Domestic violence is an incredibly dangerous crime, and abusive behaviors can be very difficult to detect, especially for victims. It can be as subtle as an unkind word or as blatant as a slap across the face. Insecurities are masked, and what appears in the beginning stages as attentive, generous, and concerned behavior; becomes possessive, extremely jealous, and controlling.

It is important to evaluate relationships daily and to take inventory of situations that may have given you pause. You might be experiencing domestic violence if your partner:

1. Monitors your phone calls, emails, text messages, social media accounts; micromanages your time; make you account for every minute of your time (when you run errands, visit friends, commute to work);

2. Is overly critical; insulting; humiliates you (public or private); makes threats; blackmails you to expose private/sensitive personal information;

3. Acts insanely jealous; possessive; constantly accusing you of being unfaithful; smothers you/is "clingy"; shows up unannounced (home, job, gym); stalks you; calls excessively;

4. Is hypersensitive; has unpredictable, radical mood changes; explosive temper; denies/minimizes the abuse/blames you for the violent behavior (your fault); and

5. Threatens you with weapons; hits, kicks, shoves, slaps, strangles, spits, or otherwise hurts you, your children, or

pets; causes visible injuries (bruises, cuts, burns); destroys/ vandalizes property (cell phone, car, home).

Your partner might offer reasonable explanations, apologies, promise to change, attend counseling, or make spiritual commitments; however, it is crucial to understand that domestic violence is cyclical, becoming more frequent and severe over time.

Despite many valiant efforts, victims cannot stop their partner's abusive behavior, and ultimatums don't make people change. Abuse isn't a couple's issue, but rather the choice of the abuser. Know your strength. Know your limitations.

Section 4.3

Signs to Check—Am I Being Abused?

This section includes text excerpted from "Am I Being Abused?" Office on Women's Health (OWH), U.S. Department of Health and Human Services (HHS), September 13, 2018.

Signs of Abuse

There are many types of violence and abuse. Some of the following are signs of physical abuse or domestic violence. Some are signs of emotional and verbal abuse or sexual abuse.

Signs of abuse include:

- Keeping track of everything you do:
  - Monitoring what you're doing all the time or asking where you are and who you're with every second of the day
  - Demanding your passwords to social media sites and email accounts
  - Demanding that you reply right away to texts, emails, or calls
  - Preventing or discouraging you from seeing friends or family
  - Preventing or discouraging you from going to work or school

- Being jealous, controlling, or angry:
  - Acting very jealous, including constantly accusing you of cheating
  - Having a quick temper, so you never know what you will do or say that may cause a problem
  - Controlling how you spend your money
  - Controlling your use of medicines or birth control
  - Making everyday decisions for you that you normally decide for yourself (like what to wear or eat)
- Demeaning you:
  - Putting you down, such as insulting your appearance, intelligence, or activities
  - Humiliating you in front of others
  - Destroying your property or things that you care about
  - Blaming you for his or her violent outbursts
- Physically harming or threatening to hurt you or loved ones:
  - Threatening to hurt you, the children, or other people or pets in your household
  - Hurting you physically (such as hitting, beating, pushing, shoving, punching, slapping, kicking, or biting)
  - Using (or threatening to use) a weapon against you
  - Threatening to harm himself or herself when upset with you
  - Threatening to turn you into authorities for illegal activity if you report physical abuse
- Forcing you to have sex or other intimate activity:
  - Forcing you to have sex when you don't want to through physical force or threats
  - Assuming that consent for a sex act in the past means that you must participate in the same acts in the future
  - Assuming that consent for one activity means consent for a future activity or increased levels of intimacy (for example, assuming that kissing should lead to sex every time)
  - If you think someone is abusing you, get help. Abuse can have serious physical and emotional effects.

Signs of an Unhealthy Relationship

Sometimes a romantic relationship may not be abusive but may have serious problems that make it unhealthy. If you think you might be in an unhealthy relationship, try talking with your partner about your concerns. If that seems difficult, you might also talk to a trusted friend, family member, counselor, or religious leader.

You might be in an unhealthy relationship if you:

- Focus all your energy on your partner

- Drop friends, family, or activities you enjoy

- Feel pressured or controlled by this person

- Have more bad times than good in the relationship

- Often feel sad or scared when with this person

- Know that this person does not support you and what you want to do in life

- Do not feel comfortable being yourself or making your own decisions

- Cannot speak honestly to work out conflicts in the relationship

- Cannot talk about your needs or changes in your life that are important

Chapter 5

Understanding Stalking

Chapter Contents

Section 5.1

Stalking—What It Is and What You Can Do about It

This section includes text excerpted from "Stalking," Office on Women's Health (OWH), U.S. Department of Health and Human Services (HHS), September 14, 2018.

What Is Stalking?

Stalking is any repeated and unwanted contact with you that makes you feel unsafe. You can be stalked by a stranger, but most stalkers are people you know—even an intimate partner. Stalking may get worse or become violent over time. Stalking may also be a sign of an abusive relationship.

Someone who is stalking you may threaten your safety by clearly saying they want to harm you. Some stalkers harass you with less threatening but still unwanted contact. The use of technology to stalk, sometimes called "cyberstalking," involves using the Internet, email, or other electronic communications to stalk someone. Stalking is against the law.

Stalking and cyberstalking can lead to sleeping problems or problems at work or school.

What Are Some Examples of Stalking?

Examples of stalking may include:

- Following you around or spying on you
- Sending you unwanted emails or letters
- Calling you often
- Showing up uninvited at your house, school, or work
- Leaving you unwanted gifts
- Damaging your home, car, or other property
- Threatening you, your family, or pets with violence

What Are Some Examples of Cyberstalking?

Examples of cyberstalking include:

- Sending unwanted, frightening, or obscene emails, text messages, or instant messages (IMs)

- Harassing or threatening you on social media

- Tracking your computer and Internet use

- Using technology such as the global positioning system (GPS) to track where you are

Are There Laws against Stalking?

Yes. Stalking is a crime. If you are in immediate danger, call 911.

You can file a complaint with the police and get a restraining order (court order of protection) against the stalker. Federal law says that you can get a restraining order for free. Do not be afraid to take steps to stop your stalker.

What Can You Do If You Think You Are Being Stalked?

If you are in immediate danger, call 911. Find a safe place to go if you are being followed or worry that you will be followed. Go to a police station, friend's house, domestic violence shelter, fire station, or public area.

You can also take the following steps if you are being stalked:

- File a complaint with the police. Make sure to tell them about all threats and incidents.

- Get a restraining order. A restraining order requires the stalker to stay away from you and not contact you. You can learn how to get a restraining order from a domestic violence shelter, the police, or an attorney in your area.

- Write down every incident. Include the time, date, and other important information. If the incidents occurred online, take screenshots as records.

- Keep evidence such as videotapes, voicemail messages, photos of property damage, and letters.

- Get names of witnesses.

- Get help from domestic violence hotlines (DVH), domestic violence shelters, counseling services, and support groups. Put these numbers in your phone in case you need them.

- Tell people about the stalking, including the police, your employer, family, friends, and neighbors.

- Always have your phone with you so you can call for help.

- Consider changing your phone number (although some people leave their number active so they can collect evidence). You can also ask your service provider about call blocking and other safety features.

- Secure your home with alarms, locks, and motion-sensitive lights.

What Can You Do If Someone Is Cyberstalking You?

If you are being cyberstalked:

- Send the person one clear, written warning not to contact you again.

- If they contact you again after you've told them not to, do not respond.

- Print out copies of evidence such as emails or screenshots of your phone. Keep a record of the stalking and any contact with police.

- Report the stalker to the authority in charge of the site or service where the stalker contacted you. For example, if someone is stalking you through Facebook, report them to Facebook.

- If the stalking continues, get help from the police. You also can contact a domestic violence shelter and the National Center for Victims of Crime Helpline (NCVCH) for support and suggestions.

- Consider blocking messages from the harasser.

- Change your email address or screen name.

- Never post online profiles or messages with details that someone could use to identify or locate you (such as your age, sex, address, workplace, phone number, school, or places you hang out).

Section 5.2

Prevalence of Stalking in the United States

This section includes text excerpted from "Stalking: Know It. Name It. Stop It," Office of Community Oriented Policing Services (COPS), U.S. Department of Justice (DOJ), January 1, 2018.

Over seven million people a year are victims of stalking and these victims range in age from high-school students and young adults to senior citizens. In the United States, approximately 15 percent of women and 6 percent of men have been a victim of stalking during their lifetimes. January is National Stalking Awareness (NSA) month and a number of national and local events are scheduled across the country to highlight resources and encourage victims to get help.

"Stalking (is) a course of conduct (over time) directed at a specific person that would cause a reasonable person to feel fear. Stalking is serious, often violent, and can escalate (to assault and homicide)."

The crime of stalking can include following victims, repetitive unwanted contact, sending unwanted gifts, property damage, and active threats to hurt either the victims or their family members. Technology is now being used in most stalking cases and can include tracking the victim with hidden cameras or global positioning systems (GPS), use of public records and online search services to follow victims, posting negative information online, and doxing.

"There is often an intersection between stalking and other crime property crimes, sexual assault crimes, domestic violence crimes," states detective Deirdri Fishel (DDF), State College Police Department (SCPD).

Up to 95 percent of stalking victims know the offender and 67 percent of stalking victims are also the victims of domestic abuse from their intimate partner. In addition, about 20 percent of stalkers use a weapon to harm the victim. Law enforcement and community partner outreach to end stalking will increase community safety and officer safety since 20 percent of officer deaths in 2016 resulted from a response to disturbance calls, and the majority of those were domestic violence service calls.

Section 5.3

Security Tips for Stalking Victims

This section includes text excerpted from "Interstate
Stalking," U.S. Department of Justice (DOJ), April 20, 2015.
Reviewed October 2018.

Danger of Getting Stalked

If you are in danger, find a safe place to go such as:

- Police/fire department

- Homes of friends or relatives, preferably unknown to the
  stalker

- Family crisis shelters

- Crowded public buildings or places

Notify Appropriate Law-Enforcement Agencies

After you are safe, notify appropriate police agencies. Give an accurate description of the stalker, his or her vehicle, address (if known), and a recent photograph if you have one.

Notify security personnel in apartments and/or appropriate personnel at your workplace, children's schools, and other places that are a part of your normal routine. Ask law enforcement about security measures they can initiate. Some agencies have alarms available for stalking victims or "panic button" alarms can be rented from private security agencies.

As well as helping to protect you, by reporting a crime of stalking, police can keep an independent record of the incidents, which can assist them in developing a threat assessment of the stalker.

Police reports may also help you get a protection order from a court or demonstrate that an existing order has been violated.

Stop All Contact with a Stalker—Now and for Good

Consult with a victim-services provider about creating a personal safety plan and follow it.

If you believe the stalker truly poses a threat, consider obtaining a restraining order, but be aware that service of the order to the stalker may provoke a response.

Document Stalking Behavior

It is important to keep a record of incidents which may support a criminal prosecution. Record dates, times of day, and places of contact with the individual who is stalking you. Log any telephone calls and save answering-machine messages. Save any correspondence from a stalker, including the envelope. Document threats in detail. Provide names and addresses of witnesses to any incidents to law enforcement or a prosecutor.

Other Illegal Acts

If the stalker has assaulted you physically or sexually, has entered your home without permission, or has damaged or stolen your property, report it to the police. They should also photograph injuries to your person or damage to your property. These are separate crimes which can be prosecuted.

Ways to Increase Your Home and Personal Safety

You can increase your home and personal safety by:

- Telling a stalker that you don't want to talk to him if you are still talking to him or her. Stop all contact.

- Treat any threat as legitimate and call the police immediately. Install deadbolts. If you lose the key, change the locks.

- If possible, install outside lights activated by a motion detector.

- Maintain an unlisted telephone number. If harassing calls persist, contact telephone company security and they can assist you with options to trace the origin of such calls.

- Use a telephone message machine to screen calls. These document contact by a stalker for the police.

- Vary the routes you take and limit the time you spend walking.

- Keep children and pets indoors and always under supervision. If you have children in common, arrange through the court for the exchange of custody or visitation through a third party.

- Tell trusted relatives, friends, a landlord, and neighbors about the situation.

- Provide family, friends, neighbors, and your employer with a photo or description of the stalker and the car she or he drives.

- Advise your employer and coworkers of the problem and provide a picture of the stalker if available. If the stalker shows up at work, have someone contact the police, and avoid any personal contact.

- Don't park in secluded areas.

Help Is Available

If you are a victim of a stalking crime, it is normal to sometimes feel frightened and vulnerable. The following agencies exist to help victims of crime. Seek their help.

National Assistance

- National Domestic Violence Hotline (NDVH)

  Toll-Free: 800-799-SAFE (800-799-7233)

  Website: www.ndvh.org

- National Center for Victims of Crime (NCVC)

  Toll-Free: 800-FYI-CALL (800-394-2255)

  Website: www.ncvc.org

- National Organization for Victim Assistance (NOVA)

  Toll-Free: 800-TRY-NOVA (800-879-6682)

  Website: www.trynova.org

- National Coalition Against Domestic Violence (NCADV)

  Phone: 303-839-1852

If in crisis, call: 800-SUICIDE (800-784-2433) or 800-273-TALK (800-273-8255)

Local Assistance

- If you feel you are in danger, first contact your local police or sheriff department. Dial 911.

- Contact your county victim assistance program in solicitor or district attorney's office.

- Federal Bureau of Investigation (FBI): To report interstate stalking crimes 404-679-9000

- U.S. Attorney's Victim Witness Assistance Program 888-431-1918, 404-581-6102, or 404-581-6041. (For victims and witnesses of federal crime)

Section 5.4

Documenting and Reporting Stalking

This section contains text excerpted from the following sources: Text in this section begins with excerpts from "Stalking Victims in the United States—Revised," U.S. Department of Justice (DOJ), September 2012. Reviewed October 2018; Text under the heading "What to Do If You Are Being Stalked" is excerpted from "Stalking Response Tips," U.S. Department of Justice (DOJ), January 31, 2013. Reviewed October 2018.

An estimated 3.3 million persons age 18 or older were victims of stalking during a 12-month period. Stalking is defined as a course of conduct directed at a specific person that would cause a reasonable person to feel fear. The National Crime Victimization Survey (the Survey) identified seven types of harassing or unwanted behaviors consistent with a course of conduct experienced by stalking victims. The Survey classified individuals as stalking victims if they responded that they experienced at least one of these behaviors on at least two separate occasions. In addition, the individuals must have feared for their safety or that of a family member as a result of the course of conduct, or have experienced additional threatening behaviors that would cause a reasonable person to feel fear. The Survey measured the following stalking behaviors:

- Making unwanted phone calls
- Sending unsolicited or unwanted letters or e-mails
- Following or spying on the victim
- Showing up at places without a legitimate reason
- Waiting at places for the victim
- Leaving unwanted items, presents, or flowers

- Posting information or spreading rumors about the victim on the Internet, in a public place, or by word of mouth

Screener Questions for Stalking Behaviors

Some questions about any unwanted contacts or harassing behavior you may have experienced that frightened, concerned, angered, or annoyed you. This includes acts committed by strangers, casual acquaintances, friends, relatives, and even spouses and partners.

1. Not including bill collectors, telephone solicitors, or other sales people, has anyone, male or female, EVER–frightened, concerned, angered, or annoyed you by...

   a. making unwanted phone calls to you or leaving messages?

   b. sending unsolicited or unwanted letters, e-mails, or other forms of written correspondence or communication?

   c. following you or spying on you?

   d. waiting outside or inside places for you such as your home, school, workplace, or recreation place?

   e. showing up at places where you were even though she or he had no business being there?

   f. leaving unwanted items, presents, or flowers?

   g. posting information or spreading rumors about you on the Internet, in a public place, or by word of mouth?

   h. none

Actions that would cause a reasonable person to feel fear

1. In order to frighten or intimidate you, did this person attack or attempt to attack...

   a. a child

   b. another family member

   c. a friend or coworker

   d. a pet

2. During the last twelve months, did this person attack or attempt to attack you by...

    a. hitting, slapping, or knocking you down

    b. choking or strangling you

    c. raping or sexually assaulting you

    d. attacking you with a weapon

    e. chasing or dragging with a car

    f. attacking you in some other way

3. Other than the attacks or attempted attacks during the last 12 months, did this person threaten to...

    a. kill you

    b. rape or sexually assault you

    c. harm you with a weapon

    d. hit, slap, or harm you in some other way

    e. harm or kidnap a child

    f. harm another family member

    g. harm a friend or coworker

    h. harm a pet

    i. harm or kill himself/herself

4. What were you most afraid of happening as these unwanted contacts or behaviors were occurring?

    a. death

    b. physical/bodily harm

    c. harm or kidnap respondent's child

    d. harm current partner/boyfriend/girlfriend

    e. harm other family members

    f. didn't know what would happen

Questions used to measure fear

1. How did the behavior of (this person/these persons) make you feel when it FIRST started? Anything else?

    a. anxious/concerned

    b. annoyed/angry

    c. frightened

    d. depressed

 e. helpless

 f. sick

 g. suicidal

 h. some other way—specify

2. How did you feel as the behavior progressed?

 a. no change in feelings

 b. anxious/concerned

 c. annoyed/angry

 d. frightened

 e. depressed

 f. helpless

 g. sick

 h. suicidal

 i. some other way—specify

What to Do If You Are Being Stalked

1. Trust your instincts. Victims of stalking often feel pressured by friends or family to downplay the stalker's behavior, but stalking poses a real threat of harm. Your safety is paramount.

2. Call the police if you feel you are in any immediate danger. Explain why even some actions that seem harmless—like leaving you a gift—are causing you fear.

3. Keep a record or log of each contact with the stalker. Be sure to also document any police reports.

4. Stalkers often use technology to contact their victims. Save all e-mails, text messages, photos, and postings on social networking sites as evidence of the stalking behavior.

5. Get connected with a local victim advocate to talk through your options and discuss safety planning. Call the National Domestic Violence Hotline at 800-799-SAFE (800-799-7233).

Section 5.5

Beware of Stalking Mobile Apps

This section includes text excerpted from "Who's Stalking:
What to Know about Mobile Spyware," Federal Trade
Commission (FTC), September 26, 2016.

Do you think an abusive partner or ex is monitoring you through your phone? They might be using stalking apps (spyware) that secretly track your devices. Here's information about what stalking apps are, how to tell if they're on your device, and what to do if they are.

What Are Stalking Apps?

Stalking applications are apps or software that someone can download onto your phone to track or monitor you. They can share detailed information about your phone activities—like phone conversations, text and email messages, photos, and account passwords—without your knowledge. Some stalking apps also advertise that they can turn on a phone's microphone and camera remotely so that the monitoring person can see and hear what's happening around the phone, even when it's not being used.

How Can You Tell If a Stalking App Is Installed on Your Phone?

If an abuser has installed a stalking app on your phone, your phone will probably look the same. No new icon will be displayed, and most antivirus software won't detect it. But these clues may suggest that a stalking app could have been installed:

- The abuser has had physical access to your phone;
- The abuser knows a lot of very specific information about you, including your exact locations, the content of conversations you've had, what you've texted and to whom, and what you've searched for online;
- The phone's battery drains faster, without any difference in your phone usage;
- There are unexplained data usage charges on your bill; or
- You have trouble turning off the phone.

What Can You Do If You Think a Stalking App Is Installed on Your Phone?

If there's a stalking app on your phone, here are some steps to consider:

- **Get help.** Law enforcement and domestic-violence advocates can help you if you believe a stalking app has been installed on your phone.

- **Check to see if your phone has been "rooted" or "jailbroken."** Stalking apps aren't sold through typical app stores. In addition, they usually can be installed only on a phone that has been "rooted" or "jailbroken," which allows a person full control over the phone's operating system. If your phone is rooted or jailbroken and you didn't do it, a stalking app could be installed. "Root checker" apps can quickly tell you whether a phone has been rooted or jailbroken.

- **Backup your phone.** Before making any changes to your phone, consider backing it up, which could help to save any potential evidence of abusive behavior. Local law enforcement may be able to help you to preserve evidence. However, do not sync your backup to a new phone, to prevent the spyware from reinstalling.

- **Reset your phone.** The only way to effectively remove a stalking app from a phone is to reset it and re-install the manufacturer's operating system.

Remember that taking any of these steps could tip-off your abuser—especially if you use your phone to research your options, make a call, or have a conversation near your phone. If you are concerned your phone might be monitored, consider leaving it behind when you are seeking help. Do what is best in your particular situation.

Chapter 6

Sexual Harassment

Harassment is any unwelcome behavior or comments made by one person to another. "Sexual harassment" is a term usually used to describe unwanted sexual contact or behavior that happens more than once at work, home, or in school. It includes any unwelcome sexual advances or requests for sexual favors that affect a person's job, schoolwork, or housing. Street harassment is behavior or comments that can be sexual—but are not always—and may target your sex, gender, age, religion, nationality, race, ethnicity, or sexual orientation.

What Is Sexual Harassment?

Sexual harassment happens when someone in your workplace, home, or school makes unwelcome sexual advances to you or requests sexual favors. It also includes verbal or physical behaviors that may affect your job, home, or education. These acts are sexual harassment when they are without your consent or are unwanted, and interfere with your work or school performance or create a hostile or offensive environment.

Sexual harassment violates most work, housing, or school policies and may be illegal. Sometimes sexual harassment is also sexual coercion. Coercion is when you are forced in a nonphysical way into sexual activity. Sexual harassers can be anyone—men or women—and can be

This chapter includes text excerpted from "Harassment," Office on Women's Health (OWH), U.S. Department of Health and Human Services (HHS), September 13, 2018.

managers, coworkers, landlords, teachers, or other students. Sexual harassment does not mean you are in a sexual relationship with the person doing it.

How Common Is Sexual Harassment?

The exact number of people who are sexually harassed at work, home, or school is not known. This is because many people do not report sexual harassment.

Surveys show that more than half of women have experienced sexual harassment at work. However, only one in four who experienced harassment reported the behavior to a supervisor or human resources (HR) representative. Reasons for not reporting the behavior included the fear that their supervisor wouldn't believe them or wouldn't help them. It also included fear of losing their job, especially if their supervisor was the person harassing them.

Studies of sexual harassment in housing are not common, but one study shows that sexual coercion by someone in authority as a landlord is the most common type of sexual harassment experienced by women in rental housing. Studies also show that sex and gender-minority women may have a harder time finding housing compared to other women.

What Are Some Ways That Women Can Be Sexually Harassed?

There are many different types of sexual harassment that happen at work, home, or school:

Verbal or Written Sexual Harassment

- Making comments about your clothing, body, behavior, or romantic relationships

- Making sexual jokes or comments

- Repeatedly asking you out on a date after you have said no

- Asking you to engage in sexual acts, such as kissing, touching, watching a sexual act, or having sex

- Requesting sexual photos or videos of you

- Threatening you for saying no to a sexual request

- Spreading rumors about your personal or sexual life

- Whistling or catcalling

- Sending online links or photos with explicit or graphic sexual content (GSC)

Physical Sexual Harassment

- Being uncomfortably close to you

- Blocking you from moving or walking away

- Inappropriate touching

- Coercing you into sexual activity by threatening to hurt your career, grades, home, or reputation (this is a type of sexual assault) if you do not engage in sexual activity

- Physically forcing you into sexual activity without your consent (rape and sexual assault)

Visual Sexual Harassment

- Displaying or sharing sexual pictures, texts (sexting), computer wallpaper, or emails

- Showing you his or her private body parts (called "flashing")

- Masturbating in front of you

Sometimes you may experience other types of harassment that may be difficult to document or prove but that can still be threatening. These can include someone staring at your body in a sexual way or making offensive sexual gestures or facial expressions.

What Can You Do to Stop Sexual Harassment?

As with all other types of abuse, if you are being sexually harassed, it is not your fault. You can take steps to alert others to the harassment and protect yourself from the person harassing you. Many types of sexual harassment are against the law. If you are being sexually harassed, try one or all of these actions:

- **Say "no" without saying anything else.** If a harasser asks you for dates or sexual acts, just say "no." You do not need to offer excuses like "I have a boyfriend," or "I don't date people I work with." If you give a reason or an excuse, it gives the harasser a way to continue the conversation or to argue with you. Physically leave the situation if you can. If the person continues to ask you for unwanted dates or sexual behavior, report them to someone in authority whose job it is to help you stop the harassment, such as a human resources manager.

- **Tell the person to stop the harassment,** if you feel safe enough to do that. If someone is harassing you by making sexual comments or showing sexual images, tell them that the comment or image is not okay with you. Saying "Stop it" and walking away is a good way to respond also.

- **Keep a record.** When you experience harassment, write down the dates, places, times, and any witnesses to what happened. Store the record in a secure place, such as your phone. If the harassment happened online, save screenshots or emails of the interactions.

- **Report it.** It can be difficult to talk about personal topics with someone at work or school, but you should tell your manager, human resources department, a local legal aid group, rental company, or school about the harassment. Describe the harassing experiences and explain that they are unwelcome and you want them to stop. If you can, it's best to make your report in writing so you can save a record of it. Keep copies of everything you send and receive from your employer, landlord, or school about the harassment.

- **Research your company's or school's complaint procedures.** Most employers and schools should have a specific procedure on how to respond to sexual-harassment complaints. If at work, get a copy of your company's employee handbook so you can use these procedures to stop the harassment. At schools that get federal funding, you can get a copy of the sexual-harassment policy. Follow the complaint procedures and keep records of it.

- **File a government agency discrimination complaint.** You can take your workplace sexual assault case higher by filing a lawsuit in federal or state court, but note that you have to file a formal sexual harassment complaint with the federal Equal Employment Opportunity Commission (EEOC) first. To report sexual harassment in housing, call the U.S. Department of Justice (DOJ) at 844-380-6178 or e-mail fairhousing@usdoj.gov.

You can also file an online complaint with the U.S. Department of Housing and Urban Development (HUD) or call your local HUD office. You can file an online school-based sexual harassment complaint with the U.S. Department of Education (ED).

Chapter 7

Street Harassment

What You Need to Know about Street Harassment

Street harassment is unwanted comments, gestures, and actions forced on someone in a public place without that person's consent. It may or may not also be sexual harassment. The harassment usually comes from strangers and is often directed at someone because of sex, gender, religion, nationality, race, ethnicity, or sexual orientation.

In a national survey, more than 50 percent of the women reported experiencing street harassment. Women of color, lesbians, and bisexual women experienced street harassment more often than other women.

You may have experienced street harassment if anyone has ever:

- Whistled or catcalled at you

- Made negative comments about your sex, gender, religion, sexual orientation, or sexual identity

- Continued to ask for your name, phone number, or other personal information after you've said no

- Followed you or stalked you

- Showed you his or her private body parts (called "flashing")

This chapter includes text excerpted from "Harassment" Office on Women's Health (OWH), U.S. Department of Health and Human Services (HHS), September 13, 2018.

- Masturbated in front of you

- Physically touched you in private areas

How You Can Respond to Street Harassment

You may have only a few seconds to decide on the best way to react to someone harassing you or someone else. Because street harassment often happens between strangers in a public place, you may not have the same legal protection that you have for sexual harassment that takes place at work or school or in rental housing. But no one has the right to physically touch or hurt you. Physically hurting someone or touching someone else without their permission or consent is always illegal.

It's probably safest to leave the situation as quickly as possible. If you cannot physically leave the situation right away, you have some other options:

- **Ignore the person.** It can be difficult to ignore someone who is saying insulting or demeaning things, but talking or arguing may lead to physical violence. Your safety is the most important consideration.

- **Move closer to someone in uniform.** Most people unconsciously associate uniforms with authority or power. If there is anyone in your area in any type of uniform—like a security guard, doctor, police officer, or bus driver—try to stand or sit near them. Then leave the situation as soon as you can.

- **Start talking to someone else.** Harassment can be easier to ignore if you are in a group or talking to someone else. If you are alone, look for someone around you to talk to. Many people around you in public places will be willing to call 911 for you if you feel unsafe.

- **Call someone on your phone.** Pretend to talk on your phone even if the person doesn't answer. Tell the person on the phone where you are, like "I'm at the Pine Street stop on the number 42 line and should be there soon." This may discourage a harasser from continuing the harassment if they think you can tell others about it.

- **Report them.** If the harassers are in a car, write down their license plate number and call the police. If the harassers are wearing a shirt or driving a vehicle that identifies their company, call or email the company to report what the employees did. You can also report street harassment online. If you have a smartphone, record a video of the harassment and let the person being harassed know that you are doing so.

If you see someone else being harassed and feel safe doing so, try to help. You can support the person being harassed without talking to the person doing the harassing. Ask the person being harassed if they're okay, or if you can help them move away from the situation. Offer to record the harassment with a smartphone.

Part Two

Intimate Partner Abuse

Chapter 8

Types of Intimate Partner Abuse

Chapter Contents

Section 8.1

Primary Forms of Intimate Partner Abuse

This section includes text excerpted from "Intimate Partner
Violence: Definitions," Centers for Disease Control and
Prevention (CDC), August 22, 2017.

There are four main types of intimate partner violence (IPV).

1. **Physical violence** is the intentional use of physical force
    with the potential for causing death, disability, injury,
    or harm. Physical violence includes, but is not limited to,
    scratching; pushing; shoving; throwing; grabbing; biting;
    choking; shaking; aggressive hair pulling; slapping; punching;
    hitting; burning; use of a weapon; and use of restraints or
    one's body, size, or strength against another person. Physical
    violence also includes coercing other people to commit any of
    the above acts.

2. **Sexual violence** is divided into five categories. Any of
    these acts constitute sexual violence, whether attempted or
    completed. Additionally, all of these acts occur without the
    victim's freely given consent, including cases in which the
    victim is unable to consent due to being too intoxicated (e.g.,
    incapacitation, lack of consciousness, or lack of awareness)
    through their voluntary or involuntary use of alcohol or
    drugs.

    -   **Rape or penetration of victim.** This includes completed
        or attempted, forced or alcohol/drug-facilitated unwanted
        vaginal, oral, or anal insertion. Forced penetration occurs
        through the perpetrator's use of physical force against the
        victim or threats to physically harm the victim.

    -   **The victim was made to penetrate someone else.** This
        includes completed or attempted, forced or alcohol/drug-
        facilitated incidents when the victim was made to sexually
        penetrate a perpetrator or someone else without the victim's
        consent.

    -   **Nonphysically pressured unwanted penetration.** This
        includes incidents in which the victim was pressured verbally
        or through intimidation or misuse of authority to consent or
        acquiesce to being penetrated.

- **Unwanted sexual contact.** This includes intentional touching of the victim or making the victim touch the perpetrator, either directly or through the clothing, on the genitalia, anus, groin, breast, inner thigh, or buttocks without the victim's consent

- **Noncontact unwanted sexual experiences.** This includes unwanted sexual events that are not of a physical nature that occur without the victim's consent. Examples include unwanted exposure to sexual situations (e.g., pornography); verbal or behavioral sexual harassment; threats of sexual violence to accomplish some other end; and/or unwanted filming, taking or disseminating photographs of a sexual nature of another person.

3. **Stalking** is a pattern of repeated, unwanted attention and contact that causes fear or concern for one's own safety or the safety of someone else (e.g., a family member or friend). Some examples include repeated, unwanted phone calls, emails, or texts; leaving cards, letters, flowers, or other items when the victim does not want them; watching or following from a distance; spying; approaching or showing up in places when the victim does not want to see the person; sneaking into the victim's home or car; damaging the victim's personal property; harming or threatening the victim's pet; and making threats to physically harm the victim.

4. **Psychological aggression** is the use of verbal and nonverbal communication with the intent to harm another person mentally or emotionally, and/or to exert control over another person. Psychological aggression can include expressive aggression (e.g., name-calling, humiliating); coercive control (e.g., limiting access to transportation, money, friends, and family; excessive monitoring of whereabouts); threats of physical or sexual violence; control of reproductive or sexual health (e.g., refusal to use birth control; coerced pregnancy termination); exploitation of a victim's vulnerability (e.g., immigration status, disability); exploitation of a perpetrator's vulnerability; and presenting false information to the victim with the intent of making them doubt their own memory or perception (e.g., mind games).

Section 8.2

Physical Abuse

This section includes text excerpted from "Physical Abuse,"
Office on Women's Health (OWH), U.S. Department of
Health and Human Services (HHS), September 13, 2018.

Physical abuse is any physical force that injures you or puts your health in danger. Physical abuse can include shaking, burning, choking, hair-pulling, hitting, slapping, kicking, and any type of harm with a weapon such as a knife or a gun. It can also include threats to hurt you, your children, your pets, or family members. Physical abuse can also include restraining you against your will by tying you up or locking you in a space. Physical abuse in an intimate partner (romantic or sexual) relationship is also called domestic violence.

Physical abuse is:

- **A crime.** Physical abuse is a criminal act, whether it happens inside or outside of the family or an intimate relationship. The police have the power and authority to protect you from physical attack. If someone in a position of power or authority physically abuses you, there are always ways to report them. Physical abuse is a crime even if it happens just one time. You may think that the abuse will never happen again. Your partner may try to convince you that it will never happen again. The abuse may stop, but it is likely to continue. And no one has the right to harm you, even once.

- **Dangerous.** Victims whose partners physically abuse them are at a higher risk for serious injury and even death.

If you think you are in an abusive relationship, learn more about getting help. Talk to your doctor or nurse. If you're in immediate danger or are physically hurt, call 911.

How Does Physical Abuse Affect a Woman's Health in the Long Term?

Physical abuse can have lasting effects on your physical and mental health. Physical abuse can cause many chronic (long-lasting) health problems, including heart problems, high blood pressure, and digestive problems. Women who are abused are also more likely to develop depression, anxiety, or eating disorders. Women who are abused may also misuse alcohol or drugs as a way to cope.

How Do You Leave a Physically Abusive Relationship?

If you are thinking about leaving an abusive relationship, even if you don't leave right away, creating a safety plan can help you know what to do if your partner abuses you again. It can help you be more independent when you leave.

Your safety plan will help you be prepared:

- **Identify a safe friend or friends and safe places to go.** Create a code word to use with friends, family, or neighbors to let them know you are in danger without the abuser finding out. If possible, agree on a secret location where they can pick you up.

- **Keep an alternate cell-phone nearby.** Try not to call for help on your home phone or on a shared phone. Your partner might be able to trace the numbers. If you don't have a cell phone, you can get a prepaid phone. Some domestic violence shelters offer free phones.

- **Memorize the phone numbers of friends, family, or shelters.** If your partner takes your phone, you will still be able to contact loved ones or shelters for a safe place to stay.

- **Make a list of things to take if you have to leave quickly.** Important identity documents and money are probably the top priority. Get these items together and keep them in a safe place where your partner will not find them. If you are in immediate danger, leave without them.

- **If you can, hide an extra set of car keys** so you can leave if your partner takes away your usual keys.

- **Ask the doctor how to get extra medicine or glasses, hearing aids, or other medically necessary items for you or your children.**

- **Contact your local family court** (or domestic violence court, if your state has one) for information about getting a restraining order. If you need legal help but don't have much money, your local domestic violence agency may be able to help you find a lawyer who will work for free or on a sliding scale.

- **Protect your online security** as you collect information and prepare. Use a computer at a public library to download information, or use a friend's computer or cell phone. Your partner might be able to track your planning otherwise.

- **Try to take with you any evidence of abuse or violence** if you leave your partner. This might include threatening notes from your partner. It might be copies of police and medical reports. It might include pictures of your injuries or damage to your property.

- **Keep copies of all paper and electronic documents on an external thumb drive.** Advocates at the National Domestic Violence Hotline (NDVH), 800-799-SAFE (800-799-7233), can help you develop your safety plan.

Section 8.3

Sexual Assault

This section includes text excerpted from "Sexual Assault," Office on Women's Health (OWH), U.S. Department of Health and Human Services (HHS), September 13, 2018.

Sexual assault is any type of sexual activity or contact, including rape, that happens without your consent. Sexual assault can include noncontact activities, such as someone "flashing" you (exposing themselves to you) or forcing you to look at sexual images.

Sexual assault is also called sexual violence or abuse. Legal definitions of sexual assault and other crimes of sexual violence can vary slightly from state to state. If you have been assaulted, it is never your fault.

What Is Included in the Definition of Sexual Assault?

Sexual assault can include:

- Any type of sexual contact with someone who cannot consent, such as someone who is underage (as defined by state laws), has an intellectual disability, or is passed out (such as from drugs or alcohol) or unable to respond (such as from sleeping)

- Any type of sexual contact with someone who does not consent

- Rape

- Attempted rape

- Sexual coercion

- Sexual contact with a child

- Fondling or unwanted touching above or under clothes

Sexual assault can also be verbal, visual, or not involve direct contact. It is any action that forces a person to join in unwanted sexual activities or attention. Other examples can include:

- Voyeurism, or peeping (when someone watches private sexual acts without consent)

- Exhibitionism (when someone exposes himself or herself in public)

- Sexual harassment or threats

- Forcing someone to pose for sexual pictures

- Sending someone unwanted texts or "sexts" (texting sexual photos or messages)

What Does "Consent" Mean?

Consent is a clear "yes" to sexual activity. Not saying "no" does not mean you have given consent. Sexual contact without consent is sexual assault or rape.

Your consent means:

- You know and understand what is going on (you are not unconscious, blacked out, asleep, underage, or have an intellectual disability)

- You know what you want to do.

- You are able to say what you want to do or don't want to do.

- You are aware that you are giving consent (and are not impaired by alcohol or drugs)

Sometimes you cannot give legal consent to sexual activity or contact—for example, if you are:

- Threatened, forced, coerced, or manipulated into agreeing

- Not physically able to (you are drunk, high, drugged, passed out, or asleep)

- Not mentally able to (due to illness or disability)

- Under the age of legal consent, which varies by state

Remember:

- **Consent is an ongoing process,** not a one-time question. If you consent to sexual activity, you can change your mind and choose to stop at any time, even after sexual activity has started.

- **Past consent does not mean future consent.** Giving consent in the past to sexual activity does not mean your past consent applies now or in the future.

- **Saying "yes" to a sexual activity is not consent for all types of sexual activity.** If you consent to sexual activity, it is only for types of sexual activities that you are comfortable with at that time with that partner. For example, giving consent for kissing does not mean you are giving consent for someone to remove your clothes.

What Is Not Considered Consent in Sexual Activity?

- **Silence.** Just because someone does not say "no" doesn't mean she is saying "yes."

- **Previous consent.** Just because someone said "yes" in the past does not mean she is saying "yes" now. Consent must be part of every sexual activity, every time.

- **Being in a relationship.** Being married, dating, or having sexual contact with someone before does not mean that there is consent now.

- **Being drunk or high.** The influence of alcohol and drugs may result in sexual assault.

- **Not fighting back.** Not putting up a physical fight does not mean that there is consent.

- **Sexy clothing, dancing, or flirting.** What a woman or girl wears or how she behaves does not show consent for sexual activity. Only a verbal "yes" means "yes" to sexual activity.

Who Commits Sexual Assault?

Sexual assault is most often committed by someone the victim knows. This may be a friend, an acquaintance, an ex, a relative, a date, or a partner. Less often, a stranger commits sexual assault.

Women and men commit sexual assault, but more than 90 percent of people who commit sexual violence against women are men.

What Is the Average Age at Which a Woman Is Sexually Assaulted?

Four of every five women who are raped are raped before age 25. About 40 percent of women who have been raped, or two in every five, were assaulted before age 18.

Section 8.4

Emotional and Verbal Abuse

This section includes text excerpted from "Emotional and Verbal Abuse," Office on Women's Health (OWH), U.S. Department of Health and Human Services (HHS), September 13, 2018.

How Can You Tell If You Are Being Emotionally or Verbally Abused?

You may be experiencing emotional or verbal abuse if someone:

- Wants to know what you're doing all the time and wants you to be in constant contact

- Demands passwords to things like your phone, e-mail, and social media and shows other signs of digital abuse

- Acts very jealous, including constantly accusing you of cheating

- Prevents or discourages you from seeing friends or family
- Tries to stop you from going to work or school
- Gets angry in a way that is frightening to you
- Controls all your finances or how you spend your money
- Stops you from seeing a doctor
- Humiliates you in front of others
- Calls you insulting names (such as "stupid," "disgusting," "worthless," "whore," or "fat")
- Threatens to hurt you, people you care about, or pets
- Threatens to call the authorities to report you for wrongdoing
- Threatens to harm himself or herself when upset with you
- Says things like, "If I can't have you, then no one can."
- Decides things for you that you should decide (like what to wear or eat)

How Does Emotional and Verbal Abuse Start?

Emotional and verbal abuse may begin suddenly. Some abusers may start out behaving normally and then begin abuse after a relationship is established. Some abusers may purposefully give a lot of love and attention, including compliments and requests to see you often, at the beginning of a relationship. Often, the abuser tries to make the other person feel strongly bonded to them, as though it is the two of them "against the world."

Over time, abusers begin to insult or threaten their victims and begin controlling different parts of their lives. When this change in behavior happens, it can leave victims feeling shocked and confused. You may feel embarrassed or foolish for getting into the relationship. If someone else abuses you, it is never your fault.

What Are the Effects of Emotional or Verbal Abuse?

Staying in an emotionally or verbally abusive relationship can have long-lasting effects on your physical and mental health, including leading to chronic pain, depression, or anxiety.

You may also:

- Question your memory of events: "Did that really happen?"

- Change your behavior for fear of upsetting your partner or act more aggressive or more passive than you would be otherwise

- Feel ashamed or guilty

- Feel constantly afraid of upsetting your partner

- Feel powerless and hopeless

- Feel manipulated, used, and controlled

- Feel unwanted

Your partner's behavior may leave you feeling as though you need to do anything possible to restore peace and end the abuse. This can feel stressful and overwhelming.

What Is Gaslighting?

"Gaslighting" is the word used when an abuser makes you feel like you are losing your mind or memory.

An abuser might:

- Deny an event happened

- Call you crazy or overly sensitive

- Describe an event as completely different from how you remember it

Gaslighting is a form of emotional abuse that abusers use to maintain power and control. When a victim is questioning her memories or her mind, she may be more likely to feel dependent on the abuser and stay in the relationship.

Gaslighting happens over time, and you may not notice it at first.

How Can You Get Help for Emotional or Verbal Abuse?

If you are in immediate danger, call 911.

If you aren't in immediate danger, reach out to a trusted friend or family member, therapist, or volunteer with an abuse shelter or domestic violence hotline.

Section 8.5

Financial Abuse

This section includes text excerpted from "Financial Abuse,"
Office on Women's Health (OWH), U.S. Department of Health
and Human Services (HHS), September 14, 2018.

Financial abuse happens when an abuser has control over finances in a relationship and withholds money from the victim. Often, a woman does not leave an abusive relationship because she fears she will not be able to provide for herself or her children. Financial abuse can make the victim feel as if she can't leave. This fear is often the main reason women don't leave an abusive relationship.

Financial abuse of older adults is also common.

How Can You Tell If You Are Being Financially Abused?

Often, financial abuse is subtle and gradual, so it may be hard to recognize. Your partner may act as though taking over the finances is a way to make life easier for you as if she or he is doing you a favor. Your partner might explain that giving you a set amount of money will help keep your family on track financially. But slowly, the "allowance" becomes smaller and smaller, and before you know it, you are asking for money and being refused.

Some of the common ways that financial abuse happens include:

- Urging you to or demanding that you quit your job or preventing you from working

- Stalking or harassing you at work

- Refusing to give you access to bank accounts and hiding or keeping assets from you

- Giving you a set amount of money to spend and no more

- Constantly questioning purchases you make and demanding to see receipts

- Making financial decisions without consulting you

- Stealing your identity or filing fraudulent tax returns with your name attached to them

- Selling property that was yours

- Filing false insurance claims with your name on them

- Not paying child support so you can't afford rent, food, and other needed items

- Forcing you to open lines of credit

What Steps Can You Take to Protect Yourself from Financial Abuse?

If the abuser has access to your credit cards, bank accounts, or Social Security number (SSN), they may try to open accounts in your name or deliberately try to ruin your credit in order to make it harder for you to leave the relationship. But you can take steps to protect yourself and your money, whether you stay in the relationship or leave.

- **Keep your personal information safe.** Call your credit card company and bank and ask them to change your personal identification number (PIN) or access codes. Change your passwords on your personal computer or phone, including passwords you use to log into your bank or credit card accounts. Do not give the passwords to anyone else.

- **Don't cosign a loan or another financial contract with an abuser.** If the abusive partner doesn't make payments on time or at all, you may be held responsible for the debt.

- **Know the laws in your state before getting married.** Laws are different in different states about how debt, money, and other assets are handled, legally, between married partners. In some states, any money earned, or debts incurred, during marriage belong to both spouses. If you're worried about a partner taking your money or hurting your credit, do not get married. Marriage is a legally binding contract between two people. If you're worried about keeping financial independence after marriage, talk to a lawyer before getting married.

- **Get a free credit report.** A credit report can tell you if any accounts were opened using your name and SSN. Federal law says that you can get a free copy of your credit report every 12 months. Using your SSN, you can get your free credit report through the website annualcreditreport.com or by calling 877-322-8228.

- **Protect your credit.** If your credit report shows activity that you don't recognize, you can report it to one of three credit bureaus (Equifax, Experian, or TransUnion). The credit bureau will start an investigation. You can ask the credit bureaus to freeze your credit so that no one can open new accounts or loans in your name. You can also request the credit bureau to issue a "fraud alert" in your name. A fraud alert makes it harder for someone to open an account in your name.

- **Save your money.** If you can do so safely, begin to save any money you can and put it in a place the abuser cannot get to. You might hide cash or items you can later sell, or you might open a bank account the abuser doesn't know about. If you open a new account, be aware that mail associated with the account might come to your address.

- **Plan for a future job.** You may worry that you don't have enough education or job experience to get a good job without a partner. Child care or transportation might be a concern. Local domestic-violence shelters can connect you to local resources to help with child care, transportation, healthcare, and job training. Many shelters can help you find work while you get new housing, food assistance, and other support in place.

- **Know your job rights.** If you have a job, know that many states have laws that protect your right to take time off to go to court for violence and abuse issues. Many states also have laws to protect you against discrimination on the job if you have experienced domestic violence or sexual assault. The Women's Legal Defense and Education Fund (WLDEF) offers a list of state laws that may help you.

What Do You Need to Know about Money When You Are Ready to Leave?

When you are getting ready to leave an abusive relationship, money issues may seem overwhelming. But you can take steps to care for yourself and your children. Gather important documents for you and your children, such as birth certificates and Social Security (SS) cards. You might also try to get copies of health-insurance cards and bank statements. These will increase your independence, and they will help with your case if you have divorce or child-custody hearings.

In case the abuser has opened credit cards in your name or other types of illegal financial activity, you should get a copy of your credit report.

You may not have time to gather much information before you go. That's okay. Collect what you can. The highest priority is getting out of the abusive relationship as safely as possible.

How Can You Financially Recover from Financial Abuse?

Make a plan to leave the abuser. Once you are away from that person, you can take steps to repair your credit and become financially independent.

- **Protect your credit.** By freezing your credit accounts or having a credit bureau issue a fraud alert, you can make it harder for someone to open accounts in your name.

- **Talk to a financial expert.** You can get free financial education and advice about dealing with debt, a mortgage, or credit issues from the nonprofit National Foundation for Credit Counseling (NFCC) at nfcc.org. An expert can help you make a step-by-step plan to repair your credit and rebuild your finances.

- **Use available resources.** Most states have assistance programs to help survivors of domestic violence. Find the resources offered in your state at the National Coalition Against Domestic Violence (NCADV) at ncadv.org.

- **Know your job rights.** Many states have laws that protect your right to take time off from a job to go to court for violence and abuse issues. Many states also have laws to protect you against discrimination on the job if you have experienced domestic violence or sexual assault. The WLDEF at legalmomentum.org offers a list of state laws that may help you.

Section 8.6

Digital Abuse

This section includes text excerpted from "Dating Violence and Abuse," Office on Women's Health (OWH), U.S. Department of Health and Human Services (HHS), September 13, 2018.

Digital abuse is a type of abuse that uses technology, especially texting or social media.

Who Are Involved in Digital Abuse?

Digital abuse is more common among younger adults, but it can happen to anyone who uses technology, such as smartphones or computers.

What Does Digital Abuse Include?

Digital abuse can include:

- Repeated unwanted calls or texts
- Harassment on social media
- Pressure to send nude or private pictures (called "sexting")
- Using texts or social media to check up on you, insult you, or control whom you can see or be friends with
- Demanding your passwords to social media sites and email
- Demanding that you reply right away to texts, emails, and calls

What Should You Do to Safeguard Yourself from Digital Abuse?

In a healthy relationship, both partners respect relationship boundaries. You do not have to send any photos that make you uncomfortable. Once you send a revealing photo, you have no control over who sees it. The other person can forward it or show it to others.

Chapter 9

When Abuse Turns Deadly

Chapter Contents

Section 9.1

Prevalence of Intimate Partner Homicide

This section includes text excerpted from "Murder-Suicide in Families," National Institute of Justice (NIJ), U.S. Department of Justice (DOJ), April 7, 2011. Reviewed October 2018.

Cases in which one intimate partner murders another and the children and then kills him- or herself are rare and usually garner widespread media coverage. This type of murder–suicide is called familicide. In almost all of these cases, the killer is a white, non-Hispanic man.

Cases in which women kill their male partners, their children, and themselves are extremely rare and thus gain even more widespread media coverage.

Risk Factors

Common characteristics of a murder–suicide in families include:

- Prior history of domestic violence

- Access to a gun

- Threats, especially increased threats with increased specificity

- Prior history of poor mental health or substance abuse, especially alcohol

The previous history of abuse is by far the most dominant risk factor. In one study, 82 percent of the men who killed their intimate partners were known to the authorities—treatment professionals, the military or the criminal justice system, for example.

In most cases, the man exhibits possessive, obsessive, and jealous behavior. There is a gradual buildup of tensions and conflicts after which an event leads the man to act. The triggering event is often the woman's announcement that she is leaving.

The time immediately after a woman leaves an abusive partner is the most dangerous.

Role of Guns

The data are clear: More incidents of murder–suicide occur with guns than with any other weapon. Access to a gun is a major risk factor in familicide because it allows the perpetrator to act on his or her rage and impulses.

In 591 murder–suicide, 92 percent were committed with a gun. States with less-restrictive gun-control laws have as much as eight times the rate of murder–suicide as those with the most-restrictive gun-control.

Compared to Canada, the United States has three times more familicide; compared to Britain, eight times more; and compared to Australia, 15 times more.

Role of Shelters

Domestic-violence shelters are meeting the needs of abuse survivors and their children, providing services such as housing, mental-health counseling, and legal assistance. Nearly three-quarters (74 percent) of domestic-violence survivors rate the assistance they received at their shelters as "very helpful," and another 18 percent rate it as "helpful."

Role of the Economy

The very low number of murder–suicide incidents makes it hard for researchers to understand exactly what role the economy plays in these cases. What is known is that economic distress is a factor, but it is only one of several factors that trigger a man to murder his family. In most cases, the couple has a history of disagreements over many issues, most commonly money, sex, and child-rearing.

Although personal economics like the loss of a job may be one of several critical factors, most experts agree that the strength or weakness of the national economy is not related to the frequency of murder–suicide, despite media coverage that suggests otherwise.

Section 9.2

Intimate Partner Strangulation

"Intimate Partner Strangulation,"
© 2019 Omnigraphics. Reviewed October 2018.

Intimate partner violence (IPV) is domestic violence by a current or former spouse or partner in an intimate relationship against the other spouse or partner. Strangulation is an extremely dangerous and fatal form of IPV. It is defined as the compression of blood vessels or air-filled passages of the neck using fingers, hands, elbows, shoulders, legs, or an object in an attempt to impede normal circulation or breathing of a person. While other physical expressions of domestic violence, such as hitting, slapping, or kicking are undoubtedly terrible, they do not bode homicide the way strangulation does. Most cases of strangulation leave little or no visible bruises and pose difficulties for law-enforcement agencies, medical professionals, family, and friends in identifying strangulation in the context of IPV. When perpetrators of IPV strangle their victims, the act is considered an extreme tactic of power and control, wherein the perpetrator physically exercises control over the victim's next breath.

Strangulation versus Choking

Most cases of strangulation are commonly reported as "choking." It is, therefore, important for law-enforcement agencies and medical professionals to acknowledge and investigate incidents of strangulation as separate from choking. Choking is different from strangulation. Choking refers to the partial or complete obstruction of the trachea (airway) through accidental swallowing of food or a foreign object, and is associated with minimal long-term injury once the object causing the obstruction is removed. Strangulation, on the other hand, is intentional pressure or compression, applied externally to the neck. Strangulation restricts the passage of blood and air to and from the brain and can result in long-term repercussions or death, even after the external pressure on the neck ceases.

Fatality of Strangulation

Death by strangulation can occur within a few minutes. In some cases, death may occur in the days or weeks following strangulation. Surveys indicate that nonfatal strangulation is a major risk factor for the future homicide of women. This underscores the importance of screening for abuse by strangulation in medical and emergency department settings. Research studies based on attempted homicide cases that are identified through law-enforcement agencies, the district attorney's office, community domestic-violence shelters and advocacy programs, or trauma centers indicate that strangulation comprises 10 percent of IPV. Research also indicates that victims of prior nonfatal strangulations are associated with over six-fold odds of becoming victims of an attempted homicide, and greater than seven-fold odds of becoming victims of completed homicides.

Common Symptoms and Signs of Strangulation

Strangulation is usually associated with a change in vision (blurriness), breathing, memory, voice, swallowing, and emotions. The victim may lose consciousness and experience loss of balance, especially of the legs. External signs include abrasions, bruises, bloody (red) eyes, or redness on the neck. There may also be ligament marks from objects used for the abuse, such as rope or fabric.

Other "hard signs" of strangulation injury include:

- Hoarseness or stridor

- Lung damage

- Vomiting and aspiration of food or fluids

- Swelling of the tongue or oropharynx

- Involuntary urination and defecation (an important indicator of homicide)

- Conjunctival or facial petechiae (small red or purple spots caused by hemorrhage under the skin)

- Pregnancy loss

Treating Nonfatal Strangulation in the Healthcare Setting

As with any traumatic injury, the primary step in treating a strangulation injury involves examining the victim's airway, breathing, and circulation in the context of symptoms, clinical signs, and/or patient's history. Resuscitative interventions are usually put into place before radiologic tests are performed. But, in the absence of any "hard signs" of a strangulation injury, laboratory and radiographic evaluations are usually not recommended and patients are discharged from emergency settings with strict precautions and advice for monitoring by family or friends. Symptomatic patients, on the other hand, are placed under observation and referred to the appropriate level of care in an emergency or hospital setting. Specialists from departments including trauma surgery, neurology, otolaryngology, and psychiatry are usually consulted for appropriate care and rehabilitation, and metabolic anomalies are addressed using specific therapeutic interventions.

Obtaining Justice for Victims

Most cases of nonfatal strangulations evade prosecution. Strangulation is minimized by both the victim and the legal system. The most common reason for this reality is the victim's reluctance or refusal to seek legal redress. While there have been increasing cases of partners reporting strangulation attempts, a majority of the victims of strangulation find themselves trapped in the vicious cycle of power and control in which abusers manipulate their victims, demean their self-esteem, and exercise absolute control over them. Abusers often promise their victims that they will reform, and the victims often live in denial of the abuse perpetrated on them.

It is common for victims of strangulation to retract their statements after initially cooperating with the investigation and to then express their unwillingness to testify against the abuser. This seems to happen because the victims fear retaliation. The abusers also appeal to the victim's weaknesses and insecurities, including their love for their children and fear of losing financial support or social standing. Whatever be the reason, unwillingness to participate in the legal process results in challenges to the criminal justice system while allowing abusers to evade arrest and prosecution.

As mentioned earlier, the greatest obstacle to prosecuting strangulation cases is the absence of visible injuries. This, further compounded by the reluctance of victims to provide information about the abuse, makes it difficult for medical personnel and law- enforcement officials to collect and document evidence of strangulation. Over the years, however, the focus has shifted from victim participation in the legal process to a reliance on hearsay evidence by victims or witnesses. All this notwithstanding, the lack of evidence and the limitations placed by the courts on the type of hearsay evidence permissible at the trial continue to remain major stumbling blocks in the successful prosecution of such domestic-violence cases, and of strangulation cases in particular.

Because of the particularly dangerous nature of strangulation crimes, efforts are being made to develop new investigation protocols for collecting evidence and prosecuting abusers. Until more effective protocols are in place, however, strangulation may continue to remain a manifestation of an ongoing pattern of abuse and IPV homicide.

References

1. "Domestic Violence and Strangulation: A Guide for Victims and Professionals," New York State Office for the Prevention of Domestic Violence (OPDV), July 14, 2016.

2. "Non-Fatal Strangulation Is an Important Risk Factor for Homicide of Women," U.S. National Library of Medicine (NLM), October 1, 2009.

3. "A Systematic Review of the Epidemiology of Nonfatal Strangulation, a Human Rights and Health Concern," U.S. National Library of Medicine (NLM), November 2014.

Section 9.3

Firearms and Domestic Violence

"Firearms and Domestic Violence," © 2016
Omnigraphics. Reviewed October 2018.

When domestic violence occurs in households where firearms are present, the violence is much more likely to be deadly. Research has shown that the presence of a gun in the household increases the risk of homicide by 500 percent for women in domestic violence situations. Firearms also frequently play a role in nonlethal domestic violence incidents. A survey of female domestic violence survivors in California shelters found that the abuser had used a gun to threaten or harm the victim in 64 percent of households that contained firearms.

Congress has attempted to address the link between firearms and domestic-violence deaths by passing laws aimed at restricting the purchase and possession of guns by perpetrators of domestic violence. One such law, known as the Lautenberg Amendment, prohibits firearms sales to people who have been convicted of misdemeanor domestic violence offenses involving the use of physical force or the threatened use of a deadly weapon. It also covers people who are subject to domestic violence personal protection orders. Under federal law, the offender must be a spouse (current or former), parent, or guardian of the victim; share a child in common with the victim; or have lived with the victim as an intimate partner.

Over 109,000 people were denied the purchase of a firearm from 1998–2014 because records showed that they had been convicted of a misdemeanor crime of domestic violence. More than 46,000 people who were subject to domestic-violence protection orders had their gun-purchase applications denied during that same period. Research also suggests that the law served as a deterrent to prevent other people involved in domestic-violence cases from applying to purchase firearms.

Preventing Gun Violence

Critics contend, however, that the federal laws concerning firearms and domestic violence have significant limitations. For instance, federal law does not protect people in certain types of relationships, such as people who are dating but do not live together or have a child together. Yet dating relationships carry a high risk of domestic violence. Data from 2008 showed that people who were currently dating made up nearly half of all homicide victims involving intimate partner abuse. In addition, federal law does not prohibit gun purchases by people convicted of domestic violence against family members other than spouses or children. Therefore, parents and siblings who are victims of domestic abuse are not protected.

Another shortcoming mentioned by critics is that the federal prohibitions on firearm possession by domestic abusers fail to ensure that abusers relinquish any guns that they already own. As a result, many people who are subject to protective orders or who have been convicted on domestic violence charges continue to possess firearms in violation of the law. Studies have shown that perpetrators who continued to possess firearms after they were prohibited from doing so were more likely to attempt homicide or threaten their partners with guns than those who had relinquished their firearms.

Critics also point out that laws prohibiting domestic-violence perpetrators from possessing firearms cannot be effective without requiring a federal criminal background check prior to the sale of any gun. Sales by unlicensed, private sellers are not subject to federal background checks, however, and many states do not report comprehensive information about domestic-violence convictions and protection orders to federal databases. As a result, many domestic abusers are able to obtain guns in violation of the law. Studies show that they often use these guns against their intimate partners. In states that require a background check before every handgun sale, 38 percent fewer women are shot to death in domestic violence incidents.

Although many gun-control proposals are controversial, policies that aim to protect victims of domestic violence receive widespread public support. A 2013 poll found that over 80 percent of the people surveyed, including 75 percent of people who owned guns, supported laws prohibiting people who violate a domestic-violence restraining order from owning firearms for ten years. The poll also indicated that more than 72 percent of both gun owners and nongun owners supported laws prohibiting people who are convicted of domestic violence from owning firearms for ten years.

References

1. "Domestic Violence and Firearms Policy Summary," Law Center to Prevent Gun Violence, May 11, 2014.

2. Sugarmann, Josh. "For Women, Gun Violence Often Linked to Domestic Violence," Huffington Post, January 10, 2014.

Section 9.4

Assessing Risk of Lethality: Are You in Danger?

This section contains text excerpted from the following sources: Text in this section begins with excerpts from "A Closer Look at the Lethality Assessment Program," National Institute of Justice (NIJ), U.S. Department of Justice (DOJ), July 26, 2015. Reviewed October 2018; Text under the heading "How Effective Are Lethality Assessment Programs for Addressing Intimate Partner Violence?" is excerpted from "How Effective Are Lethality Assessment Programs for Addressing Intimate Partner Violence?" National Institute of Justice (NIJ), U.S. Department of Justice (DOJ), June 11, 2018.

A Closer Look at the Lethality Assessment Program

The dual goals of the Lethality Assessment Program (LAP) are to educate intimate partner violence (IPV) victim–survivors about risk factors for homicide and to connect them with support and safety-planning services. Collaboration, education, and self-determination are the touchstones of this intervention.

Near the end of an investigation at an IPV incident scene, the police officer will administer a brief risk-assessment screen to the victim–survivor. This "Lethality Screen" is an 11-item questionnaire that assesses the victim–survivor's level of risk for being killed by the IPV offender. It is suggested that the officer use the Lethality Screen when a past or current intimate-partner relationship is involved and a "manifestation of danger" is evidenced by at least one of the following:

1. The officer believes that an assault or other violent act has occurred, whether or not there was probable cause for arrest,

2. The officer is concerned for the victim–survivor's safety once the officers leave the incident scene,

3. The officer is responding to a domestic-violence call from a victim-survivor or at a location where IPV has occurred in the past, or

4. The officer has a gut feeling that the victim–survivor is in danger.

If a victim–survivor screens in as "high risk," which means an increased risk of homicide, the police officer responds proactively with the "Protocol Referral." The police officer conveys to the high-risk victim–survivors the danger that they are in—and lets them know that people in similar situations have been killed. The officer also calls the local 24-hour domestic-violence hotline at the collaborating advocacy organization for information on planning for the victim–survivor's safety and gives the victim–survivor the choice of speaking directly with the hotline advocate.

After initiating the call, the officer provides the hotline advocate with basic information that will help the advocate develop safety suggestions for the victim–survivor. If the victim–survivor chooses not to speak on the telephone, the hotline advocate provides the officer with some immediate safety-planning tips for the next 24 hours to share with the victim–survivor.

If the victim–survivor chooses to speak with the hotline advocate, the conversation is brief and focused, both because the officer must return to service and because the victim–survivor might not be in a position to absorb a great deal of information. Being on the phone with the victim–survivor at an IPV incident scene is a different type of call for a hotline advocate: Time is limited, and the victim–survivor might not have come to terms with the seriousness of the situation yet. Hotline counselors are trained to use special guidelines to:

1. Gain the victim–survivor trust,

2. Reinforce the officer's warning about the danger that the victim–survivor is in (and thus reinforce the partnership with law enforcement),

3. Educate the victim–survivor in immediate safety-planning, and

4. Actively encourage the victim–survivor to seek available services.

How Effective Are Lethality Assessment Programs for Addressing Intimate Partner Violence?

Research on risk-screening programs for victims of domestic violence (DV) shows that the programs can increase the likelihood that victims of IPV and DV seek help and create safety plans—which, ultimately, can result in a decrease in violence. Research showed mixed results on predicting lethal violence, however.

Intimate partner violence is a pervasive issue across the United States, with a significant (30 to 70 percent) portion of femicides occurring as a result of IPV. Beginning in 2003, the Maryland Network

Against Domestic Violence developed the Lethality Assessment Program as a way for first responders to identify victims of intimate partner violence who are at the greatest risk of being killed. The program emphasizes self-determination and is designed to empower victim–survivors toward decisions of self-care.

A previous Lethality Assessment Program study focused on specific populations and sought to expand the body of evidence on the program's utility. This quasi-experimental study had four goals:

1. **Evaluation:** Examine the effectiveness of the program in reducing intimate partner violence, increasing rates of emergency planning, and increasing help-seeking by victims.

2. **Validation:** Assess the predictive capability of the Lethality Screen tool.

3. **Implementation fidelity:** Track how many high-risk women actually spoke to a service provider in accordance with Lethality Assessment Program's protocol.

4. **Satisfaction:** Assess victim satisfaction with the police response and the Lethality Assessment Program itself.

Researchers collected data on victims of IPV in seven police jurisdictions in Oklahoma. The researchers initially faced some difficulties in recruiting participants, but over a period of approximately three-and-a-half years, several hundred women agreed to participate and were reached for follow-up interviews. The age of participants varied greatly (ages 18–79) and the participants were racially diverse; about 43 percent were white, 30 percent were African American, 10 percent were Native American, and 8 percent were Latina. About two-thirds of participants had children living in their homes, and about half had completed high school or earned a GED (General Educational Development).

Results

The researchers found that, although the program did not appear to have a significant effect on reducing the frequency of IPV, at follow-up, it appeared to significantly reduce the severity and frequency of the violence that the victim–survivors experienced.

In addition to reducing the severity and frequency of violence, the Lethality Assessment Program also appeared to increase the likelihood that the victim–survivors sought help and developed safety plans. Women who participated in the program were significantly more likely to remove or hide their partner's weapons, to obtain formal services for domestic violence, to establish safety strategies with friends and family, and to obtain some form of protection against their partner.

Given these results, the researchers recommended the Lethality Assessment Program as a collaborative police—social service intervention with an emerging evidence base.

In terms of its ability to predict violence, the Lethality Screen performed well in predicting that serious or lethal violence would not occur, though it did not perform as well when predicting that serious or lethal violence would occur. This discrepancy is by design, to minimize the possibility that a woman who screens at low risk for severe violence, in fact, becomes a victim of severe violence (i.e., a false negative). That intentional design resulted in a high ratio of women who screen at high risk for violence but do not experience the predicted violence (i.e., false positives).

The study also found that the Lethality Screen has a 92.86 percent sensitivity for predicting near-fatal violence, meaning that for every 13 women correctly screened as high risk for near-fatal violence, only one woman is incorrectly screened as low risk.

The study also found that the Lethality Screen has a positive predictive value of 13.27 percent, meaning that for every woman correctly screened as high risk for near-fatal violence, between six and seven additional women are incorrectly screened as high risk and will not experience the predicted violence. Again, the study's authors emphasize that this is by design. Results of the Lethality Screen correlate significantly with survivors' own assessment of the likelihood that their partner will physically abuse or seriously hurt them in the next year.

To test the implementation fidelity of the Lethality Assessment Program, researchers tracked how many of the women classified as high risk actually spoke to a hotline counselor. By the end of the intervention, 61.6 percent of high-risk women had spoken to a counselor.

Researchers uncovered two factors associated with who spoke to a hotline counselor: the severity of the violence of the incident that preceded the Lethality Screen, and the severity of posttraumatic stress disorder (PTSD) symptoms. Researchers found that the more severe the preceding incident of violence was, the more likely the victim would speak to the hotline counselor. They also found that women reporting more PTSD symptoms were less likely to speak to a hotline counselor; for each additional PTSD symptom that women experienced, they were 15 percent less likely to speak to the hotline counselor. The study's authors suggest that increased training for police on PTSD symptoms and the mental-health effects of IPV could help police implement the Lethality Assessment Program more effectively to better connect victims to needed services.

Researchers found that victims who received assistance through the Lethality Assessment Program reported being more satisfied with the police response. Researchers suggested that the program is particularly promising because "a collaborative response that provides offender accountability (through criminal-justice sanctions) and survivor safety (through social-service intervention) makes available a broader scope of intervention." To confirm the positive effects of the Lethality Assessment Program, researchers encouraged replication of this study in other jurisdictions.

Chapter 10

Physical Effects of Domestic Violence

Chapter Contents

Section 10.1

Types of Domestic Violence Injuries

"Types of Domestic Violence Injuries,"
© 2016 Omnigraphics. Reviewed October 2018.

Certain types and patterns of physical injuries are more commonly caused by domestic violence assaults than by accidents, participation in sports, or other means. Examples include some types of bruises and scrapes on the head, face, neck, arms, or abdomen; injuries to the genitals or rectum; broken or loose teeth; and ruptured eardrums. Being aware of these types of injuries and watching for suspicious patterns can help identify and protect people who are experiencing physical abuse.

Most of the physical injuries associated with domestic violence are caused by blunt-force trauma. This type of trauma can occur when a moving object (such as a fist, foot, or weapon) strikes the body, or when a moving body strikes a fixed object (such as a wall, floor, or table). Injuries can also result from actions such as grabbing, choking, pinching, and biting. All of these sources of injury leave physical signs that may raise suspicions of domestic violence.

Types of Injuries

Bruises are among the most common types of injuries found in survivors of domestic violence. Although bruises can have many accidental causes, certain locations and distributions of bruises may raise concerns about physical abuse. Bruising occurs when physical trauma causes blood to leak out of small blood vessels and pool in surrounding tissues. This blood shows through the surface of the skin as discoloration and swelling. The size, shape, and color of bruises vary, so their appearance cannot be reliably used to determine the date of an injury or the degree of force involved. Bruises in the following locations, however, are often caused by domestic violence:

- Tiny "pinpoint" bruises, or petechiae, around the eyes or mouth may result from choking or strangulation attempts.

- Finger-shaped bruises on the throat, face, arms, or thighs are often caused by forceful grabbing, holding, or pinching.

- Counter-pressure bruises on the spine or hipbones often result from forceful restraint on the ground or against a wall.

- Black eyes are often caused by a punch to the face or a skull fracture.

Abrasions are injuries affecting the top layers of the skin that are typically caused by scraping, rubbing, or crushing. They appear red in color and may bleed or ooze slightly. Abrasions can provide medical professionals with valuable clues about physical abuse because they always occur at the site of impact, and they sometimes indicate the direction of impact or retain an imprint of the causative object. For instance, an abrasion from a kick may retain an imprint of the tread of a shoe.

Lacerations occur when the skin and other soft body tissues are torn, split, stretched, or compressed as a result of blunt-force trauma. Lacerations differ from cuts, which are caused by impacts with sharp objects rather than blunt objects or surfaces. Laceration wounds tend to be irregular and jagged. Lacerations to the lips and mouth from being smashed against the teeth are often caused by domestic violence. Although the rate of healing depends on many factors, doctors can sometimes estimate the date of injury by examining a laceration.

Some other injuries that are considered characteristic of domestic violence include cigarette burns, rope burns, bite marks, and welts that retain an imprint of a hand or an object used as a weapon.

Patterns of Injury

The location and distribution of physical injuries on the body can also provide indications of domestic violence. Certain patterns of injury are commonly found in cases of physical abuse, including:

- Frequent injuries to the head and neck, which are the location of 50 percent of domestic violence injuries.

- Injuries distributed among the body parts covered by a bathing suit—such as the breasts, buttocks, and genitals—which are usually hidden under clothing.

- Bilateral injuries affecting both sides of the body, and especially the arms and legs.

- Defensive injuries to the palms, forearms, feet, back, or buttocks from trying to block punches or protect against an attack.

- Bruises or other injuries in various stages of healing, or evidence of both old and new injuries, which may suggest repeated or ongoing abuse.

- Unexplained injuries or injuries that do not fit the stated cause.

- Untreated injuries, or injuries for which the victim has delayed seeking medical attention.

References

1. Dryden-Edwards, Roxanne. "Domestic Violence Signs and Symptoms," eMedicineHealth, 2016.

2. "Injuries Associated with Assault and Abuse," Forensics Talk, September 2006.

Section 10.2

Medical Consequences of Domestic Violence

This section includes text excerpted from "Intimate Partner Violence: Consequences," Centers for Disease Control and Prevention (CDC), August 22, 2017.

The Cost of Intimate Partner Violence to Society

The costs of intimate partner violence (IPV) against women alone in 1995 exceeded an estimated $5.8 billion. These costs included nearly $4.1 billion in the direct costs of medical and mental healthcare and nearly $1.8 billion in the indirect costs of lost productivity. This is generally considered an underestimate because the costs associated with the criminal justice system were not included.

In 2003, IPV costs exceeded $8.3 billion, which included $460 million for rape, $6.2 billion for physical assault, $461 million for stalking, and $1.2 billion in the value of lost lives.

The increased annual healthcare costs for victims of IPV can persist as much as 15 years after the cessation of abuse. Victims of severe IPV lose nearly eight million days of paid work—the equivalent of more than 32,000 full-time jobs—and almost 5.6 million days of household productivity each year.

Women who experience severe aggression by men (e.g., not being allowed to go to work or school, or having their lives or their children's lives threatened) are more likely to have been unemployed in the past, have health problems, and be receiving public assistance.

Consequences of Intimate Partner Violence

Approximately 27 percent of women and 11 percent of men in the United States have experienced contact sexual violence, physical violence, or stalking by an intimate partner and reported at least one measured impact related to these or other forms of violence in that relationship. In general, victims of repeated violence over time experience more serious consequences than victims of one-time incidents. The following list describes some, but not all, of the consequences of IPV.

Physical

Nearly one in four women (23%) and one in seven men (14%) aged 18 and older in the United States have been the victim of severe physical violence by an intimate partner in their lifetime. Nearly, 14 percent of women and four percent of men have been injured as a result of IPV that included contact sexual violence, physical violence, or stalking by an intimate partner in their lifetime. In 2010, 241 males and 1,095 females were murdered by an intimate partner.

Apart from deaths and injuries, physical violence by an intimate partner is associated with a number of adverse health outcomes. Several health conditions associated with intimate partner violence may be a direct result of the physical violence (for example, bruises, knife wounds, broken bones, traumatic brain injury (TBI), back, or pelvic pain, headaches). Other conditions are the result of the impact of intimate partner violence on the cardiovascular, gastrointestinal, endocrine, and immune systems through chronic stress or other mechanisms.

Examples of health conditions associated with IPV include:

- Asthma
- Bladder and kidney infections
- Circulatory conditions
- Cardiovascular disease (CVD)
- Fibromyalgia (FM)

- Irritable bowel syndrome (IBS)
- Chronic pain syndromes (CPS)
- Central nervous system disorders (CNS)
- Gastrointestinal disorders
- Joint disease
- Migraines and headaches

Children might become injured during IPV incidents between their parents. A large overlap exists between IPV and child maltreatment.

- Reproductive
- Gynecological disorders
- Pelvic inflammatory disease (PID)
- Sexual dysfunction
- Sexually transmitted infections (STIs), including human immunodeficiency virus (HIV)/acquired immunodeficiency syndrome (AIDS)
- Delayed prenatal care
- Preterm delivery
- Pregnancy difficulties like low birth weight babies and perinatal deaths
- Unintended pregnancy

Psychological

Physical violence is typically accompanied by emotional or psychological abuse. IPV–whether sexual, physical, or psychological–can lead to various psychological consequences for victims.

- Anxiety
- Depression
- Symptoms of posttraumatic stress disorder (PTSD)
- Antisocial behavior
- Suicidal behavior in females
- Low self-esteem

- Inability to trust others, especially in intimate relationships
- Fear of intimacy
- Emotional detachment
- Sleep disturbances
- Flashbacks
- Replaying assault in the mind

Social

Victims of IPV sometimes face the following social consequences:

- Restricted access to services
- Strained relationships with health providers and employers
- Isolation from social networks
- Homelessness

Health Behaviors

Women with a history of IPV are more likely to display behaviors that present further health risks (e.g., substance abuse, alcoholism, suicide attempts) than women without a history of IPV.

IPV is associated with a variety of negative health behaviors. Studies show that the more severe the violence, the stronger its relationship to negative health behaviors by victims.

- Engaging in high-risk sexual behavior
- Unprotected sex
- Decreased condom use
- Early sexual initiation
- Choosing unhealthy sexual partners
- Multiple sex partners
- Trading sex for food, money, or other items
- Using harmful substances
- Smoking cigarettes
- Drinking alcohol

- Drinking alcohol and driving

- Illicit drug use

- Unhealthy diet-related behaviors

- Fasting

- Vomiting

- Abusing diet pills

- Overeating

- Overuse of health services

Section 10.3

Domestic Abuse and Traumatic Brain Injury

"Domestic Violence and Traumatic Brain Injury,"
© 2016 Omnigraphics. Reviewed October 2018.

Traumatic brain injury (TBI) is a type of damage to the brain that results from an external physical force being applied to the head. TBI may occur when the head strikes a stationary object, such as the ground or a wall, or when the head is struck by a hard object, such as a baseball bat. TBI can also result from forceful shaking of the head, which causes the brain to move around within the skull, or from penetration of the skull by a foreign object, such as a bullet or a knife. Brain injury may also occur from the deprivation of oxygen through choking or near drowning.

Although media attention has raised awareness of the risk of TBI among athletes and military veterans, little consideration has been given to the prevalence of TBI among women who are survivors of domestic violence. Yet research has shown that 90 percent of all injuries from domestic violence occur to the face, head, or neck. One study found that 30 percent of women who sought emergency medical treatment for domestic violence injuries had lost consciousness at least once, and 67 percent showed symptoms of TBI. Another study found that

75 percent of the battered women in three domestic-violence shelters reported receiving a brain injury from an intimate partner, while 50 percent had sustained multiple brain injuries.

Many of the common acts of physical aggression that are used by perpetrators of domestic violence can cause brain injuries, including beating someone on the head with fists or other objects, pushing someone down stairs or into a solid object, shaking someone strenuously, choking or holding someone underwater, and shooting or stabbing someone in the face or head. Victims of domestic violence may not realize that they have sustained a brain injury, especially if they do not seek or receive medical treatment. But a history of TBI leads to a substantially greater risk of sustaining further brain injuries, and repeated brain injuries are known to have a cumulative effect.

Effects of Traumatic Brain Injury (TBI)

TBI affects people differently, so the symptoms may vary depending on the individual. There are some initial symptoms that are fairly common, however, including a brief loss of consciousness, dizziness, headaches, loss of short-term memory, slower processing of information, fatigue, and sensitivity to light and sound. With repeated injuries or lack of medical treatment, people with TBI may experience increasing levels of physical, cognitive, and functional disabilities. Some of the most common problems include:

- Weakness, clumsiness, and motor control difficulties

- Communication difficulties, including slurring of speech and problems with word finding

- Issues involving balance, vision, and hearing

- Difficulty concentrating or paying attention, along with increased distractibility

- Issues with problem-solving and task completion

- Difficulty with long-term goal setting, prioritizing, planning, and organization

- Increased tension, anxiety, and irritability

- Impulsiveness and lapses in judgment

- Increased risk of depression and substance abuse

Survivors of domestic violence may experience a wide range of challenges related to TBI. Slower reaction time and inattentiveness, for instance, may increase the risk that physical abuse will result in further brain injuries. Abusive partners may also try to use the symptoms of a brain injury as tools to manipulate and control their victims. For instance, they may take advantage of short-term memory loss to make victims doubt their memories and perceptions of past abuse.

Survivors with TBI may also find it more difficult to assess situations, make plans for their own safety, leave an abusive partner, and live independently or in a domestic-violence shelter. They may also have trouble accessing support services, remembering appointments, and navigating the criminal justice system. Testifying in child custody or criminal court proceedings requires survivors to remember details of abuse and communicate them clearly and sequentially. Yet these abilities may be compromised in individuals with TBI, which may reduce their credibility in court and negatively affect their outcomes. Domestic-violence survivors with TBI may also experience problems caring for children or maintaining employment.

Supporting Survivors with TBI

Advocates and service providers for survivors of domestic violence must be aware of the high risk of TBI among their clients. Shelters and counseling facilities should put screening procedures in place to identify people with TBI, train staff to address their special needs and challenges, and implement organizational policies to better support them. Some additional tips for helping domestic-violence survivors with TBI include:

- Treat people as individuals. Strive to understand and accommodate their unique challenges and strengths, provide positive and respectful feedback, and empower them to make necessary changes in their lives.

- Be aware that an abuse survivor may have TBI even in the absence of a formal diagnosis. If TBI has been diagnosed, however, do not assume that the individual has cognitive or functional disabilities.

- Recognize that behavioral concerns and noncompliance with shelter rules may be linked to an underlying TBI. Provide accommodations as needed—such as a planner to help a person with memory deficits remember communal responsibilities—to enable abuse survivors to adapt to the shelter environment.

- Keep in mind that recovery from a brain injury takes time and does not necessarily happen in a linear or sequential manner. As a result, people's needs may change frequently.

- Adapt safety-planning to make it more appropriate for people living with TBI. Many safety-planning discussions require domestic-violence survivors to envision hypothetical circumstances or remember long lists of actions to be executed in a crisis. But these discussions can be challenging for people with TBI who struggle with abstract thought or memory problems. To make the discussions more productive, experts recommend minimizing outside distractions, holding shorter meetings more frequently, focusing on a single topic at each meeting, making action items simple and concrete, and concluding by summarizing the information and checking for understanding.

- Educate others about TBI and its intersection with domestic violence.

References

1. "The Intersection of Brain Injury and Domestic Violence," New York State Coalition Against Domestic Violence, n.d.

2. "Traumatic Brain Injury and Domestic Violence Facts," Alabama Department of Rehabilitation Services, 2012.

Section 10.4

Domestic Violence and HIV Risk

This section includes text excerpted from "Intersection of Intimate Partner Violence and HIV in Women," Centers for Disease Control and Prevention (CDC), February 2014. Reviewed October 2018.

What We Know about Intimate Partner Violence and Human Immunodeficiency Virus (HIV) in Women

Intimate partner violence (IPV) includes physical violence, sexual violence, threats of physical or sexual violence, stalking, and psychological aggression (including coercive tactics) by a current or former intimate partner.

Findings from the 2010 National Intimate Partner and Sexual Violence Survey (NISVS) indicate that 35.6 percent of women in the United States have experienced rape, physical violence, or stalking by an intimate partner in their lifetime, and 5.9 percent or 6.9 million women experienced these forms of violence in the year prior to the survey.

In addition, one in five women has experienced an attempted, completed, or alcohol-drug facilitated rape (defined as a physically forced or threatened vaginal, oral, and/or anal penetration) in their lifetime, mostly by a current or former partner.

Approximately 80 percent of female victims of rape experienced their first rape before the age of 25. Nearly one in two women have experienced other forms of sexual violence in their lifetime (e.g., sexual coercion, unwanted sexual contact). Over 1.1 million people in the United States are estimated to be living with the human immunodeficiency virus (HIV) and nearly one in five is unaware of their infection. Approximately 50,000 Americans become infected with HIV each year. Women and adolescent girls accounted for 20 percent of new HIV infections in the United States in 2010 and represented approximately 21 percent of HIV diagnoses among adults and adolescents in 2011.

African Americans bear the greatest burden of HIV among women; Hispanic women are disproportionately affected. Of new infections in 2010, 64 percent occurred in blacks, 18 percent were in whites, and 15 percent were in Hispanics/Latinas. The rate of new infections among black women was 20 times that of white women and over four times the rate among Hispanic/Latina women.

The most common methods of HIV transmission among women are high-risk heterosexual sexual contact (87 percent for black women, 86 percent for Hispanic women) and injection drug use.

Links between Intimate Partner Violence and HIV

The association between violence against women and risk for HIV infection has been the focus of a growing number of studies. Findings from these studies indicate:

- Women and men who report a history of IPV victimization are more likely than those who do not to report behaviors known to increase the risk for HIV, including injection drug use, treatment for a sexually transmitted infection (STI), giving or receiving money or drugs for sex, and anal sex without a condom in the past year. This is true even when other factors such as demographic characteristics, other unhealthy behaviors (smoking, heavy drinking, high body mass index (BMI)) and negative health conditions (e.g., stroke, disability, and asthma) are similar.

- HIV-positive women in the United States experience IPV at rates that are higher than for the general population. Across a number of studies, the rate of IPV among HIV-positive women (55 percent) was double the national rate, and the rates of childhood sexual abuse (39 percent) and childhood physical abuse (42 percent) were more than double the national rate.

- Rates of violence victimization among HIV-positive women are comparable to those for HIV-negative women drawn from similar populations and with similar levels of HIV risk behaviors. However, HIV-positive women may experience abuse that is more frequent and more severe.

- Women in relationships with violence have four times the risk of contracting STIs, including HIV, than women in relationships without violence. Fear of violence can influence whether some women get tested for HIV. However, in one U.S. study, fear of partner notification and partner violence were not statistically associated with women's decisions to get or not get an HIV test.

- Sexual abuse in childhood and forced sexual initiation in adolescence are associated with increased HIV risk-taking behaviors, including sex with multiple partners, sex with unfamiliar partners, sex with older partners, alcohol-related risky sex, anal sex, and low rates of condom use among 17–20 year olds as well as HIV infection in adult women.

Studies of HIV-Positive Women

Several studies have examined the relationship between violence and the timing of becoming infected with HIV or disclosing HIV status. These studies suggest that IPV can be both a risk factor for HIV and a consequence of HIV.

A history of victimization is a significant risk factor for unprotected sex for both HIV-positive women and men. HIV-positive women and gay/bisexual men reporting a history of violence perpetration are also more likely to report engaging in unprotected sex, particularly when drugs were used in conjunction with sex.

HIV serostatus disclosure may be an initiating or contributing factor for partner violence. In U.S. samples, 0.5–4 percent of HIV-positive women report experiencing violence following HIV serostatus disclosure. Violence perceived to be triggered by HIV disclosure was as high in the years following diagnosis as in the initial year of diagnosis.

Relationship violence and trauma history can compromise the health and prevention practices of women living with HIV. Abused women have more than four times the rate of antiretroviral therapy failure (ATF), and of not practicing safe sex, as women who have not experienced abuse recently.

Studies of Women with a History of Abuse

Forced sex occurs in approximately 40–45 percent of physically violent intimate relationships and increases a woman's risk for STIs by two to ten times that of physical abuse alone. Women who had ever experienced forced sex were more likely to report HIV risky behaviors but less likely to have been tested for HIV despite the greater perceived likelihood of having HIV than nonabused women.

Women who had been physically abused as adults were only one-fifth as likely to report consistent condom use after two safer sex counseling sessions as women who had not been abused.

Women who had experienced both physical and sexual violence, compared to women who reported physical violence alone, were more likely to have had a recent STI (14 versus 4 percent), to have had an STI during the relationship (43 versus 20 percent), to use alcohol as a coping behavior (72 versus 47 percent), and to have been threatened when negotiating condom use (35 versus 10 percent).

Women who experience IPV or sexual violence are at greater risk for a range of adverse health consequences, including increased prevalence of stress, depression, and chronic anxiety than their nonabused counterparts. A national study found that women who experienced rape or stalking by any perpetrator or physical violence by an intimate partner in their lifetime were more likely than women who did not experience these forms of violence to report having asthma, diabetes, and irritable bowel syndrome (IBS), and both women and men who experienced these forms of violence were more likely to report frequent headaches, chronic pain, difficulty sleeping, activity limitations, poor physical health, and poor mental health than women and men who did not experience these forms of violence.

Significant associations have also been found between IPV and altered red blood cell and decreased T-cell function, and relationships between stress, depression, and other psychosocial factors with disease progression have been found in HIV infected persons.

Women with HIV have nearly six times the national rate of post-traumatic stress disorder (PTSD). Chronic depression has been associated with a greater decline in CD4 cell count in women living with HIV, and HIV-positive women with chronic depression are more than twice as likely to die than HIV-positive women with limited or no depression, even when other health and social factors are similar.

Chapter 11

Emotional and Socioeconomic Effects of Domestic Violence

Chapter Contents

Section 11.1

Violence against Women Can Take Lifelong Toll

This section includes text excerpted from "Effects of Violence against Women," Office on Women's Health (OWH), U.S. Department of Health and Human Services (HHS), September 13, 2018.

What Are the Short-Term Physical Effects of Violence against Women?

The short-term physical effects of violence can include minor injuries or serious conditions. They can include bruises, cuts, broken bones, or injuries to organs and other parts inside your body. Some physical injuries are difficult or impossible to see without scans, X-rays*, or other tests done by a doctor or nurse.

* *A type of high-energy radiation. In low doses, X-rays are used to diagnose diseases by making pictures of the inside of the body.*

Short-term physical effects of sexual violence can include:

- Vaginal bleeding or pelvic pain

- Unwanted pregnancy

- Sexually transmitted infections (STIs), including human immunodeficiency virus (HIV)

- Trouble sleeping or nightmares

If you are pregnant, a physical injury can hurt you and the unborn child. This is also true in some cases of sexual assault.

If you are sexually assaulted by the person you live with, and you have children in the home, think about your children's safety as well as your own. Violence in the home often includes child abuse. Many children who witness violence in the home are also victims of physical and suffer emotional harm from witnessing domestic violence abuse.

What Are the Long-Term Physical Effects of Violence against Women?

Violence against women, including sexual or physical violence, is linked to many long-term health problems. These can include:

- Arthritis

- Asthma

- Chronic pain

- Digestive problems, such as stomach ulcers

- Heart problems

- Irritable bowel syndrome (IBS)

- Nightmares and problems sleeping

- Migraine headaches

- Sexual problems, such as pain during sex

- Stress

- Problems with the immune system

Many women also have mental-health problems after violence. To cope with the effects of the violence, some women start misusing alcohol or drugs or engage in risky behaviors, such as having unprotected sex. Sexual violence can also affect someone's perception of their own bodies, leading to unhealthy eating patterns or eating disorders. If you are experiencing these problems, know that you are not alone. There are resources that can help you cope with these challenges.

How Is Traumatic Brain Injury (TBI) Related to Domestic Violence?

A serious risk of physical abuse is a concussion and traumatic brain injury (TBI) from being hit on the head or falling and hitting your head. TBI can cause:

- A headache or a feeling of pressure

- Loss of consciousness

- Confusion

- Dizziness

- Nausea and vomiting

- Slurred speech

- Memory loss

- Trouble concentrating

- Sleep loss

Some symptoms of TBI may take a few days to show up. Over a longer time, TBI can cause depression and anxiety. TBI can also cause problems with your thoughts, including the ability to make a plan and carry it out. This can make it more difficult for a woman in an abusive relationship to leave. Even if you think you are okay after head trauma, talk to your doctor or nurse if you have any of these symptoms. Treatment for TBI can help.

What Are the Mental-Health Effects of Violence against Women?

If you have experienced a physical or sexual assault, you may feel many emotions—fear, confusion, anger, or even being numb and not feeling much of anything. You may feel guilt or shame over being assaulted. Some people try to minimize the abuse or hide it by covering bruises and making excuses for the abuser.

If you've been physically or sexually assaulted or abused, know that it is not your fault. Getting help for assault or abuse can help prevent long-term mental-health effects and other health problems.

Long-term mental health effects of violence against women can include:

- **Posttraumatic stress disorder (PTSD).** This can be a result of experiencing trauma or having a shocking or scary experience, such as sexual assault or physical abuse. You may be easily startled, feeling tense or on edge, have difficulty sleeping, or have angry outbursts. You may also have trouble remembering things or have negative thoughts about yourself or others. If you think you have PTSD, talk to a mental-health professional.

- **Depression.** Depression is a serious illness, but you can get help to feel better. If you are feeling depressed, talk to a mental-health professional.

- **Anxiety.** This can be general anxiety about everything, or it can be a sudden attack of intense fear. Anxiety can get worse over time and interfere with your daily life. If you are experiencing anxiety, you can get help from a mental-health professional.

Other effects can include shutting people out, not wanting to do things you once enjoyed, not being able to trust others, and having low self-esteem.

Many women who have experienced violence cope with this trauma by using drugs, drinking alcohol, smoking, or overeating. Research shows that about 90 percent of women with substance-use problems had experienced physical or sexual violence.

Substance use may make you feel better in the moment, but it ends up making you feel worse in the long term. Drugs, alcohol, tobacco, or overeating will not help you forget or overcome the experience. Get help if you're thinking about or have been using alcohol or drugs to cope.

Who Can Help Women Who Have Been Abused or Assaulted?

After you get help for physical injuries, a mental-health professional can help you cope with emotional concerns. A counselor or therapist can work with you to deal with your emotions in healthy ways, build your self-esteem, and help you develop coping skills. You can ask your doctor for the name of a therapist, or you can search an online list of mental-health services.

Victims of sexual assault can also talk for free with someone who is trained to help through the National Sexual Assault Hotline over the phone at 800-656-HOPE (800-656-4673) or online.

What Are Some Other Effects of Violence against Women?

Violence against women has physical and mental health effects, but it can also affect the lives of women who are abused in other ways:

- **Work.** Experiencing a trauma such as sexual violence may interfere with someone's ability to work. Half of the women who experienced sexual assault had to quit or were forced to leave their jobs in the first year after the assault. Total lifetime income loss for these women is nearly $250,000 each.

- **Home.** Many women are forced to leave their homes to find safety because of violence. Research shows that half of all homeless women and children became homeless while trying to escape intimate partner violence.

- **School.** Women in college who are sexually assaulted may be afraid to report the assault and continue their education. But Title IX laws require schools to provide extra support for sexual-assault victims in college. Schools can help enforce no-contact orders with an abuser and provide mental-health counseling and school tutoring.

- **Children.** Women with children may stay with an abusive partner because they fear losing custody or contact with their children.

Sometimes, violence against women ends in death. More than half of women who are murdered each year are killed by an intimate partner. One in ten of these women experienced violence in the month before their death.

Section 11.2

Domestic Violence and Homelessness

This section includes text excerpted from "Domestic Violence and Homelessness," Administration for Children and Families (ACF), U.S. Department of Health and Human Services (HHS), July 9, 2015. Reviewed October 2018.

According to the Status Report on Hunger and Homelessness, U.S. Conference of Mayors (2012), domestic violence is the third leading cause of homelessness among families in the United States. Research shows that housing is one of the main needs identified by survivors at the time of shelter entry.

Domestic violence is devastating and costly for the families served by the U.S. Department of Health and Human Services (HHS) as well as for the local communities striving to help anyone in crisis. The experiences of domestic violence, poverty, and homelessness can seriously disrupt the well-being of a family, including their connections to community support.

The Administration for Children and Families (ACF) has an important role in helping families struggling with domestic violence. The toll of domestic violence on a child's well-being is life changing; unfortunately, children who witness domestic violence in their homes often experience other adverse childhood events, increasing the risk of subsequent health and behavioral difficulties.

The most meaningful steps that state and federal program administrators can take to address domestic violence include ensuring that all health and human-service providers have the capacity to:

- Recognize the impact of domestic violence

- Respond effectively with trauma-informed strategies; and

- Safely link families to domestic-violence services

The Family Violence Prevention and Services Act (FVPSA) funds life-saving domestic-violence shelter and other support services in states, territories, and tribes. The Family Violence Prevention and Services Program (FVPSA Program) in the Family and Youth Services Bureau (FYSB) administers these funds.

For Immediate Help

If you are in danger or need a place to stay, please call 800-799-SAFE (800-799-7233) or visit www.thehotline.org to connect to a domestic-violence shelter or program in your area.

Chapter 12

Children and Exposure to Domestic Violence

Chapter Contents

Section 12.1

Effects of Domestic Violence on Children

This section includes text excerpted from "Effects of
Domestic Violence on Children," Office on Women's
Health (OWH), U.S. Department of Health and
Human Services (HHS), September 13, 2018.

Many children exposed to violence in the home are also victims of
physical abuse. Children who witness domestic violence or are victims of abuse themselves are at serious risk for long-term physical
and mental-health problems. Children who witness violence between
parents may also be at greater risk of being violent in their future
relationships. If you are a parent who is experiencing abuse, it can be
difficult to know how to protect your child.

What Are the Short-Term Effects of Domestic Violence or Abuse on Children?

Children in homes where one parent is abused may feel fearful
and anxious. They may always be on guard, wondering when the next
violent event will happen. This can cause them to react in different
ways, depending on their age:

- **Children in preschool.** Young children who witness intimate
  partner violence may start doing things they used to do
  when they were younger, such as bedwetting, thumbsucking,
  increased crying, and whining. They may also develop difficulty
  falling or staying asleep; show signs of terror, such as stuttering
  or hiding; and show signs of severe separation anxiety.

- **School-aged children.** Children in this age range may feel
  guilty about the abuse and blame themselves for it. Domestic
  violence and abuse hurt children's self-esteem. They may not
  participate in school activities or get good grades, have fewer
  friends than others, and get into trouble more often. They also
  may have a lot of headaches and stomachaches.

- **Teens.** Teens who witness abuse may act out in negative ways,
  such as fighting with family members or skipping school. They
  may also engage in risky behaviors, such as having unprotected
  sex and using alcohol or drugs. They may have low self-esteem
  and have trouble making friends. They may start fights or bully

others and are more likely to get in trouble with the law. This type of behavior is more common in teen boys who are abused in childhood than in teen girls. Girls are more likely than boys to be withdrawn and to experience depression.

What Are the Long-Term Effects of Domestic Violence or Abuse on Children?

More than 15 million children in the United States live in homes in which domestic violence has happened at least once. These children are at greater risk for repeating the cycle as adults by entering into abusive relationships or becoming abusers themselves. For example, a boy who sees his mother being abused is ten times more likely to abuse his female partner as an adult. A girl who grows up in a home where her father abuses her mother is more than six times as likely to be sexually abused as a girl who grows up in a nonabusive home.

Children who witness or are victims of emotional, physical, or sexual abuse are at higher risk for health problems as adults. These can include mental-health conditions, such as depression and anxiety. They may also include diabetes, obesity, heart disease, poor self-esteem, and other problems.

Can Children Recover from Witnessing or Experiencing Domestic Violence or Abuse?

Each child responds differently to abuse and trauma. Some children are more resilient, and some are more sensitive. How successful a child is at recovering from abuse or trauma depends on several things, including having:

- A good support system or good relationships with trusted adults

- High self-esteem

- Healthy friendships

Although children will probably never forget what they saw or experienced during the abuse, they can learn healthy ways to deal with their emotions and memories as they mature. The sooner a child gets help, the better his or her chances for becoming a mentally and physically healthy adult.

How Can You Help Your Children Recover after Witnessing or Experiencing Domestic Violence?

You can help your children by:

- **Helping them feel safe.** Children who witness or experience domestic violence need to feel safe. Consider whether leaving the abusive relationship might help your child feel safer. Talk to your child about the importance of healthy relationships.

- **Talking to them about their fears.** Let them know that it's not their fault or your fault.

- **Talking to them about healthy relationships.** Help them learn from the abusive experience by talking about what healthy relationships are and are not. This will help them know what is healthy when they start romantic relationships of their own.

- **Talking to them about boundaries.** Let your child know that no one has the right to touch them or make them feel uncomfortable, including family members, teachers, coaches, or other authority figures. Also, explain to your child that she or he doesn't have the right to touch another person's body, and if someone tells them to stop, they should do so right away.

- **Helping them find a reliable support system.** In addition to a parent, this can be a school counselor, a therapist, or another trusted adult who can provide ongoing support. Know that school counselors are required to report domestic violence or abuse if they suspect it.

- **Getting them professional help.** Cognitive behavioral therapy (CBT) is a type of talk therapy or counseling that may work best for children who have experienced violence or abuse. CBT is especially helpful for children who have anxiety or other mental-health problems as a result of the trauma. During CBT, a therapist will work with your child to turn negative thoughts into more positive ones. The therapist can also help your child learn healthy ways to cope with stress.

Your doctor can recommend a mental-health professional who works with children who have been exposed to violence or abuse. Many shelters and domestic-violence organizations also have support groups for kids. These groups can help children by letting them know they are not alone and helping them process their experiences in a non-judgmental place.

Is It Better to Stay in an Abusive Relationship Rather Than Raise Your Children as a Single Parent?

Children do best in a safe, stable, and a loving environment, whether that's with one parent or two. You may think that your kids won't be negatively affected by the abuse if they never see it happen. But children can also hear the abuse, such as screaming and the sounds of hitting. They can also sense tension and fear. Even if your kids don't see you being abused, they can be negatively affected by the violence they know is happening.

If you decide to leave an abusive relationship, you may be helping your children feel safer and making them less likely to tolerate abuse as they get older. If you decide not to leave, you can still take steps to protect your children and yourself.

How Can You Make Yourself and Your Children Safe Right Now If You Are Not Ready to Leave an Abuser?

Your safety and the safety of your children are the biggest priorities. If you are not yet ready or willing to leave an abusive relationship, you can take steps to help yourself and your children now, including:

- Making a safety plan for you and your child

- Listening and talking to your child and letting them know that abuse is not okay and is not their fault

- Reaching out to a domestic-violence support person who can help you learn your options

If you are thinking about leaving an abusive relationship, you may want to keep quiet about it in front of your children. Young children may not be able to keep a secret from an adult in their life. Children may say something about your plan to leave without realizing it. If it would be unsafe for an abusive partner to know ahead of time that you're planning to leave, talk only to trusted adults about your plan. It's better for you and your children to be physically safe than for your children to know ahead of time that you will be leaving.

Section 12.2

Domestic Abuse and Childhood Obesity

"Domestic Abuse and Childhood Obesity,"
© 2016 Omnigraphics. Reviewed October 2018.

Of the many negative impacts of domestic violence on children, one of the most surprising is that it can damage their DNA—the basic genetic code contained in cells that makes each person unique. A 2014 study found that children who were exposed to domestic violence, suicide, or the incarceration of a family member showed evidence of chromosomal damage.

Specifically, children who had experienced or witnessed domestic violence had significantly shorter telomeres than children raised in more stable family environments. Telomeres are caps that protect the ends of chromosomes from deterioration when cells replicate. In this way, telomeres help preserve the genetic information stored in chromosomes. A small amount of telomeric DNA is lost as part of the normal process of cell division, so telomeres gradually become shorter as people age. When the extent of telomere shortening reaches a certain limit, the cell is programmed to stop dividing or die. As a result, scientists consider telomere length to be a biological indicator of a person's general health and projected lifespan.

The rate at which telomeres shorten is influenced by many factors, including certain elements of the person's lifestyle. Lifestyle factors such as smoking, obesity, unhealthy eating habits, lack of exercise, and exposure to environmental pollution can increase the rate of telomere shortening. Another factor that can accelerate the process of telomere shortening is stress, which may explain why children who are exposed to domestic violence tend to have shorter telomeres than their peers.

The study showed that the children who had the greatest exposure to traumatic family situations had the shortest telomeres, even after controlling for age, socioeconomic status, and other factors. The impact of domestic violence was more pronounced in girls than in boys. The researchers found that girls who were exposed to family trauma had the shortest telomeres, and thus the most genetic damage.

Shorter telomeres have been linked to a higher risk for early onset of age-associated health problems, including heart disease, obesity, diabetes, cognitive decline, mental illness, and premature death. Research has also shown, however, that improving diet, exercise, and other lifestyle factors has the potential to reduce the rate of telomere shortening, which may delay the onset of age-related diseases and prolong lifespan. This finding suggests that interventions aimed at stopping domestic violence and promoting stable home environments can help children live longer, healthier lives.

References

1. Brannon, Keith. "Domestic Violence Scars Kids' DNA," *Futurity*, June 16, 2014.

2. Griffiths, Sarah. "Domestic Violence Can 'Scar' a Child's DNA," Daily Mail, June 18, 2014.

Part Three

Abuse in Specific Populations

Chapter 13

Child Abuse

Chapter Contents

Section 13.1

Types of Child Abuse

This section includes text excerpted from "What Is Child Abuse and Neglect? Recognizing the Signs and Symptoms," Child Welfare Information Gateway, U.S. Department of Health and Human Services (HHS), July 2013. Reviewed October 2018.

How Is Child Abuse and Neglect Defined in Federal Law?

The federal legislation lays the groundwork for state laws on child maltreatment by identifying a minimum set of acts or behaviors that define child abuse and neglect. The Federal Child Abuse Prevention and Treatment Act (CAPTA), (42 U.S.C.A. §5106g), as amended and reauthorized by the CAPTA Reauthorization Act of 2010, defines child abuse and neglect as, at minimum: "Any act or failure to act on the part of a parent or caretaker which results in death, serious physical or emotional harm, sexual abuse or exploitation; or an act or failure to act which presents an imminent risk of serious harm." Most federal and state child protection laws primarily refer to cases of harm to a child caused by parents or other caregivers; they generally do not include harm caused by other people, such as acquaintances or strangers. Some state laws also include a child's witnessing of domestic violence as a form of abuse or neglect.

What Are the Major Types of Child Abuse and Neglect?

Within the minimum standards set by CAPTA, each state is responsible for providing its own definitions of child abuse and neglect. Most states recognize the four major types of maltreatment: physical abuse, neglect, sexual abuse, and emotional abuse. Signs and symptoms for each type of maltreatment are listed below. Additionally, many states identify abandonment and parental substance abuse as abuse or neglect. While these types of maltreatment may be found separately, they often occur in combination.

Physical abuse is nonaccidental physical injury (ranging from minor bruises to severe fractures or death) as a result of punching, beating, kicking, biting, shaking, throwing, stabbing, choking, hitting (with a hand, stick, strap, or another object), burning, or otherwise harming a child, that is inflicted by a parent, caregiver, or other people who have responsibility for the child. Such injury is considered abuse regardless of whether the caregiver intended to hurt the child. Physical discipline, such as spanking or paddling, is not considered abuse as long as it is reasonable and causes no bodily injury to the child.

Neglect is the failure of a parent, guardian, or another caregiver to provide for a child's basic needs. Neglect may be:

- Physical (e.g., failure to provide necessary food or shelter, or lack of appropriate supervision)

- Medical (e.g., failure to provide necessary medical or mental-health treatment)

- Educational (e.g., failure to educate a child or attend to special education needs)

- Emotional (e.g., inattention to a child's emotional needs, failure to provide psychological care, or permitting the child to use alcohol or other drugs)

Sometimes cultural values, the standards of care in the community, and poverty may contribute to maltreatment, indicating the family is in need of information or assistance. When a family fails to use information and resources, and the child's health or safety is at risk, then child welfare intervention may be required. In addition, many states provide an exception to the definition of neglect for parents who choose not to seek medical care for their children based on religious beliefs.

Sexual abuse includes activities by a parent or caregiver such as fondling a child's genitals, penetration, incest, rape, sodomy, indecent exposure, and exploitation through prostitution or the production of pornographic materials. Sexual abuse is defined by CAPTA as "the employment, use, persuasion, inducement, enticement, or coercion of any child to engage in, or assist any other person to engage in, any sexually explicit conduct or simulation of such conduct for the purpose of producing a visual depiction of such conduct; or the rape, and in cases of caretaker or inter-familial relationships, statutory rape, molestation, prostitution, or other form of sexual exploitation of children, or incest with children."

Emotional abuse (or psychological abuse) is a pattern of behavior that impairs a child's emotional development or sense of self-worth. This may include constant criticism, threats, or rejection, as well as withholding love, support, or guidance. Emotional abuse is often difficult to prove, and therefore, child protective services may not be able to intervene without evidence of harm or mental injury to the child. Emotional abuse is almost always present when other types of maltreatment are identified.

Abandonment is now defined in many states as a form of neglect. In general, a child is considered to be abandoned when the identity or whereabouts are unknown of the parent or parents, the child has been left alone in circumstances in which the child suffers serious harm, or the parent has failed to maintain contact with the child or provide reasonable support for a specified period of time. Some states have enacted laws—often called safe-haven laws—that provide safe places for parents to relinquish newborn infants.

Substance abuse is an element of the definition of child abuse or neglect in many states. Circumstances that are considered abuse or neglect in some states include the following:

- Prenatal exposure of a child to harm due to the mother's use of an illegal drug or other substance

- Manufacture of methamphetamine in the presence of a child

- Selling, distributing, or giving illegal drugs or alcohol to a child

- Use of a controlled substance by a caregiver that impairs the caregiver's ability to adequately care for the child

Section 13.2

Child Abuse and Neglect: Risk and Protective Factors

This section includes text excerpted from "What Is Child Abuse and Neglect? Recognizing the Signs and Symptoms," Child Welfare Information Gateway, U.S. Department of Health and Human Services (HHS), July 2013. Reviewed October 2018.

Recognizing Signs of Abuse and Neglect

In addition to working to prevent a child from experiencing abuse or neglect, it is important to recognize high-risk situations and the signs and symptoms of maltreatment. If you do suspect a child is being harmed, reporting your suspicions may protect him or her and get help for the family. Any concerned person can report suspicions of child abuse or neglect. Reporting your concerns is not making an accusation; rather, it is a request for an investigation and assessment to determine if help is needed.

Some people (typically certain types of professionals, such as teachers or physicians) are required by state law to make a report of child maltreatment under specific circumstances—these are called mandatory reporters. Some states require all adults to report suspicions of child abuse or neglect.

Some children may directly disclose that they have experienced abuse or neglect.

The following signs may signal the presence of child abuse or neglect.

The Child

- Shows sudden changes in behavior or school performance

- Has not received help for physical or medical problems brought to the parents' attention

- Has learning problems (or difficulty concentrating) that cannot be attributed to specific physical or psychological causes

- Is always watchful, as though preparing for something bad to happen

- Lacks adult supervision

- Is overly compliant, passive, or withdrawn
- Comes to school or other activities early, stays late, and does not want to go home
- Is reluctant to be around a particular person
- Discloses maltreatment

The Parent

- Denies the existence of—or blames the child for—the child's problems in school or at home
- Asks teachers or other caregivers to use harsh physical discipline if the child misbehaves
- Sees the child as entirely bad, worthless, or burdensome
- Demands a level of physical or academic performance the child cannot achieve
- Looks primarily to the child for care, attention, and satisfaction of the parent's emotional needs
- Shows little concern for the child

The Parent and Child

- Rarely touch or look at each other
- Consider their relationship entirely negative
- State that they do not like each other

The above list may not be all the signs of abuse or neglect. It is important to pay attention to other behaviors that may seem unusual or concerning. In addition to these signs and symptoms, Child Welfare Information Gateway (CWIG) provides information on the risk factors and perpetrators of child abuse and neglect fatalities.

Signs of Physical Abuse

Consider the possibility of physical abuse when the child:

- Has unexplained burns, bites, bruises, broken bones, or black eyes
- Has fading bruises or other marks noticeable after an absence from school

- Seems frightened of the parents and protests or cries when it is time to go home
- Shrinks at the approach of adults
- Reports injury by a parent or another adult caregiver
- Abuses animals or pets

Consider the possibility of physical abuse when the parent or another adult caregiver:

- Offers conflicting, unconvincing, or no explanation for the child's injury, or provides an explanation that is not consistent with the injury
- Describes the child as "evil" or in some other very negative way
- Uses harsh physical discipline with the child
- Has a history of abuse as a child
- Has a history of abusing animals or pets

Signs of Neglect

Consider the possibility of neglect when the child:

- Is frequently absent from school
- Begs or steals food or money
- Lacks needed medical or dental care, immunizations, or glasses
- Is consistently dirty and has severe body odor
- Lacks sufficient clothing for the weather
- Abuses alcohol or other drugs
- States that there is no one at home to provide care

Consider the possibility of neglect when the parent or another adult caregiver:

- Appears to be indifferent to the child
- Seems apathetic or depressed
- Behaves irrationally or in a bizarre manner
- Is abusing alcohol or other drugs

Signs of Sexual Abuse

Consider the possibility of sexual abuse when the child:

- Has difficulty walking or sitting

- Suddenly refuses to change for gym or to participate in physical activities

- Reports nightmares or bedwetting

- Experiences a sudden change in appetite

- Demonstrates bizarre, sophisticated, or unusual sexual knowledge or behavior

- Becomes pregnant or contracts a venereal disease, particularly if under age 14

- Runs away

- Reports sexual abuse by a parent or another adult caregiver

- Attaches very quickly to strangers or new adults in their environment

Consider the possibility of sexual abuse when the parent or another adult caregiver:

- Is unduly protective of the child or severely limits the child's contact with other children, especially of the opposite sex

- Is secretive and isolated

- Is jealous or controlling with family members

Signs of Emotional Maltreatment

Consider the possibility of emotional maltreatment when the child:

- Shows extremes in behavior, such as overly compliant or demanding behavior, extreme passivity, or aggression

- Is either inappropriately adult (parenting other children, for example) or inappropriately infantile (frequently rocking or head-banging, for example)

- Is delayed in physical or emotional development

- Has attempted suicide

- Reports a lack of attachment to the parent

Consider the possibility of emotional maltreatment when the parent or another adult caregiver:

• Constantly blames, belittles, or berates the child

• Is unconcerned about the child and refuses to consider offers of help for the child's problems

• Overtly rejects the child

Section 13.3

Consequences of Child Abuse and Neglect

This section includes text excerpted from "Child Abuse and Neglect: Consequences," Centers for Disease Control and Prevention (CDC), April 10, 2018.

Child abuse and neglect affect children's health now and later, and the costs to our country are significant. Child abuse and neglect can lead to poor physical and mental health well into adulthood. The physical, psychological, behavioral, and economic consequences of child maltreatment are explained below.

One in Four Children Suffers Abuse

• An estimated 676,000 children were confirmed by child protective services as being victims of abuse and neglect in 2016.

• At least one in four children have experienced child neglect or abuse (including physical, emotional, and sexual) at some point in their lives, and one in seven children experienced abuse or neglect in 2017.

Physical

• In 2016, about 1,750 children died from abuse and neglect across the country.

- Abuse and neglect during infancy or early childhood can cause regions of the brain to form and function improperly with long-term consequences on cognitive and language abilities, socioemotional development, and mental health. For example, the stress of chronic abuse may cause a "hyperarousal" response in certain areas of the brain, which may result in hyperactivity and sleep disturbances.

- Children may experience severe or fatal head trauma as a result of abuse. Nonfatal consequences of abusive head trauma include varying degrees of visual impairment (e.g., blindness), motor impairment (e.g., cerebral palsy) and cognitive impairments.

- Children who experience abuse and neglect are also at increased risk for adverse health effects and certain chronic diseases as adults, including heart disease, cancer, chronic lung disease, liver disease, obesity, high blood pressure, high cholesterol, and high levels of C-reactive protein.

Psychological

- In one long-term study, as many as 80 percent of young adults who had been abused as children met the diagnostic criteria for at least one psychiatric disorder at age 21. These young adults exhibited many problems, including depression, anxiety, eating disorders, and suicide attempts.

- The stress of chronic abuse may result in anxiety and may make victims more vulnerable to problems, such as posttraumatic stress disorder (PTSD), conduct disorder, and learning, attention, and memory difficulties.

- Youth who have experienced child abuse and neglect receive more medications for depression, anxiety, and other issues than other youth in psychiatric care.

Behavioral

- Children who experience abuse and neglect are at increased risk of smoking, alcoholism, and drug abuse as adults, and are more likely to engage in high-risk sexual behaviors.

- Those with a history of child abuse and neglect are 1.5 times more likely to use illicit drugs, especially marijuana, in middle adulthood.

- Abused and neglected children are about 25 percent more likely to experience problems such as delinquency, teen pregnancy, and low academic achievement. One study found that physically abused children were at greater risk of being arrested as juveniles, being a teen parent, and not graduating high school.

- A National Institute of Justice (NIJ) study indicated that being abused or neglected as a child increased the likelihood of arrest as a juvenile by 59 percent. Abuse and neglect also increased the likelihood of an adult criminal behavior by 28 percent and violent crime by 30 percent.

- Child abuse and neglect can have a negative effect on the ability of people to establish and maintain healthy intimate relationships in adulthood.

Economic

- The total lifetime economic burden resulting from new cases of fatal and nonfatal child abuse and neglect in the United States in 2008 is approximately $124 billion in 2010 dollars. This economic burden rivals the cost of other high-profile public health problems, such as stroke and type 2 diabetes.

- The estimated average lifetime added cost per victim of nonfatal child abuse and neglect was $210,012 (in 2010 dollars), including:
  - Childhood healthcare costs
  - Adult medical costs
  - Productivity losses
  - Child welfare costs
  - Criminal justice costs
  - Special education costs

The estimated average lifetime added cost per death is $1,272,900, including medical costs and productivity losses.

Research suggests the benefits of effective prevention likely outweigh the costs of child abuse and neglect.

Chapter 14

Teen Dating Violence

Chapter Contents

Section 14.1

What Is Teen Dating Violence?

This section includes text excerpted from "Teen
Dating Violence," Centers for Disease Control and
Prevention (CDC), June 11, 2018.

Unhealthy relationships can start early and last a lifetime. Teens
often think some behaviors, such as teasing and name-calling, are a
"normal" part of a relationship. However, these behaviors can become
abusive and develop into more serious forms of violence.

Teen dating violence is defined as the physical, sexual, psychological, or emotional aggression within a dating relationship,
including stalking. It can occur in person or electronically and
might occur between a current or former dating partner. Several
phrases are used to describe teen dating violence. Below are just
a few:

• Relationship abuse

• Intimate partner violence

• Relationship violence

• Dating abuse

• Domestic abuse

• Domestic violence

Teen dating violence is widespread with serious long- and short-
term effects. Many teens do not report it because they are afraid
to tell friends and family. The 2015 National Youth Risk Behavior
Survey (NYRBS) found that nearly 12 percent of high-school females
reported physical violence and nearly 16 percent reported sexual
violence from a dating partner in the 12 months before they were
surveyed. For high-school males, more than seven percent reported
physical violence and about five percent reported sexual violence
from a dating partner.

The Centers for Disease Control and Prevention (CDC) report found
that among victims of contact sexual violence, physical violence, or
stalking by an intimate partner, nearly 23 percent of females and
14 percent of males first experienced some form of violence by that
partner before age 18.

What Are the Consequences of Teen Dating Violence?

As teens develop emotionally, they are heavily influenced by experiences in their relationships. Healthy relationship behaviors can have a positive effect on a teen's emotional development. Unhealthy, abusive, or violent relationships can have short- and long-term negative effects on a developing teen. Youth who experience dating violence are more likely to:

- Experience symptoms of depression and anxiety
- Engage in unhealthy behaviors, such as using tobacco, drugs, and alcohol
- Exhibit antisocial behaviors
- Think about suicide

Additionally, youth who are victims of dating violence in high school are at higher risk for victimization during college.

Why Does Teen Dating Violence Happen?

Teens receive messages about how to behave in relationships from peers, adults, and the media. All too often these examples suggest that violence in a relationship is normal, but violence is never acceptable.

Violence is related to certain risk factors. The risk of having unhealthy relationships increases for teens who:

- Believe that dating violence is acceptable
- Are depressed, anxious, or have other symptoms of trauma
- Display aggression toward peers or display other aggressive behaviors
- Use drugs or illegal substances
- Engage in early sexual activity and have multiple sexual partners
- Have a friend involved in teen dating violence
- Have conflicts with a partner
- Witness or experience violence in the home

Communicating with your partner, managing uncomfortable emotions such as anger and jealousy, and treating others with respect are a few ways to keep relationships healthy and nonviolent. Dating violence can be prevented when teens, families, organizations, and communities work together to implement effective prevention strategies.

Section 14.2

Types of Teen Dating Violence and Consequences

This section includes text excerpted from "Dating Matters,"
Centers for Disease Control and Prevention (CDC),
July 2015. Reviewed October 2018.

Teens often think that some behaviors, such as teasing or name-calling, are a normal part of a relationship. However, these behaviors can often become abusive—and even develop into more serious forms of violence.

It is sometimes hard to tell when a behavior has crossed the line and is not only unhealthy, but also unsafe. Educators can help youth explore and understand when this line has been crossed and connect youth with resources and support.

Teen dating violence (TDV) is defined as any physical, sexual, and/or emotional/psychological violence within a dating relationship, including stalking. Dating violence can take place both in person and electronically.

Involvement in dating violence can lead to potentially severe and long-lasting consequences.

The impact of violent behaviors has been shown to reach far beyond just those involved in the relationship. Evidence suggests that other students or bystanders to a conflict are impacted as well. Any kind of violence among youth affects all kids in the school. Teens who feel unsafe or unhappy have difficulty focusing on learning.

Types of Teen Dating Violence

- **Physical**—When a partner is physically attacked, such as being pinched, hit, shoved, or kicked

- **Emotional/psychological**—Threatening a partner or harming his or her sense of self-worth. Examples include name-calling, coercion, shaming, bullying, embarrassing on purpose, or keeping him/her away from friends and family. This form of teen dating violence can happen in person or online, such as through email or social media.

- **Sexual**—Forcing a partner to engage in a sex act when she or he does not or cannot consent. Sexual violence is not just rape. It includes forcing any type of sexual act, including touching or kissing. People can force others into sexual contact by using physical force, or by using words—such as threats or pressure. Some forms of sexual violence do not involve physical contact and include acts like exposing sexual body parts to someone else.

Prevalence of Teen Dating Violence

- A survey of U.S. high-school students suggests that one in five female students and 1 in 10 male students who date have experienced some form of physical and/or sexual teen dating violence during the past 12 months.

- Among adult victims of rape, physical violence, and/or stalking by an intimate partner, one in five women and nearly one in seven men first experienced some form of partner violence between 11 and 17 years of age.

- We know that emotional/psychological violence is the most common type of dating violence. Numbers range depending on the survey and type of population surveyed (e.g., just girls or just boys), but about a third to three-quarters of youth who date report perpetrating this type of violence against a dating partner at least once.

- Sexual dating violence is often reported at lower rates than the other types of dating violence.

Consequences for Victims of Teen Dating Violence

- Increased absenteeism
- Problems in nondating relationships
- Decline in well-being
- Failure to participate in school activities

- Poor academic performance
- Thoughts of suicide
- Fear
- Depression and/or anxiety
- Drug, alcohol, and tobacco use
- Injury
- Delinquent behavior
- Experiencing violence in subsequent relationships

Consequences of Engaging in Teen Dating Violence

- Loss of friend's respect
- Poor academic performance
- Alienation from friends and family
- Physical and health problems
- Juvenile or criminal record/confinement
- Loneliness
- Expulsion from school
- Loss of job

Section 14.3

Teen Dating Violence: Risk Factors

This section includes text excerpted from "Risk and
Protective Factors, Psychosocial Health Behaviors and Teen
Dating Violence," National Institute of Justice (NIJ),
U.S. Department of Justice (DOJ), January 6, 2015.
Reviewed October 2018.

Demographic, Individual, Relational, and Cultural Factors

One important goal of research on teen dating violence is to understand which youth are more vulnerable to experiencing violence in their relationships. Identifying youth at risk for violence increases the likelihood of early intervention and prevention. Researchers seek to identify the risk factors indicating an increased likelihood for dating violence and the protective factors that buffer against dating violence. Risk factors and protective factors can be found across multiple contexts or domains, including factors specific to an individual, peer group, or social group, relationship, or community/environment. Multiple risk factors and protective factors may be at play within a relationship. Researchers have begun to focus on identifying which risk factors and protective factors most strongly relate to teen dating violence.

In a National Institute of Justice (NIJ)-funded study of 5,647 teens (51.8 percent female, 74.6 percent Caucasian) from 10 middle schools and high schools (representing grades 7–12) throughout New York, New Jersey, and Pennsylvania, researchers identified several factors related to increased risk for dating violence. The researchers focused especially on cyber abuse, but found that the following factors related to multiple forms of abuse:

- **Gender:** Female teens reported more cyber, psychological, and sexual violence, while male teens reported more physical dating violence.

- **Sexual activity:** Teens who had been involved in sexual activity were more likely to experience cyber, physical, psychological, and sexual dating abuse.

- **Delinquency:** The more delinquent activities that teens engaged in, the more likely they were to experience cyber, physical, psychological, and sexual dating abuse.

Another NIJ-funded study examined multiple risk factors among 223 at-risk, low-income teens in central Virginia. The study first examined potential risk factors that each partner could bring to a relationship. These factors could be grouped into four broad categories:

- Precarious sexual history

- Risky family background

- Poor self-regulation skills

- Risky social environment

When examined together, risk factors that could be changed (e.g., having delinquent peers) related more strongly to dating violence than risk factors that could not be changed (e.g., exposure to maltreatment in childhood).

The study also examined certain relationship-specific factors that might be associated with increased violence within the relationship:

- In relationships involving high levels of delinquent behaviors by both partners, higher levels of violence were exhibited.

- The older the teens' romantic partners were, the more likely the teens were to experience dating violence and engage in risky sexual behaviors. This finding was explained, in part, by the fact that the larger the age gap between teens and their older partners, the more likely both partners were to engage in delinquent behaviors during the relationship.

A NIJ-funded longitudinal study of 1,162 students in the Midwest examined factors that led teens to engage in bullying, sexual harassment and dating violence while in middle and high school.

The researchers found that youth who bullied other students while in middle school were more likely to engage in more serious forms of interpersonal aggression connected with dating and romantic relationships as they grew older. But the connection between bullying others in middle school and perpetrating teen dating violence in high school was not direct. Instead, bullying behavior in middle school predicted bullying behavior in high school—which, in turn, was linked to perpetrating teen dating violence.

In middle school, aggression toward a sibling was a predictor of bullying behavior for both girls and boys. For girls, family conflict and having delinquent friends were also predictors of bullying behavior. For boys, family conflict was not a predictor of bullying behavior, but both having delinquent friends and self-reported delinquency were predictors.

Among high-school students, researchers found direct links between those who bullied and those who perpetrated teen dating violence. Female teens who bullied others were likely to perpetrate sexual, verbal, and physical dating violence. Male teens who bullied others were likely to perpetrate verbal, and physical dating violence.

NIJ-funded research also examined factors related to victimization among a national sample of 1,525 Latino teens. Results revealed that being a victim of one type of violence might place teens at risk for other forms of violence. Many victims of dating violence also were victims of crime or of peer/sibling violence. In addition, even after accounting for the fact that young people were often victims of multiple forms of violence, dating violence, in particular, was associated with delinquency.

- **Violent delinquency** was associated with greater psychological and physical dating violence.

- **Nonviolent delinquency** — specifically, property damage — and drug delinquency were associated with greater psychological dating violence.

This study also identified two factors that might help to protect against dating violence among Latino teens:

- **Cultural orientation:** Teens who were more oriented toward their Latino culture were less likely to experience physical or psychological dating violence.

- **Social support:** Teens who reported greater social support were less likely to experience stalking or psychological, physical, or sexual dating violence

Overall, findings from NIJ-funded studies suggest a need to screen for teen dating violence and provide intervention programming among youth who have experienced other forms of violence or who have engaged in delinquent behaviors.

Psychosocial Health Behaviors

Teen dating violence has been associated with negative psychosocial health behaviors, but we cannot say definitively that teen dating violence causes negative health outcomes. Much of the research is correlational. Nevertheless, research can determine whether youth who experience dating violence are also at risk for negative psychosocial health behaviors. Knowing what types of health behaviors are associated with teen dating violence can help service providers better recognize and adequately respond to the needs of teens who experience dating violence.

The NIJ-funded study of dating violence among 5,647 teens from middle schools and high schools (representing grades 7–12) throughout New York, New Jersey, and Pennsylvania identified two psychosocial health behaviors associated with teen dating violence:

- **Depression:** Teens who reported more cyber, psychological, physical, and sexual dating violence reported more frequent feelings of depression.

- **Anger/hostility:** Teens who reported more cyber, psychological, and physical dating violence reported more frequent feelings of anger or hostility.

Similar findings emerged from a national study of relationships among 1,525 Latino teens. Researchers controlled for a total count of the number of different types of victimization that the participants experienced, including conventional crime and peer/sibling victimization. After controlling for total victimization, dating violence remained associated with depression and hostility:

- Experiencing sexual dating violence was associated with clinical levels of depression.

- Experiencing psychological dating violence was associated with greater hostility.

Section 14.4

How Peers Can Affect Risk and Protective Factors

This section includes text excerpted from "Teen Dating Violence—
How Peers Can Affect Risk and Protective Factors," National
Criminal Justice Reference Service (NCJRS), November 2014.
Reviewed October 2018.

Compared to childhood, adolescence is a period marked by significant changes in the nature and importance of interpersonal relationships. Relationships with friends become more autonomous and central to personal well-being and, for the first time, many youths become involved in romantic relationships. Although the initiation of romantic relationships is a positive and healthy experience for many youths, it is a source of violence and abuse for others. Approximately nine percent of high-school students report being hit, slapped, or physically hurt on purpose by their boyfriend or girlfriend in the past year. Teen dating violence rates appear to be even higher among certain populations, such as youth who have a history of exposure to violence.

Recognizing a large number of youth who experience dating violence, policymakers at the federal and state levels have worked to raise awareness of dating violence, prevent violence from occurring, and offer more protection and services to victims. In response to this increased focus on teen dating violence, research has begun to flourish. Since 2008, the National Institute of Justice (NIJ) has provided close to $15 million in funding for basic, applied and policy-level research on dating violence. These projects have led to increased knowledge about risk and protective factors and psychosocial health behaviors associated with teen dating violence, and the development and evaluation of dating violence prevention programs targeting diverse samples of youth. Research has also examined adolescents' knowledge of and barriers to using protection orders against violent partners. This research in brief looks at the research from the perspective of one key emerging theme: Peers and the contexts in which peers interact can contribute to their risk for and protection against dating violence. Although the research focuses primarily on findings from NIJ-funded research, it also draws upon the broader literature on adolescent development and romantic relationships to show ways that teens shape each other's experiences across the spectrum of entering into and leaving violent romantic relationships.

Peer Roles in Teen Dating Violence

Peer roles are best understood within a multisystemic framework. That is when teens begin dating, each partner enters into the relationship with his or her own set of perceptions, attitudes, and behaviors shaped, in part, by the broader social "contexts," or environments, in which they live. Teens interact with peers in many different social contexts, for example, schools, social clubs, sports teams, neighborhood parks or community centers. Each social context can promote attitudes and behaviors that encourage or discourage dating violence. For example, teens' and their peers' perceptions of whether violence is acceptable within romantic relationships might depend on the level of violence they witness at school or in their neighborhood.

Thus, when considering how peers might shape dating experiences, it is important to consider not only the context of teens' close peer group but also the larger school and community contexts in which teens and their peers interact.

Teens' peers have the potential to considerably shape their dating experiences. Teens spend most of their days in school with peers and, in their free time, spend proportionally more time with peers than with parents or any other adults. The desire to fit in and be liked by peers heightens in adolescence, and teens begin to rely on peers as a primary source of support and guidance. In addition, peer groups often set norms and offer social rewards for dating; for example, youth who date are often perceived as more socially acceptable or popular than youth who do not date. As such, peers are likely to have a significant impact on teens' decisions about whether to date, whom to date, and when to break up with romantic partners. Furthermore, the experiences that teens witness or perceive their peers to have within romantic relationships might shape teens' perceptions of what is normal or acceptable in their own romantic relationships. It is critical to consider the very public nature of teens' romantic relationships. Teen couples often interact in the presence of peers at school or in other social settings where other teens and adults are present, such as a mall, a movie theatre, or at home. Because of this, interactions that occur in public, or that happen in private but are shared with peers, might quickly become public knowledge to the larger peer network. Even when teens are not physically together, they are often still interacting by cell phone, text messages, social media sites, online video games and other electronic outlets that allow them to disseminate information quickly and widely. As a result, when relationships become violent or unhealthy in other ways, teens are at risk for experiencing embarrassment, being publicly ridiculed, or developing negative reputations among their peers. These concerns are very real to teens; they have to contend with their image among close friends and the larger peer network on a daily basis.

Of particular interest to service providers is that the presence of peers might instigate, elevate, or reduce the likelihood of teen dating violence, depending on the situation. For example, if a girl hits a boy in front of his friends, the boy might feel pressure to "save face" and hit her in return. On the other hand, if peers are present when a couple is arguing, the peers might help defuse the situation and prevent the argument from escalating to violence—or peers who witness or hear about violence occurring also might seek help from an adult.

Clearly, teens' orientation toward peers and the significant amount of time spent with them affords numerous opportunities for peers to impact teens' behaviors and decisions within romantic relationships. Findings emerging from NIJ-funded research on peer roles in teen dating violence can be viewed in terms of three overarching questions:

1. Do risky peer contexts increase the likelihood that teens will experience dating violence?

2. What roles do peers play in seeking help after teens experience violence?

3. Can group interventions or those focused on social contexts reduce the risk for teen dating violence?

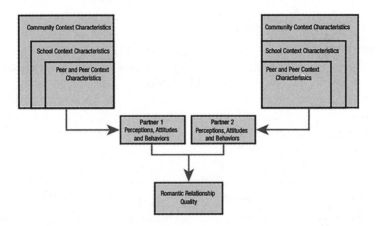

Figure 14.1. *Peer Roles in Teen Dating Violence: A Multisystemic Framework*

This figure illustrates the theoretical framework guiding the review of research on peers, peer contexts, and teen dating violence. It is not intended to depict all potential influences on the quality of the romantic relationships among teens; there are a number of individual- and family-level factors, for example, that are not depicted in this figure.

Do Risky Peer Contexts Increase the Likelihood That Teens Will Experience Dating Violence?

Research consistently shows the tendency for dating violence to overlap with peer victimization, suggesting that youth who are victims or perpetrators of peer violence tend to be the same youth at risk for experiencing violence within romantic relationships. As such, researchers have begun to identify risky or antisocial characteristics of teens' broader peer social environments that increase the risk for dating violence.

Peer Violence and Dating Violence Tend to Co-Occur

Two studies using community-based samples directly examined the links between dating violence and peer violence, including the associations between bullying among peers and dating violence. One study of 1,162 teens attending high school in Illinois revealed concurrent links between youth who bully and youth who perpetrate teen dating violence, suggesting an overlap in teens who victimize peers and those who victimize dating partners. Specifically, female teens who bullied others were also likely to perpetrate sexual harassment and sexual, verbal, and physical dating violence. Similarly, male teens who bullied others were also likely to perpetrate sexual harassment, physical dating violence, and verbal dating violence. A survey of 5,647 teens across three northeastern states focused more specifically on the co-occurrence of cyberbullying and teen dating violence. Results revealed significant overlaps in who perpetrated cyberbullying and cyberdating violence—26 percent of teens who perpetrated cyberbullying also perpetrated cyberdating violence, compared with only seven percent of teens who did not perpetrate cyberbullying. Overlap also existed in victimization experiences. Teens who experienced cyberbullying by peers were more than three times as likely to experience cyberdating violence, compared with those who did not experience cyberbullying (38 percent versus 13 percent, respectively).

Furthermore, a national study of 1,525 Latino teens revealed links between victimization by dating partners and a wide range of other forms of victimization. About 71 percent of dating violence victims experienced peer/sibling violence, sexual victimization, stalking, conventional crime, or another form of victimization in the prior year. Dating violence and peer/sibling violence were the two most common forms of victimization to co-occur. About 57 percent of teen victims of dating violence were also victims of peer/sibling violence.

The consistency with which peer violence and teen dating violence have been found to co-occur illustrates that teens who struggle with establishing healthy peer relationships also have difficulties in romantic relationships. Although only a little is known about how this occurs, these findings are in line with theories that suggest that outcomes in one relationship tend to be shaped by experiences, beliefs, and attitudes learned in other relationships.

Youth in Risky, Antisocial Environments Are at Significant Risk for Teen Dating Violence

Practitioners often must provide services to teens who have multiple risk factors for dating violence and thus would benefit by knowing which risk factors are most important to address in situations where time and resources might be limited. One study simultaneously examined multiple risk factors, including social context, within a sample of low-income teens who were receiving community-based services allocated to at-risk populations. Among the 223 youth in that study, there were 11 known risk factors for dating violence, divided into four categories: risky social environment, risky sexual history, risky family background and poor ability to self-regulate. Risky social environment represented a combination of teens' ratings of peer delinquency, exposure to peer dating abuse, negative neighborhood quality, and attitudes toward relationship abuse.

When the four categories of risk factors were examined simultaneously, the risky social environment was the strongest correlate of physical and emotional dating violence victimization and perpetration within a romantic relationship. Teens from risky family backgrounds were also more likely to experience and perpetrate emotional and physical dating violence. However, this finding was partly explained by the fact that the more high-risk the teens' family backgrounds were, the more likely they were to become involved in risky social contexts, such as having delinquent peers or witnessing dating violence among their peers. Studies consistently show that teens who engage in delinquent behaviors are at risk for experiencing and perpetrating dating violence. Indeed, teens' own participation in delinquent behaviors is a likely indicator that they are embedded within a risky social environment. The vast majority of adolescent delinquency is committed in groups of peers, and teens' and their peers' levels of delinquency tend to be similarly aligned. Moreover, teens who engage in delinquency are also likely to choose delinquent romantic partners, creating risky romantic relationship contexts that are, in turn, associated with higher levels of dating violence and other health-risk behaviors.

Findings from NIJ-funded studies contribute to a growing body of literature suggesting that a diverse set of peer attributes are linked to whether teens experience or perpetrate dating violence, including close peers' and the broader peer group's behaviors, attitudes, and guidance; teens' social standing among the broader peer group; and the quality of relationships with close peers. Moreover, peer risk factors tend to be more strongly associated with dating violence perpetration and victimization in adolescence than with family risk factors.

What Roles Do Peers Play in Help-Seeking after Teens Experience Violence?

Teen dating violence has been associated with negative psychosocial health outcomes, including delinquency, hostility, and depression. Once teens experience violence in one relationship, they are at significant risk for experiencing violence in another relationship. Thus, it is important that teens who experience dating violence seek help soon after, so they can receive services to protect against the potential psychosocial impacts of violence and reduce the likelihood of future violence. Peers also can have a significant impact on how teens respond to dating violence. Studies have identified two ways in which peers play a role in the aftermath of dating violence: (1) Peers often serve as first responders to dating violence, and (2) peers can hinder or encourage legal help-seeking in the form of a protection order.

Peers as First Responders to Dating Violence

It is difficult to determine how many teens seek help after violence occurs because researchers often ask different questions about help-seeking and dating abuse. For example, some researchers examine the percentage of teens who sought help after experiencing certain forms of serious physical or sexual abuse, whereas others examine help-seeking among teens who experienced any form of dating violence. Regardless, one clear message has emerged: Many teens do not seek help from anyone after violence has occurred, and those who do seek help most frequently turn to a friend.

In a study of 2,173 teens who reported being the victim of cyber, physical, psychological, or sexual dating abuse, only 8.6 percent reported seeking help from at least one person; more females (11%) sought help than males (5.7%). Very few teens—only 4.1 percent of females and two percent of males—sought help after they experienced dating abuse for the first time. Among the teens who did seek help, more than three-quarters (77.2%) turned to a friend for help and 48.5 percent turned to parents. Less than 10 percent sought help from other service providers, such as a teacher or police officer. For those who did seek help, both males (69.2%) and females (82%) were most likely to seek help from friends. Somewhat higher rates were reported in another study that asked only about help-seeking after experiencing physical, sexual, or stalking dating violence in the past year. Of the roughly 90 Latino teens who had experienced such violence, about 63 percent sought help afterward (60% of males and 69% of females).

Compared with psychological or cyber forms of abuse, it is possible that teens are more likely to recognize physical, sexual, and stalking dating violence as abuse and thus seek help. Nonetheless, few teens (15.6%) sought help from formal sources such as school, social services, or legal professionals. Instead, male and female teens were most likely to turn to friends for help (43.6% and 41.4%, respectively). These findings add to the growing evidence that peers tend to be the most frequent first responders to teen dating violence among male and female teens, teens of varying racial and ethnic backgrounds, and teens who experience different forms of dating violence.

Peers Play a Role in Teens' Help-Seeking

An exploratory study examined teens' use of protection orders, also called civil orders of protection or restraining orders. In July 2008, New York state law was modified to give teens access to protection orders without parental consent and without having a child in common with their partner. The study examined all petitions filed by dating violence victims age 18 and younger throughout 2009 and 2010—a two-year period shortly after the law took effect. The study found that the orders were not being used widely; victims filed only 1,200 petitions during the two-year period. To better understand potential barriers to obtaining protection orders, the researchers conducted focus groups and interviewed teens who were potentially at risk for dating violence or had begun the process of filing for a protection order. These conversations revealed that many youth were hesitant to obtain protection orders because they were afraid of escalating violence, were reluctant to end the relationship, or felt overwhelmed with other responsibilities. Another common barrier to seeking a protection order was how family and friends would feel about it. For example, teens were concerned about being viewed as a "snitch" or as responsible for the violence. Some teens felt ashamed to admit their victimization to others, as shown in the following examples: "I feel like you'd get talked about at school. 'Cause, like, I feel like we live in a small town, so everyone would know and figure out, and they'd talk about you." "Your friends whatever, like, might look at you a different way they see it as you went to the police and you couldn't handle it—that's really not for guys." Teens also were concerned that protection orders place victims at risk for retaliation by the abusive partners' peer network and might lead to social isolation resulting from losing mutual friends after the breakup. For example, one teen's decision to end the relationship and seek a protective order led to the dissolution of nearly her entire peer network: "It's like I don't have anybody." Another teen stated, "[His] friends target you. When I was with him he got some other girls, and they were all, like, gang member . . . and now there's, like, a whole group of girls after me and, like, I don't feel safe at all." On the other hand, teens' social networks can also be a source of motivation to seek legal protection. Teens reported that moral support from their friends and family is what helped them make it through the process of obtaining a protection order. Teens who had obtained a protection order recommended making peer support networks available for those who are considering taking legal action against an abusive partner. Although research on protection orders in abusive teen relationships is nascent, preliminary work illustrates that teens' decisions to bring legal action against an abusive partner are shaped by more than the abusiveness of the relationship and guidance from caring adults. Teens also weigh the potential benefits of the protection order against the potential negative consequences such legal action might have on their image and social well-being among peers.

Can Group Interventions or Those Focused on Social Contexts Reduce the Risk for Teen Dating Violence?

Researchers, practitioners, and policymakers are invested in identifying and implementing interventions that decrease the likelihood of dating violence among teen partners. Growing evidence supports the finding that teens tend to weigh the perceptions of peers when making decisions about romantic relationships. Such knowledge raises the question of whether interventions conducted on a group level—that is, among groups of peers within a school or other social setting—would be effective at reducing the risk for teen dating violence. Practically speaking, interventions in schools and other community-based peer settings are worthwhile because they offer opportunities to reach large numbers of teens in the environments where they spend a significant amount of their time.

Most of the effective teen dating violence interventions identified to date have been school-based programs. The majority of these programs take a universal preventive approach—where all students in a school receive the intervention—and have been developed for implementation among high-school students. Yet, many youth have already started dating and have experienced dating violence before high school. As such, the new generation of teen-dating violence-prevention programs is beginning to focus on middle-school youth, which will increase the likelihood of reaching teens before they begin dating or when they first start to date. Start Strong: Building Healthy Teen Relationships and Dating Matters™ are two examples of comprehensive, multicomponent teen-dating violence-prevention initiatives implemented with middle-school-aged youth and their families across the United States.

Between 2005 and 2011, NIJ funded the development and evaluation of Shifting Boundaries, one of the first teen-dating violence-intervention programs designed for middle-school students. Shifting Boundaries was developed and tested in an early study in Cleveland, Ohio, and then modified and re-evaluated in 117 sixth- and seventh-grade classes (30 public middle schools) in New York City. Schools and classrooms were randomly assigned to

1. a classroom intervention with both a personal interaction and a law-and-justice curriculum, including discussions on relational boundaries, laws, and legal penalties; or

2. a school building intervention that consisted of building-based restraining orders, a display of posters about the reporting of dating violence and harassment, and monitoring of violence "hot spots"; or

3. a combined classroom and building intervention; or

4. a control group.

Compared with teens in the control group, teens who received the school building intervention seemed to benefit in many ways, regardless of whether they had the classroom intervention.

Specifically, six months after the intervention, teens who received the school building intervention showed significant reductions in sexual and other types of victimization by dating partners compared with teens in the control group. At that time, teens were presented with example cases of dating violence and asked if they would intervene. Teens who received only the school building intervention were significantly more likely than teens in the control group to report that they would intervene if they witnessed dating violence.

Community-based interventions can also reduce dating violence risk among high-risk youth. Youth who have been exposed to known risk factors might need specialized intervention that aligns with their pattern of risk. Moreover, high-risk youth might be less likely to participate fully in school-based interventions, compared with lower-risk teens. For example, they might miss more days of school or be less engaged in learning opportunities. One study developed and evaluated two community-based group interventions to prevent dating violence victimization of teen girls involved in the child welfare system. Specifically, it compared the incidence of dating violence among female teens who did not receive an intervention with female teens who completed either

1.   a social learning/feminist group intervention focused on gendered attitudes, beliefs about relationships, and relational skills, or

2.   a risk detection/executive-functioning group intervention focused on noticing contextual danger cues, regulating emotions, and knowing how to respond in difficult situations.

Teens who received one of the group-treatment interventions were two to five times less likely to report being sexually or physically victimized by romantic partners over the course of the study, compared with teens who did not participate in one of the group interventions.

Additional research is needed to determine exactly why the Shifting Boundaries building-wide intervention and the community-based social learning/feminist and risk detection/executive-functioning group interventions reduced the likelihood of dating violence among teens. The interventions are similar in that they use structured peer contexts—school-based and group interventions—to deliver programming. In addition, they focus on improving teens' knowledge, attitudes, and norms regarding dating violence, and they aim to teach teens how to recognize and respond to violence that occurs between youth. The findings regarding Shifting Boundaries are consistent with other research that shows positive school environments—including positive norms, values, and expectations—are associated with lower levels of student aggression and bullying behaviors.

Section 14.5

Safety Planning for Teens

This section includes text excerpted from "In Relationships,"
girlshealth.gov, Office on Women's Health (OWH), August 24, 2018.

As a teen, you will have relationships with a lot of people. These
relationships will probably include friendships and dating relationships. Most of the time, these relationships are fun and healthy, and
they make us feel good about ourselves. Sometimes, though, these
relationships can be unhealthy. Unhealthy relationships result in
someone getting hurt physically or emotionally. The questions and
answers below will help you understand how to spot an unhealthy
relationship and how to change a bad situation.

What Is a Healthy Relationship?

In healthy relationships, you and your friend or the person you are
dating feel good about each other and yourselves. You do activities
together, like going to movies or out with other friends, and you talk
to one another about how you feel. These relationships can last a few
weeks, a few months, or even years.

In healthy relationships, there is respect and honesty between both
people. This means that you listen to each other's thoughts and opinions and accept each other's right to say no or to change your mind
without giving each other a hard time. You should be able to let the
other person know how you are feeling. You might disagree or argue
sometimes, but in healthy relationships, you should be able to talk
things out to solve problems.

What Is Abuse?

Some people think that their relationship isn't abusive unless there
is physical fighting. There are other types of abuse, though. Below is
a list of different types of abuse.

- **Physical abuse** is when a person touches your body in an
  unwanted or violent way. This may include hitting, kicking,
  pulling hair, pushing, biting, choking, or using a weapon or
  other item to hurt you.

- **Verbal/emotional abuse** is when a person says something
  or does something that makes you feel afraid or bad about

yourself. This may include yelling, name-calling, saying mean things about your family and friends, embarrassing you on purpose, telling you what to do, or threatening to hurt you or hurt themselves. Pressuring you to use drugs or alcohol is also abuse, as is keeping you from spending time with your friends and family.

- **Sexual abuse** is any sexual contact that you do not want. You may have said "no" or may be unable to say no because the abuser has threatened you, stopped you from getting out of the situation, or has physically stopped you from leaving. This may include unwanted touching or kissing, or forcing you to have sex. Sexual abuse includes date rape.

What Are the Signs That I Am in an Abusive or Unhealthy Relationship?

There are many signs that you could be in an abusive or unhealthy relationship. Take a look at the list of warning signs below and see if any of these describe your relationship.

Your friend or the person you are going out with:

- Gets angry when you talk or hang out with other friends or other dating partners
- Bosses you around
- Often gets in fights with other people or loses his or her temper
- Pressures you to have sex or to do something sexual that you don't want to do
- Uses drugs and alcohol, and tries to pressure you into doing the same thing
- Swears at you or uses mean language
- Blames you for his or her problems or tells you that it is your fault that she or he hurt you
- Insults or tries to embarrass you in front of other people
- Has physically hurt you
- Makes you feel scared of their reactions to things
- Always wants to know where you are going and who you are with

My Friend Gets Mad If I Hang out with Other People. What Should I Do?

Be honest and stick to your decision. Tell your friend you like spending time with him or her but that you also want to spend time with other friends and family. Whether you are in a close friendship or a dating relationship, it is important for both of you to stay involved with the activities and interests you enjoyed before you became close. In a healthy relationship, you both need time to hang out with other friends and spend time alone.

What Are Unhealthy Relationships?

In an unhealthy relationship, you usually feel the exact opposite of how you feel when you're in a "healthy relationship." You and your friend do not usually feel good about each other and yourselves. Not all unhealthy relationships are abusive, but sometimes they can include verbal, physical, emotional, or sexual abuse. This can involve both people being violent or abusive toward each other or can involve only one person doing this to the other. Many times, a relationship is not unhealthy in the very beginning, but becomes so over time.

Why Are Some People Violent?

There are many reasons why a person could be violent or abusive to someone in any relationship. For example, a person who has grown up in a violent family may have learned that violence, like hitting or verbal control, was the way to solve a problem. They may be violent because they feel bad about themselves and think they will feel better if they make someone else feel worse. Others may get pressured by their friends to prove how strong they are. Sometimes people have trouble controlling their anger. Yet, violence never solves problems.

Drugs and alcohol can also play a part in abusive behavior. There are some people who lose control and hurt someone after they have been drinking or taking drugs. But this is no excuse! Just because someone is under the influence of drugs and alcohol or has a bad temper does not mean that their abusive behavior is okay.

Why Do Some People Stay in Unhealthy or Violent Relationships?

Sometimes it may be hard to get out of an abusive relationship because violence in relationships is often cyclical. After a person is violent, she or he may apologize and promise never to hurt you again. They may even say that they will work on the relationship, and it may be a while before that person acts violently again. These ups and downs can make it hard to leave a relationship.

It's also hard to leave someone you care about. You may be scared or ashamed to admit that you are in an abusive relationship, or you may be simply scared to be alone without that person. You may be afraid that no one will believe you, or that your friend or partner will hurt you more if you tell someone. Whatever the reasons, leaving an unhealthy relationship is hard, but it is something you should do.

Why Should I Leave?

Abusive relationships are unhealthy for you. Staying in one could cause you to experience difficulty sleeping and to suffer from headaches and stomachaches. You might feel depressed, sad, anxious, or nervous, and you may lose or gain weight. You may also blame yourself, feel guilty, and have trouble trusting other people in your life. Staying in an abusive relationship may hurt your self-esteem and make it hard for you to believe in yourself. If you are being physically abused, then you also run the risk of being permanently harmed or even killed if you stay. You should definitely leave the relationship if you are getting hurt, or if you are being threatened with physical harm in any way.

But the most important reason to leave an unhealthy relationship is that you deserve to be in a relationship that is healthy and fun.

How Do I Get out of an Unhealthy or Abusive Relationship?

First, if you think that you are in an unhealthy relationship, you should talk to a parent/guardian, friend, counselor, doctor, teacher, coach, or other trusted person about your relationship. Tell them why you think the relationship is unhealthy and exactly what the other person has done (hit, pressured you to have sex, tried to control you). See the question "What are the signs that I am in an unhealthy or abusive relationship?" for information that can help you explain your situation to an adult. If need be, this trusted adult can help you contact your parent/guardian, counselors, school security, or even the police about the violence. With help, you can get out of an unhealthy relationship.

Sometimes, leaving an abusive relationship can be dangerous, so it is very important for you to make a safety plan. Leaving the relationship will be a lot easier and safer if you have a plan.

What Do I Do If I Am Being Hurt by a Parent/Guardian or Another Family Member?

Sadly, there are times when people whose role it is to care for us instead abuse us. Child abuse is when any person caring for a child fails to take care of the child, physically hurts the child, or treats the child in a sexual way. No matter what, parents, guardians, and caregivers are supposed to protect and care for their children. The term 'child abuse' doesn't just refer to young children. Child abuse can happen to a child of any age, from infants to teenagers.

What Do I Do If a Friend Tells Me That She or He Is in an Abusive Relationship?

If your friend talks to you about his or her abuse, you can help by:

- Listening without judging or blaming
- Telling your friend that you believe him or her
- Telling your friend that it is NOT his or her fault
- Telling your friend that you are always there to listen if he or she wants to talk about it
- Reminding your friend of all the friends and family who care about him or her
- Letting your friend know that you are worried about his or her safety
- Telling your friend that you want to help him or her talk to a parent/guardian or other trusted adult right away
- Offering to go with your friend to talk to an adult
- Helping your friend make a safety plan. (See the question "How do I get out of an unhealthy or abusive relationship?" above for tips on making a safety plan.)
- Sharing the number of the 24-hour National Domestic Violence Hotline (NDVH): 800-799-SAFE (800-799-7233) or 800-787-3224 (TDD)
- Suggesting your friend take a self-defense class

Be sure not to take this on alone. Talk with a trusted adult, such as a school counselor, about how to help your friend.

Should I Have My Friend Talk to His or Her Parents/ Guardians or Another Adult?

Yes! The most important thing that you can do for your friend is to try to get him or her to talk to an adult right away. This adult could be a parent/guardian, coach, teacher, school counselor, doctor, nurse, or spiritual or community leader. Offer to go with your friend to talk to an adult about the abusive relationship. If your friend is nervous about going to talk to an adult, remind him or her that an adult can:

- Listen and give advice on how to handle the situation

- Help get him or her to a safe place

- Help contact the right people, such as the police, the school principal, or a counselor

What If My Friend Won't Listen to Me and Wants to Keep the Abuse a Secret?

After you urge your friend to talk to an adult about the abuse, you should also tell an adult. It is too much for you to handle alone. You may think you need to keep your friend's secret, but it is important for you to tell a trusted adult—especially if you are afraid that your friend could get hurt. Your friend will need help even if she or he doesn't think so.

Do not tell your friend to choose between his or her abusive partner and you. Be supportive, no matter what your friend decides to do. Don't tell your friend's secrets to others.

What Else Do I Need to Know?

At least 1 in 10 teens experience physical violence in their relationships. Even if you have not experienced physical, sexual, or verbal and emotional abuse, one of your friends may be in an unhealthy relationship with another friend or dating partner. If you are in an unhealthy relationship, or if your friend is, it is important to get help right away before someone gets hurt! Relationships are an important part of life and are supposed to be fun and special!

Section 14.6

Teen Dating Violence Statistics

This section includes text excerpted from "Prevalence of
Teen Dating Violence," National Institute of Justice (NIJ),
U.S. Department of Justice (DOJ), July 22, 2016.

Estimates of teen dating violence prevalence vary widely because
studies define and measure violence differently over different periods
of time for different populations.

Nationally Representative Surveys

Youth Risk Behavior Survey (YRBS), a nationally representative
annual survey of youth in grades 9–12, found that, of those students
who dated someone in the last 12 months, approximately one in 10
reported being a victim of physical violence from a romantic partner
during that year.

The National Longitudinal Study of Adolescent Health (NLSAH),
analyzing a nationally representative sample of adolescents in grades
7–12 who were then followed over time, showed that approximately 30
percent of people ages 12–21 in heterosexual relationships reported experiencing psychological abuse in the past 18 months; 20 percent of youth
in same-sex relationships reported experiencing the same type of abuse.

About 10 percent of students in the Youth Risk Behavior Study
who had dated someone in the last 12 months reported that they had
been kissed, touched or physically forced to have sexual intercourse
against their will by a dating partner during that year.

To date, there are no nationally representative data on the perpetration of dating violence.

Study of Middle and High Schools in New York, New Jersey, and Pennsylvania

One National Institute of Justice (NIJ)-funded study examined the
prevalence of dating violence among 5,647 teens (51.8 percent female,
74.6 percent Caucasian) from 10 middle schools and high schools (representing grades 7–12) throughout New York, New Jersey, and Pennsylvania. Findings indicated that within the past year:

- 18.0 percent of respondents reported experiencing cyber dating
  abuse (e.g., "my partner used my social networking account

without permission" or "my partner sent texts/emails to engage in sexual acts I did not want").

- 20.7 percent experienced physical dating violence (e.g., reporting that a partner "pushed" or "kicked" the respondent).

- 32.6 percent experienced psychological dating abuse (e.g., "my partner threatened to hurt me" or "my partner would not let me do things with other people").

- 9.0 percent experienced sexual coercion (e.g., "my partner pressured me to have sex when [she or he] knew I didn't want to").

The study also specifically examined dating violence rates among teens who had dated within the past year (66 percent of total teens; $n = 3,745$). The following percentages of dating teens reported experiencing forms of abuse:

- Cyber dating abuse: 26.3 percent

- Physical dating violence: 29.9 percent

- Psychological dating abuse: 47.2 percent

- Sexual coercion: 13.0 percent

Longitudinal Study of Students in the Midwest

An NIJ-funded longitudinal study of 1,162 students in the Midwest examined the prevalence of several kinds of abuse that male and female middle- and high-school students experienced and perpetrated in teen dating relationships.

Physical violence. About one-third of girls and boys (35 percent and 36 percent, respectively) reported experiencing physical violence in a teen dating relationship. More girls reported perpetrating physical dating violence than boys (34 percent versus 17 percent).

Verbal emotional abuse. Verbal emotional abuse was the most common form of abuse in teen dating relationships for both girls and boys: 73 percent of girls and 66 percent of boys reported experiencing at least one instance of verbal abuse in a dating relationship in high school. In addition, 64 percent of girls and 45 percent of boys reported perpetrating verbal emotional abuse toward a dating partner.

Sexual coercion. Nearly one in four girls and one in seven boys reported being victims of sexual coercion in a teen dating relationship.

Study of Dating Violence among Latino Adolescents

NIJ-funded research has also examined the prevalence of dating violence among a national sample of Latino adolescents. Phone interviews were conducted with 1,525 Latino teens, ranging in age from 12–18, most of whom (76.1 percent) were born in the United States. Respondents reported experiencing the following within the past year:

- At least one form of dating violence: 19.5 percent
- Psychological dating violence: 14.8 percent
- Physical dating violence: 6.6 percent
- Sexual dating violence: 5.6 percent
- Stalking: 1.0 percent

Chapter 15

Date Rape

Chapter Contents

Section 15.1

What Is Date Rape?

This section includes text excerpted from "What Are
Date Rape Drugs and How Do You Avoid Them?" National
Institute on Drug Abuse (NIDA) for Teens, March 16, 2015.
Reviewed October 2018.

You may have been warned that sometimes people secretly slip drugs into other people's drinks to take advantage of them sexually. These drugs are called "date rape drugs."

Date rape, also known as "drug-facilitated sexual assault," is any type of sexual activity that a person on a date does not agree to. It may come from someone you know, someone you may have just met, and/ or someone you thought you could trust.

Date-rape drugs can make people become physically weak or pass out. This is why people who want to rape someone use them—because they leave individuals unable to protect themselves.

Many of these drugs have no color, smell, or taste, and people often do not know that they have taken anything. Many times people who have been drugged (usually girls or women, but not always) are unable to remember what happened to them.

The Dangerous Three

The three most common date rape drugs are Rohypnol® (flunitrazepam), GHB (gamma hydroxybutyric acid), and ketamine.

- **Rohypnol** (also known as roofies, forget-me-pill, and R-2) is a type of prescription pill known as a benzodiazepine—it is chemically similar to drugs such as Valium or Xanax, but unlike these drugs, it is not approved for medical use in this country.

  - It has no taste or smell and is sometimes colorless when dissolved in a drink.

  - People who take it can feel very sleepy and confused and forget what happens after its effects kick in.

  - It can also cause weakness and breathing difficulties and can make it difficult for those who have taken it to move their body.

  - The effects of Rohypnol can be felt within 30 minutes of being drugged and can last for several hours.

- To prevent misuse of Rohypnol, the manufacturer changed the pill to look like an oblong olive green tablet with a speckled blue core. When dissolved in light-colored drinks, the new pills dye the liquid blue and alert people that their drink has been tampered with. Unfortunately, generic versions of Rohypnol may not contain the blue dye.

- **Gamma-hydroxybutyrate (GHB)** (also known as cherry meth, scoop, and goop) is a type of drug that acts as a central nervous system (CNS) depressant and is prescribed for the treatment of narcolepsy (a sleep disorder).

  - It can cause a person to throw up; it can also slow their heart rate and make it hard to breathe.

  - At high doses, it can result in a coma or death.

  - It's a tasteless, odorless drug that can be a powder or liquid. It's colorless when dissolved in a drink.

  - Mixing it with alcohol makes these effects worse.

  - GHB can take effect in 15–30 minutes, and the effects may last for three to six hours.

- **Ketamine** (also known as cat valium, k-hole, and purple) is a dissociative anesthetic. That means it distorts perceptions of sight and sound and makes a person feel detached from their environment and themselves. It also reduces pain and overall feeling. Like other anesthetic drugs, it's used during surgical procedures in both humans and animals.

  - It's a tasteless, odorless drug that can be a powder or liquid.

  - It can cause hallucinations and make people feel totally out of it.

  - It can also increase heartbeat, raise blood pressure, and cause nausea.

  - The effects of ketamine may last for 30–60 minutes.

All Drugs Lower Your Defenses

It's important to remember that all drugs affect how well your mind and body operate. In fact, alcohol is linked to far more date rapes than the drugs mentioned here. And nearly all drugs of abuse make people vulnerable to being taken advantage of—by impairing their judgment, reducing their reaction time, and clouding their thinking.

And as disgusting as it is to think about, when you don't have your wits about you, someone may take that as an opportunity to push themselves on you.

How Can You Avoid Date Rape Drugs?

If you're at a party where people are drinking alcohol, you should be aware that there could be predators hoping to make you drunk or vulnerable. No matter what you're drinking, even if it's soda or juice, people can slip drugs in your drinks—so pour all drinks yourself and never leave them unattended (even if you have to take them into the bathroom with you).

Also, be sure to stick with your friends. There's safety in numbers.

But even if you leave your drink or leave your friends behind, know this for certain: if you are drugged and taken advantage of, it's not your fault.

Bottom line: People who date rape other people are committing a crime.

Section 15.2

Date Rape Drugs

This section includes text excerpted from "Date Rape Drugs," Office on Women's Health (OWH), U.S. Department of Health and Human Services (HHS), May 22, 2018.

What Are the Most Common Date Rape Drugs?

The three most common date rape drugs are:

- **Rohypnol.** Rohypnol is the trade name for flunitrazepam. Abuse of two similar drugs appears to have replaced Rohypnol abuse in some parts of the United States. These are clonazepam (marketed as Klonopin in the United States and Rivotril in Mexico) and alprazolam (marketed as Xanax). Rohypnol is also known as:

  - Circles

- Forget Pill
- LA Rochas
- Lunch Money
- Mexican Valium
- Mind Erasers
- Poor Man's Quaalude
- R-2
- Rib
- Roach
- Roach-2
- Roches
- Roofies
- Roopies
- Rope
- Rophies
- Ruffies
- Trip-and-Fall
- Whiteys
- **Gamma-hydroxybutyrate (GHB)**, which is short for gamma-hydroxybutyric acid. GHB is also known as:
  - Bedtime Scoop
  - Cherry Meth
  - Easy Lay
  - Energy Drink
  - G
  - Gamma 10
  - Georgia Home Boy
  - G-Juice
  - Gook
  - Goop

- Great Hormones
- Grievous Bodily Harm (GBH)
- Liquid E
- Liquid Ecstasy
- Liquid X
- PM
- Salt Water
- Soap
- Somatomax
- Vita-G
- **Ketamine**, also known as:
  - Black Hole
  - Bump
  - Cat Valium
  - Green
  - Jet
  - K
  - K-Hole
  - Kit Kat
  - Psychedelic Heroin
  - Purple
  - Special K
  - Super Acid

What Do the Drugs Look Like?

- Rohypnol comes as a pill that dissolves in liquids. Some are small, round, and white. Newer pills are oval and green-gray in color. When slipped into a drink, a dye in these new pills makes clear liquids turn bright blue and makes dark liquids turn cloudy. But this color change might be hard to see in a dark drink, like cola, or dark beer, or in a dark room. Also, the pills with no dye are still available. The pills may be ground up into a powder.

- GHB has a few forms: a liquid with no odor or color, white powder, and the pill. It might give your drink a slightly salty taste. Mixing it with a sweet drink, such as fruit juice, can mask the salty taste.

- Ketamine comes as a liquid and a white powder.

What Effects Do These Drugs Have on the Body?

These drugs are very powerful. They can affect you very quickly and without your knowledge. The length of time that the effects last varies. It depends on how much of the drug is taken and if the drug is mixed with other drugs or alcohol. Alcohol makes the drugs even stronger and can cause serious health problems—even death.

Rohypnol

The effects of Rohypnol can be felt within 30 minutes of being drugged and can last for several hours. If you are drugged, you might look and act like someone who is drunk. You might have trouble standing. Your speech might be slurred. Or you might pass out. Rohypnol can cause these problems:

- Muscle relaxation or loss of muscle control

- The difficulty with motor movements

- Drunk feeling

- Problems talking

- Nausea

- Can't remember what happened while drugged

- Loss of consciousness

- Confusion

- Problems seeing

- Dizziness

- Sleepiness

- Lower blood pressure

- Stomach problems

- Death

GHB

GHB takes effect in about 15 minutes and can last three or four hours. It is very potent: A very small amount can have a big effect. So it's easy to overdose on GHB. Most GHB is made by people in home or street "labs." So, you don't know what's in it or how it will affect you. GHB can cause these problems:

- Relaxation
- Drowsiness
- Dizziness
- Nausea
- Problems seeing
- Loss of consciousness
- Seizures
- Can't remember what happened while drugged
- Problems breathing
- Tremors
- Sweating
- Vomiting
- Slow heart rate
- Dream-like feeling
- Coma
- Death

Ketamine

Ketamine is very fast-acting. You might be aware of what is happening to you, but unable to move. It also causes memory problems. Later, you might not be able to remember what happened while you were drugged. Ketamine can cause these problems:

- Distorted perceptions of sight and sound
- Lost sense of time and identity
- Out-of-body experiences
- Dream-like feeling

- Feeling out of control

- Impaired motor function

- Problems breathing

- Convulsions

- Vomiting

- Memory problems

- Numbness

- Loss of coordination

- Aggressive or violent behavior

- Depression

- High blood pressure

- Slurred speech

Are These Drugs Legal in the United States?

Some of these drugs are legal when lawfully used for medical purposes. But that doesn't mean they are safe. These drugs are powerful and can hurt you. They should only be used under a doctor's care and order.

- Rohypnol is **not** legal in the United States. It is legal in Europe and Mexico, where it is prescribed for sleep problems and to assist anesthesia before surgery. It is brought into the United States illegally.

- Ketamine is legal in the United States for use as an anesthetic for humans and animals. It is mostly used on animals. Veterinary clinics are robbed for their ketamine supplies.

- GHB was made legal in the United States to treat problems from narcolepsy (a sleep disorder). Distribution of GHB for this purpose is tightly restricted.

Is Alcohol a Date Rape Drug? What about Other Drugs?

Any drug that can affect judgment and behavior can put a person at risk for unwanted or risky sexual activity. Alcohol is one such drug.

In fact, alcohol is the drug most commonly used to help commit sexual assault. When a person drinks too much alcohol:

- It's harder to think clearly

- It's harder to set limits and make good choices

- It's harder to tell when a situation could be dangerous

- It's harder to say "no" to sexual advances

- It's harder to fight back if a sexual assault occurs

- It's possible to blackout and to have memory loss

The club drug "ecstasy" 3,4-methylenedioxymethamphetamine (MDMA) has been used to commit sexual assault. It can be slipped into someone's drink without the person's knowledge. Also, a person who willingly takes ecstasy is at greater risk of sexual assault. Ecstasy can make a person feel "lovey-dovey" toward others. It also can lower a person's ability to give reasoned consent. Once under the drug's influence, a person is less able to sense danger or to resist a sexual assault.

Even if a victim of sexual assault drank alcohol or willingly took drugs, the victim is not at fault for being assaulted. It is never okay to have sexual contact with someone without their consent. Sexual assault is always the responsibility of the person who commits the assault. Sexual assault is never the victim's fault, regardless of the circumstances.

How Can I Protect Myself from Being a Victim?

- Don't accept drinks from other people.

- Open containers yourself.

- Keep your drink with you at all times, even when you go to the bathroom.

- Don't share drinks.

- Don't drink from punch bowls or other common, open containers. They may already have drugs in them.

- If someone offers to get you a drink from a bar or at a party, go with the person to order your drink. Watch the drink being poured and carry it yourself.

- Don't drink anything that tastes or smells strange. Sometimes, GHB tastes salty.

- Have a nondrinking friend with you to make sure nothing happens.

- If you realize you left your drink unattended, pour it out.

- If you feel drunk and haven't consumed any alcohol—or, if you feel like the effects of drinking alcohol are stronger than usual—get help right away.

Are There Ways to Tell If I Might Have Been Drugged and Raped?

It is often hard to tell. Most victims don't remember being drugged or assaulted. The victim might not be aware of the attack until 8 or 12 hours after it occurred. These drugs also leave the body very quickly. Once a victim gets help, there might be no proof that drugs were involved in the attack. But there are some signs that you might have been drugged:

- You felt drunk but did not consume any alcohol—or, you feel like the effects of drinking alcohol were stronger than usual.

- You wake up feeling very hungover and disoriented or having no memory of a period of time.

- You remember having a drink but cannot recall anything after that.

- You find that your clothes are torn or not on right.

- You feel like you had sex, but you cannot remember it.

What Should I Do If I Think I've Been Drugged and Raped?

Get medical care right away. Call 911 or have a trusted friend take you to a hospital emergency room (ER). Don't urinate, douche, bathe, brush your teeth, wash your hands, change clothes, eat, or drink before you go. These things may give evidence of the rape. The hospital will use a "rape kit" to collect evidence.

Call the police from the hospital. Tell the police exactly what you remember. Be honest about all your activities. Remember, nothing you did—including drinking alcohol or doing drugs—can justify rape.

Ask the hospital to take a urine (pee) sample that can be used to test for date rape drugs. The drugs leave your system quickly. Rohypnol stays in the body for several hours and can be detected in the urine up to 72 hours after taking it. GHB leaves the body in 12 hours. Don't urinate before going to the hospital.

Don't pick up or clean up where you think the assault might have occurred. There could be evidence left behind—such as on a drinking glass or bed sheets.

Get counseling and treatment. Feelings of shame, guilt, fear, and shock are normal. A counselor can help you work through these emotions and begin the healing process. Calling a crisis center or a hotline is a good place to start. One national hotline is the National Sexual Assault Hotline (NSAH) at 800-656-HOPE (800-656-4673).

Chapter 16

Digital Dating Abuse

Chapter Contents

Section 16.1

Sexting

This section contains text excerpted from the following
sources: Text in this section begins with excerpts from "Kids:
Texting and Sexting," Federal Trade Commission (FTC),
September 2011. Reviewed October 2018; Text beginning with the
heading "What Harm Does Sexting Do?" is excerpted from
"Much Ado about Sexting," National Criminal Justice Reference
Service (NCJRS), June 2010. Reviewed October 2018.

Anyone with a cell phone probably uses it to send and receive text
messages and images. It's similar to using e-mail or instant messaging
and most of the same etiquette and safety rules apply.

What Is Texting?

If your kids are texting, encourage them to respect others. Texting
shorthand can lead to misunderstandings. Tell them to think about
how a text message might be read and understood before sending it.
Also, encourage your kids to:

- Ignore texts from people they don't know

- Learn how to block numbers from their cell phone

- Avoid posting their cell phone number online

- Never provide financial information in response to a text

What Is Sexting?

Sending or forwarding sexually explicit photos, videos, or messages
from a mobile phone is known as "sexting." Tell your kids not to do
it. In addition to risking their reputation and their friendships, they
could be breaking the law if they create, forward, or even save this
kind of message. Teens may be less likely to make a bad choice if they
know the consequences.

What Harm Does Sexting Do?

Sexting engenders a number of potential harms. Some are fairly
immediate; others are more remote. Some involve only family and
friends; others pertain to larger populations. The most immediate

harm arises from the humiliation of discovery—by parents, authority figures, and unintended recipients. Besides humiliation, such discoveries may lead to punishments, such as loss of cell phone privileges or suspensions from school.

Other forms of humiliation can occur if recipients are not pleased or if they forward the photos to others. Subsequent harm may also occur through bullying or harassment by recipients. In extreme cases, suicides have resulted.

Some cases of sexting have resulted in criminal prosecution because the transmission of sexually explicit images of children constitutes child pornography in the United States. For instance, six Pennsylvania high-school students were charged with a combination of manufacturing, possessing, and distributing pornography when the three girls were discovered to have sent nude and semi-nude photos to three boys. Another Pennsylvania case involved child pornography charges for 16 students.

In one of the best-known cases, an 18-year-old boy distributed nude photographs of his former girlfriend after a heated breakup. The boy was convicted of distributing pornography, placed on probation for five years, and must spend 25 years on Florida's sex offender list. Such forms of unwanted notoriety may have long-term consequences. A conviction for a felony or a serious misdemeanor, for example, may create obstacles to college admissions. Sexually explicit photos on social media pages may come to the attention of prospective employers. Such photos may also prove embarrassing for future romantic relationships.

Is Sexting Illegal?

There is no legal definition of sexting, making it a legal gray area. State law enforcement has charged teens under child pornography laws for sexting because sexting falls within the purview of many states' child pornography laws.

Section 16.2

Cyberbullying

This section contains text excerpted from the following
sources: Text in this section begins with excerpts from "What Is
Cyberbullying?" StopBullying.gov, U.S. Department of Health and
Human Services (HHS), July 26, 2018; Text under the heading
"What Teens Can Do" is excerpted from "What Teens Can Do,"
StopBullying.gov, U.S. Department of Health and Human
Services (HHS), February 7, 2018.

Cyberbullying is bullying that takes place over digital devices
such as cell phones, computers, and tablets. Cyberbullying can occur
through short message service (SMS), text, and apps, or online in
social media, forums, or gaming where people can view, participate in,
or share content. Cyberbullying includes sending, posting, or sharing
negative, harmful, false, or mean content about someone else. It can
include sharing personal or private information about someone else,
causing embarrassment or humiliation. Some cyberbullying crosses
the line into unlawful or criminal behavior.

The most common places where cyberbullying occurs are:

- Social media, such as Facebook, Instagram, Snapchat, and
  Twitter

- SMS, also known as text message, sent through devices

- Instant message (via devices, e-mail provider services, apps, and
  social media messaging features)

- E-mail

Special Concerns Regarding Cyberbullying

With the prevalence of social media and digital forums, comments,
photos, posts, and content shared by individuals can often be viewed by
strangers as well as acquaintances. The content an individual shares
online—both their personal content as well as any negative, mean, or
hurtful content—creates a kind of permanent public record of their
views, activities, and behavior. This public record can be thought of as
an online reputation, which may be accessible to schools, employers,
colleges, clubs, and others who may be researching an individual now
or in the future. Cyberbullying can harm the online reputations of
everyone involved—not just the person being bullied, but those doing

the bullying or participating in it. Cyberbullying has unique concerns in that it can be:

- **Persistent.** Digital devices offer an ability to immediately and continuously communicate 24 hours a day, so it can be difficult for children experiencing cyberbullying to find relief.

- **Permanent.** Most information communicated electronically is permanent and public, if not reported and removed. A negative online reputation, including for those who bully, can impact college admissions, employment, and other areas of life.

- **Hard to notice.** Because teachers and parents may not overhear or see cyberbullying taking place, it is harder to recognize.

Laws and Sanctions

Although all states have laws requiring schools to respond to bullying, many states do not include cyberbullying under these laws or specify the role that schools should play in responding to bullying that takes place outside of school. Schools may take action either as required by law, or with local or school policies that allow them to discipline or take other action. Some states also have provisions to address bullying if it affects school performance.

Frequency of Cyberbullying

The *2015 School Crime Supplement* (National Center for Education Statistics (NCES) and U.S. Bureau of Justice Statistics (BJS)) indicates that, nationwide, about 21 percent of students ages 12 to 18 experienced bullying.

The Centers for Disease Control and Prevention's (CDC) 2017 Youth Risk Behavior Surveillance System (YRBSS) indicates that an estimated 14.9 percent of high-school students were electronically bullied in the 12 months prior to the survey.

What Teens Can Do

Bullying stops us from being who we want to be, and prevents us from expressing ourselves freely, and might even make us feel unsafe. If you are bullied, say something! If you are bullying, it's not cool!

Being Bullied

You might be being bullied. You should:

- **Know what bullying is.** Get familiar with what bullying is and what it is not. If you recognize any of the descriptions, you should stay calm, stay respectful, and tell an adult as soon as possible.

- **Speak up.** If you feel uncomfortable with the comments or actions of someone—tell someone! It is better to let a trusted adult know than to let the problem continue.

- **Get help.** If you feel like you are at risk of harming yourself or others, get help now!

Being Bullied Online

When someone is bullying you online or via text message:
Remember, bullying does not only happen at school. It can happen anywhere, including through texting, the Internet, and social media.

How You Can Contribute to Antibullying Initiatives

The Federal Partners in Bullying Prevention (FPBP) invites you to take action to make a difference in your community! By following the steps in this youth engagement toolkit (www.stopbullying.gov/sites/default/files/2017-09/youthengagement_brieftoolkit_compliant.pdf), you can join other youth leaders across the country and the FPBP to organize a bullying prevention social and educational event.

Chapter 17

Abuse in Pregnancy

Chapter Contents

Section 17.1

Prevalence, Effects, Screening, and Management

This section includes text excerpted from "Intimate Partner Violence Screening," Agency for Healthcare Research and Quality (AHRQ), May 2015. Reviewed October 2018.

Nearly one in six pregnant women in the United States have been abused by a partner.

Women who experience intimate partner violence prior to and during pregnancy are at increased risk of low maternal weight gains, infections and high blood pressure, and are more likely to deliver preterm or low-birth weight babies.

Women who received prenatal counseling for intimate partner violence (IPV) had fewer recurrent episodes of IPV during and postpregnancy, as well as better birth outcomes such as lower rates of preterm birth and low birth weight.

IPV affects as many as 324,000 pregnant women each year.

Physical violence perpetrated by intimate partners is also often accompanied by emotionally abusive and controlling behavior. Although women of all ages may experience IPV, it is most prevalent among women of reproductive age and contributes to gynecologic disorders, pregnancy complications, unintended pregnancy, and sexually transmitted infections.

Due to underreporting and lack of recognition, IPV may occur more commonly among pregnant women than conditions for which they are currently being screened (i.e., gestational diabetes, preeclampsia, etc.). IPV can have direct and indirect impacts on fetal health, such as spontaneous abortion and maternal stress, which in turn can induce alcohol or drug use or smoking. These behaviors are associated with poor outcomes like low birth weight, fetal alcohol syndrome, and others. Three studies have also found possible associations between IPV and unintended pregnancies.

Research has found that IPV rates are highest in families with young children, which supports intervention during the pre- and perinatal periods. Screening is effective in the early detection and effectiveness of interventions to increase the safety of abused women.

U.S. Preventive Services Task Force (USPSTF) Recommendation

Screen women of childbearing age for IPV, such as domestic violence (DV), and provide or refer women who screen positive to intervention services. This recommendation applies to women who do not have signs or symptoms of abuse.

How Frequently Is This Preventive Service Being Provided?

Ninety-six percent of women receive prenatal care, which can consist of 12–13 prenatal visits. As such, it can be an important window of opportunity to screen. Although screening for IPV is recommended by the USPSTF, studies have shown very low screening rates ranging from 1.5–12 percent in primary care settings.

What Are the Best Screening Practices Identified in the Literature?

The American Congress of Obstetricians and Gynecologists (ACOG), in line with the United States. U.S. Department of Health and Human Services (HHS) and Institute of Medicine (IOM), recommends that IPV screening and counseling should be a core part of women's preventive health visits and at periodic intervals, including obstetric care (at first prenatal visit, at least once per trimester, and at the postpartum checkup, as disclosure may not occur at the first attempt). Providers should also offer ongoing support, and review available prevention and referral options.

All of the screening tools evaluated by the USPSTF are directed at patients and can be self-administered or used in a clinician interview format. The six tools that showed the most sensitivity and specificity were:

- HITS (Hurt, Insult, Threaten, Scream)
- OVAT (Ongoing Violence Assessment Tool)
- STaT (Slapped, Things and Threaten)
- HARK (Humiliation, Afraid, Rape, Kick)
- CTQ–SF (Modified Childhood Trauma Questionnaire–Short Form)
- WAST (Woman Abuse Screen Tool)

Studies have shown that patient self–administered or computerized screenings are as effective as clinician interviewing in terms of disclosure, comfort, and time spent screening.

What Are the Best Interventions Identified in the Literature?

Evidence from randomized trials supports a variety of interventions for women of childbearing age, including counseling, home visits, and mentoring support. Depending on the type of intervention, these services may be provided by clinicians, nurses, social workers, nonclinical mentors, or community workers. Counseling generally includes information on safety behaviors and community resources. In addition to counseling, home visits may include emotional support, education on problem-solving strategies, and parenting support.

A systematic review that evaluated the benefits of IPV interventions in primary health settings showed that 76 percent of interventions resulted in at least one statistically significant benefit—reductions of violence, improvement of physical and emotional health, safety promoting behaviors, use of IPV community-based resources. It also highlighted the following domains of successful interventions: focusing on self-efficacy and empowerment, focusing on access to IPV resources, and brief nonphysician interventions (collaborative multidisciplinary care teams).

What Barriers Exist for Providers?

- Time constraints
- Discomfort with the topic
- Fear of offending the patient or partner
- Need for privacy
- Perceived lack of power to change the problem, and
- A misconception regarding patient population's risk of exposure to IPV

What Does the Affordable Care Act Cover?

All Marketplace plans and many other plans must cover domestic and interpersonal violence screening and counseling for all women without charging a copayment or coinsurance. This is true even if the patient has not met their yearly deductible. This applies only when these services are delivered by a network provider.

Section 17.2

Intimate Partner Violence and Perinatal Depression as Comorbidities

This section includes text excerpted from "A Comprehensive Approach for Community-Based Programs to Address Intimate Partner Violence and Perinatal Depression," U.S. Department of Health and Human Services (HHS), January 2013. Reviewed October 2018.

Intimate partner violence (IPV) and perinatal depression (PD) are both extremely important public-health concerns. Women from all sexual orientations; racial, ethnic, cultural, and socioeconomic backgrounds; and of all ages are at risk for experiencing both PD and IPV. It is important to note that a majority of data specific to prevalence and trends relies mostly on self-reporting. The shame and stigma associated with both violence and depression often prevent women from reporting. As a result, prevalence data regarding rates of IPV and PD are often severely underestimated.

What Is Perinatal Depression?

Perinatal depression (PD) is a multifaceted condition which includes both physical and emotional effects that can occur before, during, and after birth. The term "PD" is used to describe a spectrum of conditions: prenatal depression, postpartum blues, postpartum depression, and postpartum psychosis.

Prenatal depression affects approximately 14 to 25 percent of pregnant women. Fifty percent of these women will then develop postpartum depression following the birth of the child, so early identification and treatment are essential. Symptoms of the mother include irritability, tearfulness, anxiety, and insomnia.

Postpartum blues is considered normal and generally occurs within the first 10 days after childbirth, affecting up to 80 percent of new mothers (American Congress of Obstetricians and Gynecologists [ACOG]). Symptoms of the mother include tearfulness, fatigue, insomnia, anxiety, and feelings of loss or being overwhelmed. However, these symptoms are generally mild, do not affect infant care, and generally resolve in the first 10 days after childbirth. Postpartum psychosis is a less common, but more severe form, of postpartum depression, which can include hallucinations, paranoia, suicide, or infanticide, requiring emergency attention. This condition is rare affecting 0.1 to 0.2 percent of women each year.

The Connection between IPV and PD

Research shows that IPV can strongly increase one's risk of experiencing depression. IPV survivors report greater medical service use and an increased mental-health burden that includes depression, posttraumatic stress disorder (PTSD), suicidal thinking, and suicide attempts. IPV was one of the most important independent risk factors for antenatal depression, increasing a woman's odds for antenatal depression by more than three times. As a study aptly concludes, IPV has been connected to mental-health issues in non-pregnant women—and as, "Pregnant women represent a population susceptible to mental-health disturbance postpartum, so it would seem logical to examine the effect of pregnancy in victims of IPV." Another study also found that women experiencing IPV during pregnancy were 2.5 times more likely to report being depressed than those not experiencing IPV. Still other research finds that IPV is strongly associated with perinatal depression in particular, along with other social stresses such as marital relations, work, finances, and housing.

In addition, depression and mental-health illness have been associated with an increased risk of experiencing IPV. A study finds that women experiencing depression or other mental illness have a higher risk of violent victimization and trauma than women without mental illness. The exact mechanism or causal relationship between co-occurring IPV/PD is not explicit, but the research clearly demonstrates a strong connection between risk factors for IPV/PD and experiences of IPV/PD. The distinctive stressors of pregnancy can exacerbate the physical, emotional, and social risk factors for experiencing both IPV and PD. Regardless of varying rates of IPV/PD prevalence, the negative effects of IPV are well documented and include preterm labor, low birth weight, future child abuse, and femicide. Survivors of intimate partner violence are more likely to experience complications during pregnancy (e.g., low maternal weight gain, infections, high blood pressure, vaginal bleeding).

IPV survivors are also less likely to have (or take advantage of) access to prenatal care and general healthcare. They are also at higher risk for substance abuse. Substance abuse and mental-health disorders can intersect and, in some cases, exacerbate outcomes. Depression alone can also lead to adverse maternal and infant health outcomes.

Specifically, maternal depression is associated with increased negative health behaviors such as substance abuse, noncompliance with a prenatal care regimen, and decreased ability to care for a newborn. Depression is also associated with preterm delivery and low birth rate.

Chapter 18

Disability and Maltreatment

Prevalence of Abuse Among Adult Individuals With Disability

In the year 2014, an estimated 35.9 percent (16,135,600) of noninstitutionalized adults ages 65+ in the United States and an estimated 10.5 percent (20,549,100) of noninstitutionalized adults ages 18 to 64 reported a disability. Unfortunately, some of these vulnerable adults are abused by family members, service providers, care assistants, and others. This abuse places the victim's health, safety, emotional well-being, and ability to engage in daily life activities at risk.

Below is a sampling of research findings relating to abuse of adults with disabilities:

- Institutionalized adult women with disabilities reported a 33 percent prevalence of having ever experienced interpersonal violence (IPV) versus 21 percent for institutionalized adult women without disabilities.

This chapter contains text excerpted from the following sources: Text beginning with the heading "Prevalence of Abuse Among Individuals with Disability" is excerpted from "Research," U.S. Administration on Aging, (AOA), May 15, 2008. Reviewed October 2018; Text beginning with the heading "Maltreatment among Children with Disabilities" is excerpted from "Childhood Maltreatment among Children with Disabilities," Centers for Disease Control and Prevention (CDC), June 22, 2018; Text under the heading "Family Violence against Women with Disabilities" is excerpted from "Violence against Women with Disabilities," Office on Women's Health (OWH), September 13, 2018.

- In a study of 342 adult men, 55 percent of men experienced physical abuse by any person after becoming disabled. Nearly 12 percent of these men stated they experienced physical abuse by a personal-assistance service provider over their lifetime.

- In the comprehensive review of literature published from 2000–2010, lifetime prevalence of any type of IPV against adult women with disabilities was found to be 26–90 percent. Lifetime prevalence of IPV against adult men with disabilities was found to be 28.7–86.7 percent. Researchers concluded that, over the course of their lives, IPV occurs at disproportionate and elevated rates among men and women with disabilities.

Abuse of Adults with Dementia

Research indicates that people with dementia are at greater risk of elder abuse. Approximately 5.1 million American elders over 65 have some kind of dementia. Close to half of all people over age 85 have Alzheimer disease or another form of dementia, making this the fastest growing segment of our population to be affected by the disease. By 2025, most states are expected to see an increase in Alzheimer prevalence.

People with dementia are particularly vulnerable to abuse because of impairments in memory, communication abilities, and judgment. Prevalence estimates are influenced, and possibly underestimated, by the fact that many people with dementia are unable, frightened, or embarrassed to report abuse. Additionally, several studies have confirmed that as dementia progresses, so does the risk of all types of abuse. Research on elder abuse of people with dementia is inherently difficult. Abuse among this population is a hidden offense, perpetrated against vulnerable people with memory impairment, by those on whom they depend. Prevalence estimates are influenced, and possibly underestimated, by the fact that many people with dementia are unable, frightened or embarrassed to report its presence.

Below are several findings on elder abuse of people with dementia.

- Prevalence rates for abuse and neglect in people with dementia vary from study to study, ranging from 27.5 percent to 55 percent.

- A 2010 study found that 47 percent of participants with dementia had been mistreated by their caregivers. Of them, 88.5 percent experienced psychological abuse, 19.7 percent experienced physical abuse, and 29.5 percent experienced neglect. A 2009 study revealed that close to 50 percent of people with dementia experience some kind of abuse.

- A 2009 study based in the United Kingdom found that 52 percent of caregivers reported some abusive behavior toward family members with dementia.

Maltreatment among Children with Disabilities

Children with disabilities may be at higher risk for abuse or neglect than children without disabilities. There are steps that parents can take to protect children with disabilities from abuse or neglect. Safe, stable, nurturing relationships between parents and children and between parents and other adults are an important way to protect your child from harm.

Parents can prevent abuse and neglect of children:

- Know the signs of possible abuse, such as:
  - Sudden changes in, or unusual behavior
  - Cuts and bruises
  - Broken bones (not due to a medical condition)
  - Burns
  - Complaints about painful genitals
- Know the signs of possible neglect, such as:
  - Constant hunger or thirst (not due to a medical condition)
  - Dirty hair or skin
  - Chronic diaper rash (not due to a medical condition)
- Know where your child is and what she or he is doing when you are not at home.
- Get to know the people who take care of your child. Only leave your child with someone you know and who can take care of your child in a place where your child will be safe from harm and danger.
- Know that your child's school must treat your child with dignity. Your child should not be punished by being mistreated, restrained, or secluded.
- Take steps to make your house a safe place where your child will not get injured.

- Talk to your child about behavior and situations that are safe and not safe.

- Identify and remind your child of safe adults that she or he can turn to. Role-playing and practicing how to find a safe adult can help young children learn where to go.

If you think your child has been abused or neglected you can:

- Talk to your child's doctor about your concerns

- Take your child to a hospital or doctor's office to be examined

- Call the police (dial 911 on your phone)

- Call the Childhelp National Child Abuse Hotline at 800-4-A-CHILD (800-422-4453)

Take care of yourself:

Being a parent is the hardest job you will ever love. It is easy to become overwhelmed, especially if you have a child who has a disability or other special healthcare needs.

Here are some things to remember when parenting gets stressful or difficult:

- Be realistic about what your child can and cannot do.

- If you are frustrated, give yourself a time-out to calm down and refocus!

- Ask people whom you trust to help you.

- Focus on the positive.

- Make time for yourself.

- Talk to a healthcare professional like your doctor or a therapist if you don't know how to handle your child's behavior.

Family Violence against Women with Disabilities

Research suggests that women with disabilities are more likely to experience domestic violence, emotional abuse, and sexual assault than women without disabilities. Women with disabilities may also feel more isolated, and feel they are unable to report the abuse, or they may be dependent on the abuser for their care. Like many women who are abused, women with disabilities are usually abused by someone they know, such as an intimate partner or family member. But women with disabilities can also face abuse from caregivers or personal assistants. Women with disabilities who need help with daily activities such as bathing, dressing, or eating may be more at risk of abuse because they are physically or mentally more vulnerable and can have many different caregivers in their life.

Recognizing Signs of Abuse in a Loved One with a Disability

Relatives must be strong advocates for their loved ones with disabilities. If you have a relative with a disability, learn the signs of abuse, especially if your relative has trouble communicating.

Report abuse to adult protective services if you notice any of the following with a loved one who has a disability:

- Suddenly being unable to meet essential day-to-day living needs that affect health, safety, or well-being
- Lack of contact with friends or family
- Visible handprints or bruising on the face, neck, arms, or wrists
- Burns, cuts, or puncture wounds
- Unexplained sprains, fractures, or dislocations
- Signs of injuries to internal organs, such as vomiting
- Wearing torn, stained, soiled, or bloody clothing
- Appearing hungry, malnourished, disoriented, or confused

Each state has an adult protective services agency.

Chapter 19

Abuse of Men

Chapter Contents

Section 19.1

About Domestic Violence against Men

This section contains text excerpted from the following sources: Text in this section begins with excerpts from "How Fatherhood Programs Can Address Domestic Violence," U.S. Department of Health and Human Services (HHS), October 17, 2016; Text under the heading "Prevalence of Victimization" is excerpted from "Prevalence and Characteristics of Sexual Violence, Stalking, and Intimate Partner Violence Victimization—National Intimate Partner and Sexual Violence Survey, United States, 2011," Centers for Disease Control and Prevention (CDC), September 5, 2014. Reviewed October 2018.

I swore never to be silent whenever and wherever human beings endure suffering and humiliation. We must always take sides. Neutrality helps the oppressor, never the victim. Silence encourages the tormentor, never the tormented. (Elie Wiesel)

Domestic violence (DV) is a violation to a person at the core of their being. It betrays love, destroys trust, inflicts irrevocable damage, and often leaves a jaded perception of love in its wake. Many individuals who have been harmed by an intimate partner feel afraid, embarrassed, blame themselves, and believe they are unable to reveal their pain to family members, friends, or others—even when they are in dire need of assistance.

Contrary to the myth, DV is not gender-based violence solely perpetrated by men against women. According to the National Coalition Against Domestic Violence (NCADV), one in four men have been victims of some form of physical violence by an intimate partner. Due to society's general apathetic response when it comes to the abuse of men, however (despite the severity), male victims of DV are often dismissed when they seek assistance from law enforcement and social services agencies. Men are threatened; physically, emotionally, verbally, and psychologically abused; and in many instances seriously injured by their intimate partners.

Domestic violence is caused by individuals who elect to employ violent, abusive behaviors as their methods of "communication," and the hidden yet common problem of battered men must be taken seriously, and the men must be aided in understanding the brutality of their experiences.

Domestic violence is a dangerous crime, and the violent behaviors that accompany it can be difficult to detect, especially for victims. It can be as subtle as an unkind word or as blatant as a slap across the face. Insecurities are masked, and what appears in the beginning as attentive, generous, and concerned becomes possessive, extremely jealous, and controlling.

It is important to evaluate relationships daily, and to take inventory of situations that may have given you pause. You might be experiencing domestic violence if your partner:

1. Monitors your phone calls, emails, text messages, social media accounts; micromanages your time; makes you account for every minute of your time (when you run errands, visit friends, commute to work, and so on);

2. Is overly critical; insulting; humiliates you (public or private); makes threats; blackmails you and threatens to expose private or sensitive personal information;

3. Acts overly jealous and possessive; constantly accuses you of being unfaithful; smothers you/is "clingy"; shows up unannounced (at home, job, gym, and so on); stalks you; calls excessively;

4. Is hypersensitive; has unpredictable, radical mood changes and an explosive temper; denies/minimizes the abuse/blames you for the violent behavior (your fault); and

5. Threatens you with weapons; hits, kicks, shoves, slaps, strangles, spits, or otherwise hurts you, your children, or your pets; causes visible injuries (bruises, cuts, burns); destroys/vandalizes property (cell phone, car, or home).

Your partner might offer reasonable explanations apologize, promise to change, attend counseling, or make spiritual commitments; however, it is crucial to understand that domestic violence is cyclical and usually becomes more frequent and severe over time.

Victims cannot stop their partner's abusive behavior, and ultimatums don't make people change. Abuse isn't a couple's issue, but rather the choice of the abuser. Know your strength. Know your limitations.

Prevalence of Victimization
Sexual Violence Victimization

An estimated 1.7 percent of (or almost two million) men report being raped during their lifetimes; 0.7 percent of men report completed forced penetration. The case count for men reporting rape in the preceding 12 months was too small to produce a statistically reliable prevalence estimate.

An estimated 39.5 percent of multiracial men report experiencing sexual violence other than rape during their lifetimes. In addition, 26.6 percent of Hispanic men, 24.5 percent of American Indian/Alaska Native men, 24.4 percent of non-Hispanic black men, and 22.2 percent of non-Hispanic white men report experiencing sexual violence other than rape during their lifetimes, and an estimated 15.8 percent of Asian or Pacific Islander men report experiencing this type of sexual violence during their lifetimes.

Stalking Victimization

Nationally, an estimated 5.7 percent of (or nearly 6.5 million) men have report experiencing stalking victimization during their lifetimes, while an estimated 2.1 percent (or 2.4 million) men report being stalked in the 12 months before taking the survey.

An estimated 9.3 percent of multiracial men report experiencing stalking during their lifetimes, as did an estimated 9.1 percent of non-Hispanic black men, 8.2 percent of Hispanic men, and 4.7 percent of non-Hispanic white men. The estimates for the other racial/ethnic groups of men are not reported because case counts were too small to produce a reliable estimate.

An estimated 58.2 percent of male stalking victims received unwanted telephone calls, and an estimated 56.7 percent received unwanted messages. An estimated 47.7 percent of male stalking victims were approached by their perpetrator, and an estimated 32.2 percent were watched, followed, or spied on with a listening or other device.

Among male stalking victims, an estimated 43.5 percent were stalked by an intimate partner, an estimated 31.9 percent by an acquaintance, an estimated 20.0 percent by a stranger, and an estimated 9.9 percent by a family member.

Intimate Partner Violence Victimization

Nationally, an estimated 0.5 percent of men reported experiencing penetrable rape by an intimate partner during their lifetimes. However, the case count for men reporting rape by an intimate partner in the preceding 12 months was too small to produce a statistically reliable prevalence estimate. An estimated 9.5 percent of men report experiencing other forms of sexual violence by an intimate partner during their lifetimes, while an estimated 2.1 percent of men report experiencing other forms of sexual violence by an intimate partner in the 12 months before taking the survey. The lifetime prevalence of physical violence by an intimate partner was an estimated 27.5 percent for men, and in the 12 months before taking the survey, an estimated 4.8 percent of men report experiencing some form of physical violence by an intimate partner. An estimated 14.0 percent of men reported experiencing at least one act of severe physical violence by an intimate partner during their lifetimes. With respect to individual severe physical violence behaviors, being hit with a fist or something hard was reportedly experienced by an estimated 10.1 percent of men, and 4.6 percent of men reported being kicked by an intimate partner. In the 12 months before taking the survey, an estimated 2.1 percent of men reported experiencing at least one form of severe physical violence by an intimate partner. The lifetime and 12-month prevalence of stalking by an intimate partner for men was an estimated 2.5 percent and 0.8 percent, respectively. Finally, an estimated 46.5 percent of men reported experiencing at least one act of psychological aggression by an intimate partner during their lifetimes; an estimated 18.0 percent of men reported experiencing some form of psychological aggression in the 12 months preceding the survey.

Intimate Partner Violence-Related Impact

Nationally, an estimated 11.5 percent of men have reported experiencing contact sexual violence, physical violence, or stalking by an intimate partner during their lifetimes and have reported experiencing at least one measured negative impact related to these or other forms of violence in that relationship. More specifically, an estimated 6.9 percent of men were fearful; 5.2 percent were concerned for their safety; 5.2 percent experienced one or more PTSD symptoms; 3.5 percent were physically injured; 1.6 percent needed medical care; 1.0 percent needed housing services; 4.0 percent needed legal services; and 4.8 percent missed at least one day of work or school. The case counts for men needing victim advocacy services, having contacted a crisis hotline, or contracting a sexually transmitted infection as a result of these types of violence were too small to produce statistically reliable estimates.

Section 19.2

Sexual Assault of Men

This section includes text excerpted from "Men and Sexual Trauma," National Center for Posttraumatic Stress Disorder (NCPTSD), U.S. Department of Veterans Affairs (VA), April 18, 2016.

At least 1 out of every 10 (or 10 percent) of men in the United States has suffered from trauma as a result of sexual assault. Like women, men who experience sexual assault may suffer from depression, post-traumatic stress disorder (PTSD), and other emotional problems as a result. However, emotional symptoms following trauma can look different in men than they do in women.

Who Are the Perpetrators of Male Sexual Assault?

• Those who sexually assault men or boys differ in a number of ways from those who assault only females.

• Boys are more likely than girls to be sexually abused by strangers or authority figures in organizations such as schools, churches, or athletics programs.

• Those who sexually assault males usually choose young men and male adolescents (the average age is 17 years old) as their victims and are more likely to assault multiple victims, compared to those who sexually assault females.

• Perpetrators often assault young males in isolated areas where help is not readily available. For instance, a perpetrator who assaults males may pick up a teenage hitchhiker on a remote road or find some other way to isolate his intended victim.

• As is true about those who assault and sexually abuse women and girls, most perpetrators of males are men. Specifically, men are perpetrators in about 86 out of every 100 (or 86 percent) of male victimization cases.

• Despite the popular misconception that only gay men would sexually assault men or boys, most male perpetrators identify as heterosexual and often have consensual sexual relationships with women.

214

What Are Some Symptoms Related to Sexual Trauma in Boys and Men?

Particularly when the assailant is a woman, the impact of sexual assault upon men may be downplayed by professionals and the public. However, men who have early sexual experiences with adults report problems in various areas at a much higher rate than those who do not.

Emotional Disorders

Men and boys who have been sexually assaulted are more likely to suffer from PTSD, anxiety disorders, and depression than those who have never been abused sexually.

Substance Abuse

Men who have been sexually assaulted have a high incidence of alcohol and drug use. For example, the probability for alcohol problems in adulthood is about 80 out of every 100 (or 80 percent) for men who have experienced sexual abuse, as compared to 11 out of every 100 (or 11 percent) for men who have never been sexually abused.

Risk-Taking Behavior

Exposure to sexual trauma can lead to risk-taking behavior during adolescence, such as running away and other delinquent behaviors. Having been sexually assaulted also makes boys more likely to engage in behaviors that put them at risk for contracting human immunodeficiency virus (HIV) (such as having sex without using condoms).

Help for Men Who Have Been Sexually Assaulted

Men who have been sexually assaulted often feel stigmatized, which can be the most damaging aspect of the assault. It is important for men to discuss the assault with a caring and unbiased support person, whether that person is a friend, clergy member, spiritual advisor, or clinician. However, it is vital that this support person be knowledgeable about sexual assault and men.

A local rape-crisis center may be able to refer men to mental-health practitioners who are well-informed about the needs of male sexual assault victims. If you are a man who has been assaulted and you suffer from any of these difficulties, please seek help from a mental-health professional who has expertise working with men who have been sexually assaulted.

Chapter 20

Elder Abuse

Chapter Contents

Section 20.1

Facts about Elder Abuse and Neglect

This section contains text excerpted from the following sources: Text in this section begins with excerpts from "Elder Abuse," National Institute on Aging (NIA), National Institutes of Health (NIH), December 29, 2016; Text beginning with the heading "Risk Factors" is excerpted from "Elder Abuse: Risk and Protective Factors," Centers for Disease Control and Prevention (CDC), May 17, 2018.

Abuse can happen to anyone—no matter the person's age, sex, race, religion, or ethnic or cultural background. Each year, hundreds of thousands of adults over the age of 60 are abused, neglected, or financially exploited. This is called elder abuse.

Abuse can happen in many places, including the older person's home, a family member's house, an assisted-living facility, or a nursing home.

Types of Abuse

There are many types of abuse:

- **Physical abuse** happens when someone causes bodily harm by hitting, pushing, or slapping.

- **Emotional abuse**, sometimes called psychological abuse, can include a caregiver saying hurtful words, yelling, threatening, or repeatedly ignoring the older person. Keeping that person from seeing close friends and relatives is another form of emotional abuse.

- **Neglect** occurs when the caregiver does not try to respond to the older person's needs.

- **Abandonment** is leaving a senior alone without planning for his or her care.

- **Sexual abuse** involves a caregiver forcing an older adult to watch or be part of sexual acts.

Money Matters

Financial abuse happens when money or belongings are stolen. It can include forging checks, taking someone else's retirement and Social Security (SS) benefits, or using another person's credit cards and bank accounts. It also includes changing names on a will, bank account, life insurance policy, or title to a house without permission from the older person. Financial abuse is becoming a widespread and hard-to-detect issue. Even someone you've never met can steal your financial information using the telephone or email. Be careful about sharing any financial information over the phone or online—you don't know who will use it.

Healthcare fraud can be committed by doctors, hospital staff, and other healthcare workers. It includes overcharging, billing twice for the same service, falsifying Medicaid or Medicare claims, or charging for care that wasn't provided. Older adults and caregivers should keep an eye out for this type of fraud.

Who Is Being Abused?

Most victims of abuse are women, but some are men. Likely targets are older people who have no family or friends nearby and people with disabilities, memory problems, or dementia.

Abuse can happen to an older person, but often affects those who depend on others for help with activities of everyday life—including bathing, dressing, and taking medicine. People who are frail may appear to be easy victims.

What Are Signs of Abuse?

You may see signs of abuse or neglect when you visit an older person at home or in an eldercare facility. You may notice the person:

- Has trouble sleeping
- Seems depressed or confused
- Loses weight for no reason
- Displays signs of trauma, such as rocking back and forth
- Acts agitated or violent
- Becomes withdrawn
- Stops taking part in activities she or he enjoys
- Has unexplained bruises, burns, or scars
- Looks messy, with unwashed hair or dirty clothes
- Develops bed sores or other preventable conditions

If you see signs of abuse, try talking with the older person to find out what's going on. For instance, the abuse may be from another resident and not from someone who works at the nursing home or assisted-living facility. Most importantly, get help.

Who Can Help?

Elder abuse will not stop on its own. Someone else needs to step in and help. Many older people are too ashamed to report mistreatment. Or, they're afraid if they make a report it will get back to the abuser and make the situation worse.

If you think someone you know is being abused—physically, emotionally, or financially—talk with him or her when the two of you are alone. You could say you think something is wrong and you're worried. Offer to take him or her to get help, for instance, at a local adult protective services agency.

Many local, state, and national social service agencies can help with emotional, legal, and financial problems.

The Administration for Community Living (ACL) has a National Center on Elder Abuse (NCEA) where you can learn about how to report abuse, where to get help, and state laws that deal with abuse and neglect.

What Is the Long-Term Effect of Abuse?

Most physical wounds heal in time. But, any type of mistreatment can leave the abused person feeling fearful and depressed. Sometimes, the victim thinks the abuse is his or her fault. Protective services agencies can suggest support groups and counseling that can help the abused person heal the emotional wounds.

Risk Factors

A combination of individual, relational, community, and societal factors contribute to the risk of becoming a perpetrator of elder abuse. They are contributing factors and may or may not be direct causes.

Understanding these factors can help identify various opportunities for prevention.

Risk Factors for Perpetration
Individual Level

- Current diagnosis of mental illness

- Current abuse of alcohol
- High levels of hostility
- Poor or inadequate preparation or training for caregiving responsibilities
- The assumption of caregiving responsibilities at an early age
- Inadequate coping skills
- Exposure to abuse as a child

Relationship Level

- High financial and emotional dependence upon a vulnerable elder
- Past experience of disruptive behavior
- Lack of social support
- Lack of formal support

Community Level

- Formal services, such as respite care for those providing care to elders, are limited, inaccessible, or unavailable

Societal Level

A culture where:

- There are high tolerance and acceptance of aggressive behavior
- Healthcare personnel, guardians, and other agents are given greater freedom in routine care and decision making
- Family members are expected to care for elders without seeking help from others
- Persons are encouraged to endure suffering or remain silent regarding their pains
- There are negative beliefs about aging and elders

In addition to the above factors, there are also specific characteristics of institutional settings that can increase the risk for perpetration of vulnerable elders, including:

- Unsympathetic or negative attitudes toward residents

- Chronic staffing problems
- Lack of administrative oversight, staff burnout, and stressful working conditions

Protective Factors for Elder Abuse

Protective factors reduce the risk of perpetrating abuse and neglect. Protective factors have not been studied as extensively or rigorously as risk factors. However, identifying and understanding protective factors are equally as important as researching risk factors. Research is needed to determine whether these factors do indeed buffer elders from abuse.

Protective Factors for Perpetration
Relationship Level

- Having numerous, strong relationships with people of varying social status

Community Level

- Coordination of resources and services among community agencies and organizations that serve the elderly population and their caregivers
- Higher levels of community cohesion and a strong sense of community or community identity
- Higher levels of community functionality and greater collective efficacy

Protective factors within institutional settings can include the following:

- Effective monitoring systems
- Solid institutional policies and procedures regarding patient care
- Regular training on elder abuse and neglect for employees
- Education and clear guidance on durable power of attorney and how it is to be used
- Regular visits by family members, volunteers, and social workers

Section 20.2

Prevalence and Consequences of Elder Maltreatment

This section includes text excerpted from "Elder Abuse: Consequences," Centers for Disease Control and Prevention (CDC), May 17, 2018.

Prevalence of Elder Abuse

Elder abuse, including neglect and exploitation, is experienced by an estimated one out of every ten people ages 60 and older who lives at home. For every one case of elder abuse that is detected or reported, it is estimated that approximately 23 cases remain hidden.

Consequences of Elder Abuse

The possible physical and psychosocial consequences of elder abuse are numerous and varied. Few studies have extensively examined the long-term consequences of elder abuse and distinguished them from those linked to normal aging.

Physical Effects

The most immediate probable physical effects include:

- Welts, wounds, and injuries (e.g., bruises, lacerations, dental problems, head injuries, broken bones, pressure sores)

- Persistent physical pain and soreness

- Nutrition and hydration issues

- Sleep disturbances

- Increased susceptibility to new illnesses (including sexually transmitted diseases (STDs))

- Exacerbation of preexisting health conditions

- Increased risks for premature death

Psychological Effects

Established psychological effects of elder abuse include high levels of distress and depression. Other potential psychological consequences that need further scientific study are:

- Increased risks for developing fear and anxiety reactions
- Learned helplessness
- Posttraumatic stress disorder (PTSD)

Chapter 21

Abuse Reported by the Lesbian, Gay, Bisexual, and Transgender Community

Chapter Contents

Section 21.1

Domestic Violence Encounters Reported by the Lesbian, Gay, and Bisexual Community

This section includes text excerpted from "NISVS: An Overview of 2010 Findings on Victimization by Sexual Orientation," Centers for Disease Control and Prevention (CDC), June 30, 2013. Reviewed October 2018.

Key Findings on Victimization by Sexual Orientation

The Sexual Orientation Report indicates that individuals who self-identify as lesbian, gay, and bisexual have an equal or higher prevalence of experiencing intimate partner violence (IPV), sexual violence (SV), and stalking as compared to self-identified heterosexuals. Bisexual women are disproportionally impacted. They experienced a significantly higher lifetime prevalence of rape, physical violence, and/ or stalking by an intimate partner, and rape, and SV (other than rape) by any perpetrator, when compared to both lesbian and heterosexual women.

Sexual minority respondents reported levels of intimate partner violence at rates equal to or higher than those of heterosexuals.

- Forty-four percent of lesbian women, 61 percent of bisexual women, and 35 percent of heterosexual women experienced rape, physical violence, and/or stalking by an intimate partner at some point in their lifetime.

- Twenty-six percent of gay men, 37 percent of bisexual men, and 29 percent of heterosexual men experienced rape, physical violence, and/or stalking by an intimate partner at some point in their lifetime.

- Approximately one in five bisexual women (22%) and nearly one in 10 heterosexual women (9%) have been raped by an intimate partner at some point in their lifetime.

Rates of some form of sexual violence were higher among lesbian women, gay men, and bisexual women, and men compared to heterosexual women and men.

- Approximately one in eight lesbian women (13%), nearly half of bisexual women (46%), and one in six heterosexual women (17%) have been raped at some point in their lifetime. This translates to an estimated 214,000 lesbian women, 1.5 million bisexual women, and 19 million heterosexual women who have been abused at some point in their lives.

- Four in 10 gay men (40%), nearly half of bisexual men (47%), and one in five heterosexual men (21%) have experienced SV other than rape at some point in their lifetime. This translates into nearly 1.1 million gay men, 903,000 bisexual men, and 21.6 million heterosexual men who have been the victim of some form of sexual violence at some point in their lives.

Table 21.1. Lifetime Prevalence of Rape, Physical Violence, and/or Stalking by an Intimate Partner

Women		Men	
Lesbian	44%	Gay	26%
Bisexual	61%	Bisexual	37%
Heterosexual	35%	Heterosexual	29%

Among rape victims, bisexual women experienced rape earlier in life compared to heterosexual women.

- Of those women who have been raped, almost half of bisexual women (48%) and more than a quarter of heterosexual women (28%) experienced their first completed rape between the ages of 11 and 17 years.

The rate of stalking among bisexual women is more than double the rate among heterosexual women.

- One in three bisexual women (37%) and one in six heterosexual women (16%) have experienced stalking victimization at some point during their lifetime in which they felt very fearful or believed that they or someone close to them would be harmed or killed. This translates into 1.2 million bisexual women and 16.8 million heterosexual women.

A higher percentage of bisexual women reported being concerned for their safety or injured as a result of IPV than lesbian or heterosexual women.

- Approximately one-fifth of self-identified lesbian and heterosexual women (20% and 22%, respectively) and one-half of bisexual women (48%) reported they were concerned for their safety and/or reported at least one posttraumatic stress disorder (PTSD) symptom (20%, 46%, and 22%, respectively, at some point in their lifetime).

- Nearly one in three bisexual women (37%) and one in seven heterosexual women (16%) were injured as a result of rape, physical violence, and/or stalking by an intimate partner at some point in their lifetime.

Opportunities for Prevention and Action

The promotion of respectful, nonviolent relationships is key to preventing violence. Findings from the Sexual Orientation Report highlight the need for broad-based prevention efforts as well as services and support systems that address the specific needs of lesbian, gay, and bisexual women and men. It is important for all sectors of society, including individuals, families, and communities, to work together to end IPV, SV, and stalking. Opportunities for prevention and intervention include:

- Implementing prevention approaches that promote acceptance and recognition of healthy, respectful relationships regardless of sexual orientation

- Including lesbian, gay, and bisexual persons in national, state, and local violence research

- Referring victims and survivors to culturally appropriate, accessible services

Section 21.2

Mistreatment of Lesbian, Gay, Bisexual, or Transgender Elders

This section includes text excerpted from "Mistreatment of Lesbian, Gay, Bisexual, and Transgender (LGBT) Elders," Administration for Community Living (ACL), March 8, 2013. Reviewed October 2018.

Population Estimates of LGBT Elders

It has been estimated that nine million Americans identify as lesbian, gay, bisexual, or transgender (LGBT). It has also been approximated that 1.5 million adults, aged 65 or older, are LGB (no transgender estimate provided). It should be noted, however, that estimates of the LGBT population may vary depending upon measurement methods and consideration of those who may not self-identify as LGBT due to social stigma.

LGBT Elders Face Multiple Challenges

LGBT elders face the typical challenges of aging, including the possibility of elder abuse or domestic violence, in combination with the threat of discrimination and abuse due to their sexual orientation or gender identity.

In a 2006 study by Metlife Mature Market Institute (MMI), 27 percent of LGBT Baby Boomers reported that they had great concern about discrimination as they age.

What's Happening inside Institutional and Long-Term Care Facilities?
Types of Discrimination Experienced by LGBT Elders

- Denial of visitors

- Refusal to allow same-sex couples to share rooms

- Refusal to place a transgender elder in a ward that matches their gender identity

- Keeping partners from participation in medical decision making

Types of Mistreatment Experienced by Transgender Elders

- Physical abuse

- Denial of personal care services

- Psychological abuse

- Being involuntarily "outed"

- Being prevented from dressing according to their gender identity

- Refused admission

Research Findings on Occurrence of Abuse

Unfortunately, prevalence and incidence studies regarding the abuse and neglect of LGBT elders are sorely lacking. Available data and information relating to the occurrence of abuse include:

- In a survey of 416 LGB elders, aged 60 or older, 65 percent of respondents reported experiencing victimization due to sexual orientation (e.g., verbal abuse, the threat of violence, physical assault, sexual assault, the threat of orientation disclosure, discrimination) and 29 percent had been physically attacked. Men were physically attacked nearly three times more often. Those who had been physically attacked reported poorer current mental health. Many in the study were still closeted from others. Serious family or personal problems can result from disclosure of an older adult's LGB identity.

- Caregivers may not be accepting of LGBT elders. In a survey of 3,500 LGBT elders, aged 55 and older, 8.3 percent of the elders reported being abused or neglected by a caretaker because of homophobia and 8.9 percent experienced blackmail or financial exploitation.

- Prejudice and hostility encountered by LGBT elders in institutional-care facilities create difficult environments. Staff may deny an LGBT elder visitors, refuse to allow same-sex couples to share a room, refuse to place a transgender elder in a ward that matches their gender identity, or keep partners from participating in medical decision making.

- Transphobia, or social prejudice against transgendered persons, may be more intense than homophobia with a very high rate of violent victimization.

- Cross-study investigation reveals that transgender people, in general, are at high risk of abuse and violence. Initial data reported by MAP state that an average of 42 percent of transgender people have experienced some form of physical violence or abuse. Further, an average 80 percent of transgender people have experienced verbal abuse or harassment. Therefore, it is a reasonable assumption that transgender elders may have experienced some form of abuse.

- Many transgender older adults have experienced mistreatment in long-term-care facilities. Examples include physical abuse, denial of personal care services, psychological abuse, being involuntarily "outed," and being prevented from dressing according to their gender identity. Others are refused admission into long-term-care facilities. The fear of discrimination and its reality result in underutilization of services.

Research Findings on Issues Affecting Help-Seeking

- As a result of growing up in a homophobic or transphobic environment, some LGBT elders may go to extraordinary measures to hide their sexual orientation. There may be such significant stigma for these elders that they will not label themselves. This may affect an abuse victim's willingness to seek help, out of fear of needing to "out" themselves to authorities and face possible hostility. This may also affect their desire to enlist home-care services out of fear of abuse.

- Lesbian, gay, and bisexual (LGB) adults from older generations lived under severe stigmatization of their identities. Many victims of attacks based on their sexual orientation do not tell others of the attacks out of fear that their sexual orientation will be disclosed or that authorities will respond with hostility or indifference.

- Victimization based on sexual orientation can lead to internalized homophobia manifested as guilt or shame. Victims may come to believe that they are not worthy people and deserve loneliness, poor living conditions, and ill health. They may not want to seek out or accept help and are at risk of self-neglect.

- For a victim of abuse in a same-sex relationship, it may be difficult to seek help because of the personal, familial, and societal risks in coming out as gay or lesbian and as a victim of domestic violence.

- Abusers may use victim fear of homophobia or threaten to "out" their victims to others as a means of control.

- Legal discrimination may discourage elder LGBT abuse victims from leaving abusive relationships because they may have no or limited legal rights to assets shared with the partner.

Section 21.3

What Rights Do You Have as a Lesbian, Gay, Bisexual, or Transgender Victim of Domestic Violence?

"Legal Rights for LGBT Victims of Domestic Violence" © 2016
Omnigraphics. Reviewed October 2018.

Domestic violence affects all sorts of intimate relationships, including those of lesbian, gay, bisexual, and transgender (LGBT) people. In fact, research has shown that the prevalence of domestic violence among same-sex couples is between 15 and 50 percent, which is the same rate found among heterosexual couples. Yet people in same-sex relationships face a number of social and legal barriers that may limit their ability to protect themselves from domestic abuse.

One such barrier is common misconception that abuse is unlikely to occur between same-sex partners because there tends to be less disparity in their physical size and strength—or, if it does occur, then it is "mutual battering." Compounding the problem, many LGBT people are reluctant to identify themselves as victims of domestic violence because they worry about encountering homophobia and discrimination. Some LGBT people believe that reporting domestic violence to law enforcement or utilizing support services could lead to involuntary outing of their sexual orientation or gender identity to family members or employers.

Civil Protection Orders

LGBT people may also find it more difficult to obtain legal protection against domestic abuse. One of the main legal tools used by survivors of domestic violence is the civil protection order (CPO). A CPO is an order issued by a family court that is intended to prevent domestic violence. Typically, the court orders the abuser to stop threatening or hurting the victim. In addition, it may order the abuser to stay away from the victim and other members of the household or family for up to five years.

Obtaining a CPO offers many benefits to survivors of domestic violence. It informs the abuser that domestic violence is a crime, and warns that any further incidents can result in arrest. It also establishes rules that the abuser must follow while the CPO is in effect, such as vacating the family home or paying child support. Finally, a CPO can stop the cycle of violence and ensure the victim's safety while they seek support and make plans for the future.

The process of obtaining a CPO generally involves two different legal hearings before a judge or magistrate. Experts recommend that people seeking a CPO hire an attorney to represent them in these proceedings. In the first one, called the ex parte hearing, the judge gathers information about the domestic violence complaint and decides whether the CPO request meets the requirements of state law. If so, the judge issues an ex parte CPO and schedules a full hearing within a week to ten days. In the full hearing, the judge hears testimony from the victim, the accused abuser, and witnesses for both sides. If a final CPO is issued, the court clerk provides certified copies to both parties, and it remains in force until the date indicated on these documents.

Same-Sex Domestic Abuse and CPOs

CPOs are important tools that empower domestic violence victims without requiring them to file criminal charges. Although it seems fair that this form of protection should be available to all citizens, in reality it can be much more difficult for LGBT people to obtain a CPO. State laws concerning CPOs vary widely in the types of relationships that qualify for protection. Some states specify that people can only seek CPOs if they are related to the abuser by blood or marriage, if they have lived with the abuser, or if they have a child together. Some states permit people who were involved in dating relationships or who shared financial and family responsibilities with the abuser to file for a CPO. But some of this statutory language excludes LGBT people.

Only one state, Hawaii, specifically makes CPOs available to "current or former same-sex partners." Most other state laws use gender-neutral language that makes the protection of LGBT domestic violence survivors subject to interpretation by the courts. A few state laws only allow people to apply for CPOs if the domestic violence occurred in a relationship with someone of the opposite sex. These laws are changing, however, with Montana dropping the opposite-sex requirement in 2013. It remains unclear how the 2015 U.S. Supreme Court (USSC) ruling that legalized same-sex marriage throughout the United States will impact the legal protections granted to LGBT domestic violence victims.

References

1. "Civil Protection Order," *Someplace Safe*, 2012.

2. Kansler, Zach. "Same Sex Domestic Abuse and Orders of Protection," *Albany Government Law Review*, February 6, 2011.

3. "Know Your Rights: LGBT Domestic Violence Survivors," Legal Momentum, 2001.

Chapter 22

Abuse within the Military

What Is Military Sexual Trauma (MST)?

Military sexual trauma, or MST, is the term used by the U.S. Department of Veterans Affairs (VA) to refer to experiences of sexual assault or repeated, threatening sexual harassment that a veteran experienced during his or her military service.

The definition used by the VA comes from Federal law (Title 38 U.S. Code 1720D) and is "psychological trauma, which in the judgment of a VA mental health professional, resulted from a physical assault of a sexual nature, battery of a sexual nature, or sexual harassment which occurred while the veteran was serving on active duty, active duty for training, or inactive duty training."

Sexual harassment is further defined as "repeated, unsolicited verbal or physical contact of a sexual nature which is threatening in character."

More concretely, MST includes any sexual activity in which a servicemember is involved against his or her will—she or he may have been pressured into sexual activities (for example, with threats of negative consequences for refusing to be sexually cooperative or with implied better treatment in exchange for sex), may have been unable to consent to sexual activities (for example, when intoxicated), or may

---

This chapter includes text excerpted from "Military Sexual Trauma," National Center for Posttraumatic Stress Disorder (NCPTSD), U.S. Department of Veterans Affairs (VA), January 22, 2018.

have been physically forced into sexual activities. Other experiences that fall into the category of MST include:

- Unwanted sexual touching or grabbing

- Threatening, offensive remarks about a person's body or sexual activities

- Threatening and unwelcome sexual advances

The identity or characteristics of the perpetrator, whether the servicemember was on or off duty at the time, and whether she or he was on or off base at the time do not matter. If these experiences occurred while an individual was on active duty or active duty for training, they are considered by the VA to be MST.

How Common Is MST?

The VA's national screening program, in which every veteran seen for healthcare is asked whether she or he experienced MST, provides data on how common MST is among veterans seen by the VA. National data from this program reveal that about 1 in 4 women and 1 in 100 men respond "yes," that they experienced MST, when screened by their VA provider. Although rates of MST are higher among women, there are actually significant numbers of women and men seen by the VA who have experienced MST.

It is important to keep in mind that these data speak only to the rate of MST among veterans who have chosen to seek VA healthcare; they cannot be used to make an estimate of the actual rates of sexual assault and harassment experiences among all individuals serving in the United States Military. Also, although veterans who respond "yes" when screened are asked if they are interested in learning about MST-related services available, not every veteran who responds "yes" necessarily needs or is interested in treatment. MST is an experience, not a diagnosis, and the current treatment needs of veterans will vary.

How Can MST Affect Veterans?

MST is an experience, not a diagnosis or a mental-health condition, and as with other forms of trauma, there are a variety of reactions that veterans can have in response to MST. The type, severity, and duration of a difficulties will all vary based on factors such as:

- Whether she or he has a prior history of trauma

- The types of responses from others she or he received at the time of the MST

- Whether the MST happened once or was repeated over time

Although trauma can be a life-changing event, people are often remarkably resilient after experiencing trauma. Many individuals recover without professional help; others may generally function well in their life, but continue to experience some level of difficulties or have strong reactions in certain situations. For some veterans, the experience of MST may continue to affect their mental and physical health in significant ways, even many years later.

Some of the experiences both female and male survivors of MST may have included:

- **Strong emotions:** Feeling depressed; having intense, sudden emotional responses to things; feeling angry or irritable all the time

- **Feelings of numbness:** Feeling emotionally "flat"; difficulty experiencing emotions such as love or happiness

- **Trouble sleeping:** Trouble falling or staying asleep; disturbing nightmares

- **Difficulties with attention, concentration, and memory:** Trouble staying focused; frequently finding their mind wandering; having a hard time remembering things

- **Problems with alcohol or other drugs:** Drinking to excess or using drugs daily; getting intoxicated or "high" to cope with memories or emotional reactions; drinking to fall asleep

- **Difficulty with things that remind them of their experiences of sexual trauma:** Feeling on edge or "jumpy" all the time; difficulty feeling safe; going out of their way to avoid reminders of their experiences

- **Difficulties with relationships:** Feeling isolated or disconnected from others; abusive relationships; trouble with employers or authority figures; difficulty trusting others

- **Physical health problems:** Sexual difficulties; chronic pain; weight or eating problems; gastrointestinal problems

Although posttraumatic stress disorder (PTSD) is commonly associated with MST, it is not the only diagnosis that can result from

MST. For example, VA medical record data indicate that, in addition to PTSD, the diagnoses most frequently associated with MST among users of VA healthcare are depression and other mood disorders, and substance-use disorders.

Fortunately, people can recover from experiences of trauma, and the VA has effective services to help veterans do this.

How Has the VA Responded to the Problem of MST?

The VA is strongly committed to ensuring that veterans have access to the help they need in order to recover from MST.

- Every VA healthcare facility has a designated MST Coordinator who serves as a contact person for MST-related issues. This person can help veterans find and access VA services and programs. She or he may also be aware of state and federal benefits and community resources that may be helpful.

- Recognizing that many survivors of sexual trauma do not disclose their experiences unless asked directly, VA healthcare providers ask every veteran whether she or he experienced MST. This is an important way of making sure veterans know about the services available to them.

- All treatment for physical and mental-health conditions related to experiences of MST is provided free of charge.

- To receive free treatment for mental and physical health conditions related to MST, veterans do not need to be service connected (or have a VA disability rating). Veterans may be able to receive this benefit even if they are not eligible for other VA care. Veterans do not need to have reported the incident(s) when they happened or have other documentation that they occurred.

- MST-related services are available at every VA medical center and every facility has providers knowledgeable about treatment for the aftereffects of MST. MST-related counseling is also available through community-based Vet Centers. Services are designated to meet veterans where they are in their recovery, whether this involves focusing on strategies for coping with challenging emotions and memories or, for veterans who are ready, actually talking about their MST experiences in depth.

- Nationwide, there are programs that offer specialized sexual-trauma treatment in residential or inpatient settings. These are programs for veterans who need more intense treatment and support.

- To accommodate veterans who do not feel comfortable in mixed-gender treatment settings, some facilities have separate programs for men and women. All residential and inpatient MST programs have separate sleeping areas for men and women.

In addition to its treatment programming, the VA also provides training to staff on issues related to MST, including a mandatory training on MST for all mental-health and primary-care providers. The VA also engages in a range of outreach activities to veterans and conducts monitoring of MST-related screening and treatment in order to ensure that adequate services are available.

Chapter 23

Abuse within Immigrant Communities

Chapter Contents

Section 23.1

Violence against Immigrant and Refugee Women: What You Need to Know

This section includes text excerpted from "Violence against Immigrant and Refugee Women," Office on Women's Health (OWH), U.S. Department of Health and Human Services (HHS), September 13, 2018.

Female immigrants or refugees face many of the same challenges as other abused women. However, they may also face some unique challenges, such as a fear of being deported or of losing custody of their children. Physical, sexual, emotional, or other type of abuse is never okay, even if it happens within a marriage. Violence against women is also against the law, even when the abuser or victim is not a U.S. citizen.

What Can Prevent Immigrant and Refugee Women from Reporting Violence or Abuse?

Immigrant and refugee women may not report violence or abuse because they may be:

- Humiliated by their community
- Taught that family duty comes first
- Accused of leaving or failing their culture and background
- Lied to about their partner's ability to have them deported and keep their children
- Told that, in the United States, the law says a woman must have sex with her partner
- Told that their abuser is allowed to hit them or use other forms of physical punishment against them

Although immigrant and refugee women may face such challenges, they also often have strong family ties and other sources of support. If you think you are being abused, reach out to someone who cares about you.

How Can Women Who Are Immigrants Report Violence or Abuse?

You can report a crime regardless of your immigration status. Violence is against the law. If you have been abused, you do not have to respond to questions about your immigration status. If the police officers do not speak your language, ask the police to provide a translator or find someone who can translate for you.

You can also call the free National Domestic Violence Hotline, 800-799-SAFE (800-799-7233), for help and resources in your area.

Can I Be Deported If I Report Abuse?

You cannot be deported if you are a U.S. citizen or a legal resident or have a valid Visa. The only exceptions to this are if you used fake documents to enter the country, broke the rules of your Visa, or committed certain crimes.

If you are undocumented (don't have legal papers to be in the United States) or are not sure about your immigration status, you should talk to an immigration lawyer. Your local domestic-violence shelter can help you find an immigration lawyer. You may be able to get a lawyer at no charge.

You may also be able to:

• Apply for a Green Card for yourself without needing your partner to file for immigration benefits for you. This is called self-petitioning. You can apply on your own if you are a victim of domestic violence and are the child, parent, or current or former spouse of a U.S. citizen or a permanent resident (Green Card holder).

• Get a U nonimmigration status Visa (U Visa). The U Visa gives protection to victims of domestic violence or sexual assault who are not U.S. citizens. The U Visa can be a path to a Green Card.

Can I Get a Restraining Order If I Am Not a U.S. Citizen?

Yes. You can get a restraining order (or court order of protection) even if you are not a citizen or legal permanent resident of the United States. A restraining order can prevent your abusive partner from contacting or touching you. You can get an application for a restraining order at a courthouse, women's shelter, or police station. Getting a restraining order is free.

How Can I Protect My Children?

If you are worried about the safety of yourself and your children, you can:

• File a restraining order (or court order of protection)

- Apply for a custody order that says your children have to live with you. You can also ask for the order to say that your partner may not take your children back to your home country. Notify the alert program of the U.S. Department of State (DOS) if you're worried your partner will try to take your children out of the country.

If you have a protection order or custody order, give a copy of the document to your children's school. Ask the school not to release the children to the abuser or anyone else not legally allowed access to your children.

How Is Female Genital Cutting Related to Violence against Immigrant and Refugee Women?

In some countries outside of the United States, female genital cutting (FGC) is performed on girls or women for cultural or traditional reasons. FGC means piercing, cutting, removing, or sewing closed all or part of a girl's or woman's external genitals for no medical reason. As a type of violence against women, FGC is illegal in the United States and in many other countries. FGC has no health benefits and can cause long-term health problems.

In the United States, estimates suggest that more than 513,000 girls and women have experienced FGC or are at risk of FGC.

Section 23.2

Basic Questions and Answers about Residency Laws for Victims of Domestic Violence

This section contains text excerpted from the following sources:
Text in this section begins with excerpts from "Victims of Criminal
Activity: U Nonimmigrant Status," U.S. Citizenship and Immigration
Services (USCIS), June 12, 2018; Text under the heading "Questions
and Answers: Battered Spouses, Children and Parents under the
Violence Against Women Act (VAWA)" is excerpted from "Questions
and Answers: Battered Spouses, Children and Parents under
the Violence Against Women Act (VAWA)," U.S. Citizenship and
Immigration Services (USCIS), July 15, 2015.
Reviewed October 2018.

The U nonimmigrant status (U Visa) is set aside for victims of
certain crimes who have suffered mental or physical abuse. U non-
immigrants Visas are helpful to law enforcement or government officials in the investigation or prosecution of criminal activity. Congress
created the U nonimmigrant Visa with the passage of the Victims
of Trafficking and Violence Protection Act (including the Battered
Immigrant Women's Protection Act) in October 2000. The legislation
was intended to strengthen the ability of law-enforcement agencies to
investigate and prosecute cases of domestic violence, sexual assault,
trafficking of aliens, and other crimes, while also protecting victims of
crimes who have suffered substantial mental or physical abuse due to
the crime and are willing to help law-enforcement authorities in the
investigation or prosecution of the criminal activity. The legislation
also helps law-enforcement agencies to better serve victims of crimes.

U Nonimmigrant Eligibility

You may be eligible for a U nonimmigrant Visa if:

- You are the victim of qualifying criminal activity.

- You have suffered substantial physical or mental abuse as a
  result of having been a victim of criminal activity.

- You have information about the criminal activity. If you are
  under the age of 16 or unable to provide information due to a
  disability, then a parent, guardian, or friend may possess the
  information about the crime on your behalf.

- You were helpful, are helpful, or are likely to be helpful to law enforcement in the investigation or prosecution of the crime. If you are under the age of 16 or unable to provide information due to a disability, then a parent, guardian, or friend may assist law enforcement on your behalf.

- The crime occurred in the United States or violated U.S. laws.

- You are admissible to the United States. If you are not admissible, you may apply for a waiver on Form I-192, Application for Advance Permission to Enter as a Nonimmigrant (www.uscis.gov/rule/40834).

Table 23.1. Qualifying Criminal Activities

• Abduction	• Hostage	• Sexual Assault
• Abusive Sexual Contact	• Incest	• Sexual Exploitation
• Blackmail	• Involuntary Servitude	• Slave Trade
• Domestic Violence	• Kidnapping	• Stalking
• Extortion	• Manslaughter	• Torture
• False Imprisonment	• Murder	• Trafficking
• Female Genital Mutilation	• Obstruction of Justice	• Witness Tampering
• Felonious Assault	• Peonage	• Unlawful Criminal
• Fraud in Foreign Labor Contracting	• Perjury	• Restraint
	• Prostitution	• Other Related Crimes*†
	• Rape	

Includes any similar activity where the elements of the crime are substantially similar.

†*Also includes attempt, conspiracy, or solicitation to commit any of the above and other related crimes.*

Applying for U Nonimmigrant Status

To apply (petition) for a U nonimmigrant status, submit:

- Form I-918, Petition for U Nonimmigrant Status

- Form I-918, Supplement B, U Nonimmigrant Status Certification. The Form I-918, Supplement B, must be signed by an authorized official of the certifying law-enforcement agency and the official must confirm that you were helpful, and currently being helpful, or will likely be helpful in the investigation or prosecution of the case.

- If any inadmissibility issues are present, you must file a Form I-192, Application for Advance Permission to Enter as Nonimmigrant, to request a waiver of the inadmissibility.

- A personal statement describing the criminal activity of which you were a victim

- Evidence to establish each eligibility requirement

You may also apply (petition) for U nonimmigrant status if you are outside the United States. To do this, you must:

- File all the necessary forms for U nonimmigrant status with the USCIS Service Center of your state.

- Follow all instructions that are sent from the USCIS Service Center, which will include having your fingerprints taken at the nearest U.S. Embassy or Consulate.

- If your petition is approved, you must follow consular process to enter the United States, which will include an interview with a consular officer at the nearest U.S. Embassy or Consulate.

- Information about your nearest United States Embassy or Consulate can be found at www.usembassy.gov

Filing for Qualifying Family Members

Certain qualifying family members are eligible for a derivative U Visa based on their relationship to you, the principal, filing for the U Visa. The principal petitioner must have their petition for a U Visa approved before their family members can be eligible for their own derivative U Visa.

Table 23.2. Qualifying Family Members

If you, the principal, are...	Then...
Under 21 years of age	You may petition on behalf of your spouse, children, parents and unmarried siblings under age 18
21 years of age or older	You may petition on behalf of your spouse and children.

To petition for a qualified family member, you must file a Form I-918, Supplement A, Petition for Qualifying Family Member of U-1 Recipient, at the same time as your application or at a later time.

Fees to File U Nonimmigrant Status Applications U Visa Extensions

- All U nonimmigrant status applications (petitions) and other forms related to the U petition are filed with the U.S.

Citizenship and Immigration Services (USCIS) Service Center of your state.

- All U nonimmigrant status applications (petitions) are free. You may request a fee waiver for any other form that is necessary for your U nonimmigrant status application (petition) by filing a Form I-912, Request for Fee Waiver, or by including your own written request for a fee waiver with your application or petition.

U Visa Extensions

When U nonimmigrant status is granted, it is valid for four years. However, extensions are available in certain, limited circumstances if the extension is:

- Needed based on a request from law enforcement;

- Needed based on exceptional circumstances,

- Needed due to delays in consular processing, or

- Automatically extended upon the filing and pendency of an application for adjustment (application for a Green Card).

U Visa Cap

- The limit on the number of U Visas that may be granted to principal petitioners each year is 10,000. However, there is no cap for family members deriving status from the principal applicant, such as spouses, children, or other eligible family members.

- If the cap is reached before all U nonimmigrant petitions have been adjudicated, USCIS will create a waiting list for any eligible principal or derivative petitioners that are awaiting a final decision and a U Visa. Petitioners placed on the waiting list will be granted deferred action or parole and are eligible to apply for work authorization while waiting for additional U Visas to become available.

- Once additional Visas become available, those petitioners on the waiting list will receive their Visa in the order in which their petition was received. Petitioners on the waiting list do not have to take any additional steps to request the U Visa. USCIS will notify the petitioner of the approval and the accompanying U Visa.

Applying for a Green Card

You may be eligible to apply for a Green Card (adjustment of status/permanent residence) if you meet certain requirements, including:

- You have been physically present in the United States for a continuous period of at least three years while in U nonimmigrant status, and

- You have not unreasonably refused to provide assistance to law enforcement since you received your U Visa.

- To apply for permanent residence (a Green Card) for yourself or a qualifying family member, visit the Green Card for a U Nonimmigrant page (www.uscis.gov/green-card/other-ways-get-green-card/green-card-victim-crime-u-nonimmigrant).

- Note: Any qualifying family member who does not have a derivative U Visa when the principal U nonimmigrant receives a Green Card is no longer eligible for a derivative U Visa, but may still be eligible to apply for lawful permanent residence.

- For information on extending your principal U Visa to ensure your family member remains eligible for a U Visa, please visit the T and U Visa extension memorandum.

Family Members Deriving Status

If the family member deriving status based on your status has met the eligibility requirements for a Green Card, they may apply for lawful permanent residence by filing their own Form I-485, Application to Register Permanent Residence or Adjust Status.

Even if your family members never had U nonimmigrant status or a U Visa, they may still be eligible for a Green Card.

- First, you must file a Form I-929, Petition for Qualifying Family Member of U-1 Nonimmigrant, for each eligible family member.

- You may file the Form I-929 at the same time or after you file your Form I-485.

If the Form I-929 for your family member(s) is approved:

- Family members in the United States may file the Form I-485 to apply for a Green Card.

- Family members outside the United States must first visit a U.S. embassy or consulate to obtain their immigrant Visa. Information for the local U.S. embassy or consulate and the procedures for obtaining a Visa to enter the United States may be found at www.usembassy.gov.

- Note: The Form I-929 is the form that is used to establish whether your family member is eligible to apply for a Green Card based on your U Visa based lawful permanent resident status. This does not mean that your family member will receive a Green Card. Even if the Form I-929 is approved, your family member is not automatically eligible for work authorization. They are eligible to work once they have received their Green Card.

Fees to File Form I-929

- All Form I-929 applications are sent to the USCIS Service Center of your state.

- There is a filing fee for the Form I-929. If you are unable to pay the fee, you may request a fee waiver by also filing a Form I-912, or by submitting a separate written request for a fee waiver.

Questions and Answers: Battered Spouses, Children and Parents under the Violence Against Women Act (VAWA)

What If My Form I-360, Petition for Amerasian, Widow(er), or Special Immigrant, Is Denied?

If your petition is denied, the denial letter will tell you how to file an appeal. You may file a Notice of Appeal along with the required fee at the USCIS Service Center within 33 days of receiving the denial. Once the fee is collected and the form is processed at the service center, the appeal will be referred to the Administrative Appeals Office in Washington, DC.

Can a Man File a Petition for Himself under the Violence Against Women Act (VAWA)?

Yes, VAWA applies equally to victims of either sex.

Do I Have to Remain Married to My Abusive Spouse until My Form I-360 Is Approved?

Effective October 28, 2000, you may file a Form I-360 if you are still married to your abusive spouse or, in certain circumstances, if you are not still married to your abusive spouse. If you are not still married to your abusive spouse when you file Form I-360, you must meet one of the following exceptions:

- You believed you were legally married to your abusive spouse but the marriage is not legitimate solely because of the bigamy of your abusive spouse.

- Your abusive spouse died within two years of filing the petition.

- Your abusive spouse lost or renounced his citizenship or lawful resident status due to an incident of domestic violence.

- Your marriage to your abusive spouse was terminated within the two years prior to filing of the petition, and there is a connection between the termination of the marriage and the battery or extreme cruelty.

The actual grounds for the termination of the marriage do not need to explicitly cite battery or extreme cruelty. After your petition has been filed, legal termination of the marriage will not usually affect the status of your petition. Unfortunately, current USCIS regulations do not reflect these statutory changes and still state that you must be married at the time of filing. USCIS is obligated to follow the statute, and you are no longer required to be married to your abusive spouse at the time of filing. You may wish to seek advice from an immigration attorney or legal advocate regarding this provision.

Can a Divorced Spouse Seek Relief by Filing a Form I-360?

Yes. Effective October 28, 2000, you may file a Form I-360 if the marriage was terminated within two years prior to the date of filing, if you can demonstrate a connection between the termination of the marriage and the battery or extreme cruelty. A battered spouse who cannot demonstrate such a connection may be eligible for battered spouse cancellation of removal. To qualify for battered spouse cancellation of removal, you must meet the other requirements that would be necessary for approval of a self-petition. In addition, you must have been physically present in the United States for three years immediately preceding the filing of the application for cancellation of removal, and you must demonstrate that your removal from the United States would result in extreme hardship to you or your child.

Your Form I-360 will be denied if you remarry prior to the approval of the Form I-360. Remarriage after the Form I-360 has been approved will not affect the validity of the petition.

What If My Abusive U.S. Citizen or Permanent Resident Spouse or Parent (Or U.S. Citizen Son or Daughter) Filed a Form I-130, Petition for Alien Relative, on My Behalf, Which Is Still Pending or Was Withdrawn?

If you are the beneficiary of a Form I-130 filed by the abusive spouse, parent or child, you will be able to transfer the priority date of the Form I-130 to the Form I-360. This is extremely important for you, since it may result in an earlier priority date and a shorter waiting time for getting a Green Card.

Can Anyone Else Assist Me?

If you need additional advice, you may contact the USCIS field office nearest your home for a list of community-based, nonprofit organizations that may be able to assist you in applying for an immigration benefit.

You should also know that help is available to you through the National Domestic Violence Hotline at 800-799-7233 or 800-787-3224 [TDD]. The hotline has information about shelters, mental healthcare, legal advice, and other types of assistance, including information about self-petitioning for immigration status.

Chapter 24

Human Trafficking

Chapter Contents

Section 24.1

What Is Human Trafficking?

This section includes text excerpted from "Human
Trafficking," Office on Women's Health (OWH), U.S. Department of
Health and Human Services (HHS), September 13, 2018.

Human trafficking is a form of slavery. It happens when a person
is forced or tricked into working in dangerous and illegal conditions
or having sexual contact with others against their will. A person who
is trafficked may be drugged, locked up, beaten, starved, or made to
work for many hours a day. Girls and women are the most common
victims of sex trafficking, a type of human trafficking.

How Are Girls and Women Trafficked in the United States?

Traffickers control victims by:

- Threatening to hurt them or their families

- Threatening to have them deported

- Taking away their passports, birth certificates, or identity (ID) cards

- Making them work to pay back the money they claim is owed them

- Giving them drugs in order to create an addiction or control
  them and then making them perform sexually to get more drugs

- Preventing them from having contact with friends, family, or the
  outside world

Types of work a trafficked person may be forced to do include prostitution or sex work, farm work, cleaning, child care, sweatshop work,
and other types of labor.

Sometimes a woman may end up trafficked after being forced to
marry someone against her will. In a forced marriage, a woman's
husband and his family have control over her. Not all people who are
trafficked are taken across state lines or national borders.

How Common Is Human Trafficking in the United States?

Human trafficking happens in every U.S. state. In 2016, at least
7,500 people were trafficked in the United States, and up to 800,000

are trafficked worldwide each year. Half of these victims are under 18, and most are girls and women.

Who Is at Risk for Being Trafficked?

Human-trafficking victims can be from urban, suburban, or rural areas and can have varying levels of education. In the United States, most human-trafficking victims come from within this country, or from Mexico and the Philippines.

While human trafficking can happen to anyone, some people in the United States are at greater risk. These include:

- Runaways and homeless youth
- Children in the welfare or juvenile justice system
- American Indians and Alaska Natives (AI/AN)
- Migrant workers
- People who don't speak English well
- People with disabilities
- People in the lesbian, gay, bisexual, transgender, questioning (LGBTQ) community

What Are the Signs of Human Trafficking?

Recognizing the signs of human trafficking can be difficult. If a woman or girl shows several of these signs, she may be trafficked:

- Appears fearful, anxious, depressed, submissive, tense, or overly nervous or paranoid
- Seems very scared if law enforcement is talked about
- Does not make eye contact
- Is very underweight
- Shows signs of physical abuse (e.g., bruising, cuts, restraint marks on the wrists)
- Has very few or no personal possessions
- Has someone else in control and insisting on being present or translating
- Cannot say where she is staying or provide an address

- Does not know where she is (the country, state, or town or city)
- Has no sense of time of day or time of year

What Is Sex Trafficking?

Sex trafficking is a type of human trafficking. Sex trafficking is when a child or adult is forced to have sexual contact or engage in sexual activity in exchange for money or favors. In sex trafficking, someone forces or coerces a child or adult to participate in sexual activity in order to get money or other things of value from a person who pays for the sex acts.

Almost all victims of sex trafficking are women or girls.

What Are the Effects of Sex Trafficking?

The physical and mental-health effects of sexual trafficking are serious. Studies show that women who have been trafficked for sex have higher levels of fear, are more isolated, and have greater trauma and mental-health needs than other victims of crime. Women and girls who have been trafficked may also misuse alcohol or drugs as a way to cope with their situation.

What Is the Link between Sex Trafficking and HIV?

Sex-trafficking victims are at high risk of getting human immunodeficiency virus (HIV), among many other sexually transmitted infections (STIs). Sex-trafficking victims may be forced into prostitution and may be sexually assaulted, including being forced to have unprotected sex with multiple partners, many of whom may also have had unprotected sex with many partners. This increases their risk of getting HIV.

Often, trafficking victims endure the riskiest types of sexual assault, such as violent vaginal and anal rape without a condom, which puts them at higher risk of getting HIV.

How Can You Help Victims of Human Trafficking?

If you think you have come in contact with a victim of human trafficking, call the National Human Trafficking Resource Center's Hotline at 888-373-7888. You can also text HELP to BeFree (233733). Hotline staff can help you figure out whether you have seen a victim of human trafficking and can suggest local resources.

Anyone who is brought into the United States for forced labor may be able to get a special visa and other help rebuilding their lives.

Section 24.2

Sex Trafficking

This section includes text excerpted from "Sexual Violence: Definitions," Centers for Disease Control and Prevention (CDC), April 10, 2018.

What Is Sexual Violence?

Sexual violence is defined as a sexual act committed against someone without that person's freely given consent. Sexual violence includes:

- **Completed or attempted forced penetration of a victim**

  Includes unwanted vaginal, oral, or anal insertion through use of physical force or threats to bring physical harm toward or against the victim

- **Completed or attempted alcohol-or drug-facilitated penetration of a victim**

  Includes unwanted vaginal, oral, or anal insertion when the victim was unable to consent because she or he was too intoxicated (e.g., unconscious, or lacked awareness) through voluntary or involuntary use of alcohol or drugs

- **Completed or attempted forced acts in which a victim is made to penetrate someone**

  Includes situations when the victim was made to, or there was an attempt to make the victim, sexually penetrate a perpetrator or someone else without the victim's consent because the victim was physically forced or threatened with physical harm

- **Completed or attempted alcohol- or drug-facilitated acts in which a victim is made to penetrate someone**

Includes situations in which the victim was made to, or there was an attempt to make the victim, sexually penetrate a perpetrator or someone else without the victim's consent because the victim was too intoxicated (e.g., unconscious, or lacked awareness) through voluntary or involuntary use of alcohol or drugs

- **Nonphysically forced penetration which occurs after a person is pressured to consent or submit to being penetrated**

  Includes being worn down by someone who repeatedly asked for sex or showed they were unhappy; having someone threaten to end a relationship or spread rumors; and sexual pressure by misuse of influence or authority

- **Unwanted sexual contact**

  Includes intentional touching, either directly or through the clothing, of the genitalia, anus, groin, breast, inner thigh, or buttocks of any person without his or her consent, or of a person who is unable to consent. The unwanted sexual contact also includes making a victim touch the perpetrator. Unwanted sexual contact can be referred to as "sexual harassment" in some contexts, such as at a school or workplace.

- **Noncontact unwanted sexual experiences**

  Includes unwanted sexual attention that does not involve physical contact. Some examples are verbal sexual harassment (e.g., making sexual comments) or unwanted exposure to pornography. This occurs without a person's consent and sometimes, without the victim's knowledge. This type of sexual violence can occur in many different settings, such as school, the workplace, in public, or through technology.

Sexual Violence: Risk and Protective Factors

Risk factors are associated with a greater likelihood of sexual violence (SV) perpetration. They are contributing factors and might not be direct causes. Not everyone who is identified as "at risk" becomes a perpetrator of violence.

A combination of individual, relational, community, and societal factors contribute to the risk of becoming a perpetrator of SV. Understanding these multilevel factors can help identify various opportunities for prevention. Protective factors may lessen the likelihood of sexual-violence victimization or perpetration either directly or by buffering against risk. These factors can exist at the individual, relational, community, and societal levels.

The Centers for Disease Control and Prevention (CDC) conducted a systematic review of risk and protective factors for SV perpetration and identified a number of factors at the individual and relationship levels. However, research examining risk and protective factors for SV perpetration at the community and societal levels is limited. The risk factors identified at community and societal levels are based on findings from the World Health Organization's (WHO) World Report on Violence and Health (www.who.int/violence_injury_prevention/violence/global_campaign/en/chap6.pdf).

Risk Factors for Perpetration
Individual Risk Factors

- Alcohol and drug use

- Delinquency

- Lack of empathy

- General aggressiveness and acceptance of violence

- Early sexual initiation

- Coercive sexual fantasies

- Preference for impersonal sex and sexual-risk taking

- Exposure to sexually explicit media

- Hostility toward women

- Adherence to traditional gender role norms

- Hypermasculinity

- Suicidal behavior

- Prior sexual victimization or perpetration

Relationship Factors

- A family environment characterized by physical violence and conflict

- Childhood history of physical, sexual, or emotional abuse

- Emotionally unsupportive family environment

- Poor parent–child relationships, particularly with fathers

- Association with sexually aggressive, hypermasculine, and delinquent peers

- Involvement in a violent or abusive intimate relationship

Community Factors

- Poverty

- Lack of employment opportunities

- Lack of institutional support from police and judicial system

- General tolerance of sexual violence within the community

- Weak community sanctions against sexual violence perpetrators

Societal Factors

- Societal norms that support sexual violence

- Societal norms that support male superiority and sexual entitlement

- Societal norms that maintain women's inferiority and sexual submissiveness

- Weak laws and policies related to sexual violence and gender equity

- High levels of crime and other forms of violence

Protective Factors for Perpetration

- Parental use of reasoning to resolve family conflict

- Emotional health and connectedness

- Academic achievement

- Empathy and concern for how one's actions affect others

Sexual Violence: Consequences

Sexual violence can have harmful and lasting consequences for victims, families, and communities. The following list describes some of those consequences.

Physical

- More than 32,000 pregnancies result from rape every year with the highest rates of rape-related pregnancy reported by women in abusive relationships
- Some long-term consequences of sexual violence include:
  - Chronic pain
  - Gastrointestinal disorders
  - Gynecological complications
  - Migraines and other frequent headaches
  - Sexually transmitted infections (STIs)
  - Cervical cancer
  - Genital injuries

Psychological

Victims of sexual violence face both immediate and chronic psychological consequences.

Immediate psychological consequences include the following:

- Shock
- Denial
- Fear
- Confusion
- Anxiety
- Withdrawal
- Shame or guilt
- Nervousness
- Distrust of others
- Symptoms of posttraumatic stress disorder (PTSD)
  - Emotional detachment
  - Sleep disturbances
  - Flashbacks
  - A mental replay of assault

Chronic psychological consequences include the following:

- Depression

- Generalized anxiety

- Attempted or completed suicide

- Posttraumatic stress disorder

- Diminished interest/avoidance of sex

- Low self-esteem/self-blame

Social

Sexual violence also has social impacts on its victims, such as the following:

- Strained relationships with family, friends, and intimate partners

- Less emotional support from friends and family

- Less frequent contact with friends and relatives

- Lower likelihood of marriage

- Isolation or ostracism from family or community

Health Risk Behaviors

Sexual-violence victimization is associated with several health-risk behaviors. Some researchers view the following health behaviors as both consequences of sexual violence and factors that increase a person's likelihood of being victimized again in the future.

- Engaging in high-risk sexual behavior

  - Unprotected sex

  - Early sexual initiation

  - Choosing unhealthy sexual partners

  - Having multiple sex partners

  - Trading sex for food, money, or other items

- Using harmful substances

  - Smoking cigarettes

  - Drinking alcohol

- Drinking alcohol and driving
- Taking drugs
- Unhealthy diet-related behaviors
  - Fasting
  - Vomiting
  - Abusing diet pills
  - Overeating
- Delinquency and criminal behavior
- Failure to engage in healthy behaviors, such as motor vehicle seat belt use

Sexual Violence: Prevention Strategies

Sexual violence is a serious problem that can have lasting, harmful effects on victims and their family, friends, and communities. The goal of sexual violence prevention is simple—to stop it from happening in the first place. The solutions, however, are just as complex as the problem.

Preventing sexual violence requires comprehensive prevention strategies that address factors at each level of the social ecology—individual, relationship, community, and society.

Many of the strategies focus on risk and protective factors for sexual violence perpetration to reduce the likelihood that an individual will engage in sexually violent behavior. The strategies and their corresponding approaches are listed in the table below.

Table 24.1. Strategies to Stop Sexual Violence

	Strategy	Approach
S	Promote Social Norms That Protect Against Violence	• Bystander Approaches • Mobilizing men and boys as allies
T	Teach Skills to Prevent Sexual Violence	• Social-emotional learning • Teaching healthy, safe dating and intimate relationship skills to adolescents • Promoting health sexuality • Empowerment-based training
O	Provide Opportunities to Empower and Support Girls and Women	• Strengthening economic supports for women and families • Strengthening leadership and opportunities for girls

Table 24.1. Continued

	Strategy	Approach
P	Create Protective Environments	• Improving safety and monitoring in schools • Establishing and consistently applying workplace policies • Addressing community-level risks through environmental approaches
SV	Support Victims/Survivors to Lessen Harm	• Victim-centered services • Treatment for victims of SV • Treatment for at-risk children and families to prevent problem behavior including sex offending

Section 24.3

Civil Rights for Victims of Trafficking

This section includes text excerpted from "Human Trafficking/
Involuntary Servitude," Federal Bureau of Investigation (FBI),
February 24, 2016.

Human trafficking, believed to be the third-largest criminal activity in the world, is a form of human slavery which must be addressed at the interagency level. Human trafficking includes forced labor, domestic servitude, and commercial sex trafficking. It involves both U.S. citizens and foreigners alike and has no demographic restrictions. The FBI works human trafficking cases under both its Civil Rights program and its Violent Crimes Against Children program. The majority of human trafficking victims in these cases are U.S. citizens, and we take a victim-centered approach in investigating such cases, which means that ensuring the needs of the victims take precedence over all other considerations.

Here in this country, people are being bought, sold, and smuggled like modern-day slaves, often beaten, starved, and forced to work as prostitutes or to take jobs as migrant, domestic, restaurant, or factory workers with little or no pay. Over the past decade, human trafficking has been identified as a heinous crime which exploits the most vulnerable in society. Among the Civil Rights Unit's priorities is its human trafficking program, based on the passage of the 13th Amendment to the U.S. Constitution, which provided that "neither slavery nor involuntary servitude, except as a punishment for crime whereof the party shall have been duly convicted, shall exist within the United States."

Under the human trafficking program, the Bureau investigates matters where a person was induced to engage in commercial sex acts through force, fraud, or coercion, or to perform any labor or service through force, coercion, or threat of law or legal process. Typically, human trafficking cases fall under the following investigative areas:

- **Domestic sex trafficking of adults:** When persons are compelled to engage in commercial sex acts through means of force, fraud, and/or coercion.

- **Sex trafficking of international adults and children:** When foreign nationals, both adult and juveniles, are compelled to engage in commercial sex acts with a nexus to the United States through force, fraud, and/or coercion.

- **Forced labor:** When persons, domestic or foreign nationals, are compelled to work in some service or industry through force or coercion.

- **Domestic servitude:** When persons, domestic or foreign nationals, are compelled to engage in domestic work for families or households, through means of force or coercion.

Human Trafficking Task Forces

The most effective way to investigate human trafficking is through a collaborative, multi-agency approach with our federal, state, local, and tribal partners. In concert with this concept, FBI investigators participate or lead task forces and working groups in every state within the United States.

Anti-Trafficking Coordination Team (ACTeam is a multi-agency initiative aimed at building human trafficking enforcement efforts and enhancing access to specialized human trafficking subject matter experts, leads, and intelligence. Each ACTeam develops and implements a strategic action plan, which leads to high-impact federal investigations and prosecutions. The federal agencies involved in the ACTeam initiative are the Department of Justice, Federal Bureau of Investigation, Department of Homeland Security, and the Department of Labor. Twelve FBI field offices participate in the initiative, including Atlanta, Boston, Cleveland, El Paso, Kansas City, Los Angeles, Memphis, Miami, Minneapolis, Newark, Portland, and Sacramento.

Enhanced Collaborative Model to Combat Human Trafficking is a multi-agency task force initiative funded through the Office for Victims of Crime (OVC) and Bureau of Justice Assistance (BJA). These multidisciplinary task forces include members from the U.S. Attorney's office, local prosecutor's office, federal law enforcement, state/local law enforcement, and a community service provider, with the goal of proactively identifying and recovering victims of human trafficking.

FBI Human Trafficking Task Forces: The Bureau's Human Trafficking program has established FBI-funded human trafficking task forces in multiple field offices, with the purpose of working with state and local law enforcement agencies in combating human trafficking through proactive and collaborative practices. The ultimate goal of these task forces is to recover victims and investigate traffickers at the state and federal level.

Trafficking Victims Protection Act

As a result of the 2000 Trafficking Victims Protection Act (TVPA), law enforcement was given the ability to protect international victims of human trafficking through several forms of immigration relief, including Continued Presence and the T visa. Continued Presence allows law enforcement officers to request temporary legal status in the United States for a foreign national whose presence is necessary for the continued success of a human trafficking investigation. The T visa allows foreign victims of human trafficking to become temporary U.S. residents, through which they may become eligible for permanent residency after three years. The TVPA also established a law requiring defendants of human trafficking investigations to pay restitution to the victims they exploited.

The TVPA, passed to create the first comprehensive federal law to address human trafficking, provided a three-pronged approach to addressing trafficking. In addition to the protections offered through immigration relief for foreign national victims of human trafficking, it also focuses on prevention through public awareness programs, both domestically and abroad, and prosecution through new federal criminal statutes. As a result of the TVPA and subsequent reauthorizations, the FBI has been provided with statutory authority to investigate matters of forced labor; trafficking with respect to peonage, slavery, involuntary servitude, or forced labor; sex trafficking by force, fraud, or coercion; and unlawful conduct with respect to documents in furtherance of trafficking.

Investigations

FBI human trafficking investigations are conducted by agents within the human trafficking program and members of our federal human trafficking task forces, and every one of the FBI's 56 field offices has worked investigations pertaining to human trafficking. Often, investigations involving human trafficking come to the attention of field offices and task forces through:

- Citizen complaints;

- The National Human Trafficking Resource Center Hotline;

- A referral from a law enforcement agency;

- A referral from nongovernment organizations (NGOs);

- Proactive victim recovery operations; and

- Outreach to state government and community entities.

During the stages of a human trafficking investigation, the primary goal of investigators is the recovery of victims in order to remove them from an environment of violence and exploitation. Program representatives work in unison with victim advocates and NGOs, who are able to provide victims of human trafficking with the short-term resources (shelter, food, clothing) and long-term resources (counseling, education assistance, job training) they require during the road to recovery. After recovering a victim of human trafficking, field offices are then able to conduct logical, efficient, and effective investigations which lead to the eventual arrest and successful prosecution of their traffickers, as well as the potential recovery of additional victims and identification of other traffickers.

The Bureau's human trafficking program has also successfully used lawful, sophisticated techniques— such as undercover investigations and Title III wire intercepts—to take down trafficking organizations, recover victims, and intercept traffickers before they are able to victimize others.

Section 24.4

Help for Victims of Trafficking

This section includes text excerpted from "Help for Victims of
Trafficking in Persons," Federal Bureau of Investigation (FBI),
September 11, 2012. Reviewed October 2018.

Freedom is one of the most important rights afforded to every
human being. No one should be forced or coerced to act against their
will. Unfortunately, the practice of modern-day slavery exists in our
world today. Trafficking in persons (human trafficking) is a violation
of federal civil rights laws. The Federal Bureau of Investigation (FBI)
is investigating these crimes as one of its top civil rights priorities to
protect those who may be a victim of this crime.

If any of these things have happened to you, you may be a victim
of a serious crime. If you feel that you are in danger, contact local law
enforcement, the FBI, or 911.

Resources for Victims

The FBI has someone who can help victims of crime and answer
their questions. Victim Specialists are specially trained professionals
working hand in hand with the FBI case agent during an investigation.
They assist victims by providing support, information, and referrals
to resources in the community.

The Victim Specialist's primary responsibilities are: the victims'
well-being; keeping victims informed about the status of their case;
and, helping victims reclaim their freedom.

If You Are a United States Citizen or Lawful Permanent Resident of the United States

There may be immigration services available to you. It is important
to talk to an immigration attorney or community organization that can
advise you about your choices. Your Victim Specialist can help connect
you to valuable resources in the community and provide referrals to
a free or low-cost attorney.

United States citizens or lawful permanent residents of the United
States can be enslaved within or outside the borders of the United
States. It is a violation of the federal civil rights laws to traffic United
States citizens or lawful permanent residents. As a citizen or lawful

permanent resident, once you are identified as a federal crime victim you are eligible to receive services and benefits.

If You Are Not a Legal Resident of the United States

You may be eligible to stay in the United States for a determined period of time depending on your individual circumstances. Once you qualify as a victim of trafficking in persons, the law guarantees certain legal benefits and services.

Regardless of Your Legal Status, Victim Specialists Can Help You Find:

- Food, clothing, and shelter
- Medical assistance, including access to STO/HIV/TB testing and immunizations
- Interpreter services
- Mental health services and counseling
- Legal/immigration assistance
- Transportation
- Child care
- Health insurance
- Education and employment services

Part Four

Preventing and Intervening in Domestic Violence

Chapter 25

Healthy Relationships Are Key to Preventing Domestic Violence

Chapter Contents

Section 25.1

What Should You Look for in a Dating Relationship

This section includes text excerpted from "Dating," Girlshealth.gov,
Office on Women's Health (OWH), September 16, 2015.
Reviewed October 2018.

When Do Teens Start Dating?

There is no right age for teens to start dating. Every person is different. Lots of teens enjoy just hanging out in a group. Here are some tips for thinking about when you might start seeing someone:

Ask yourself:

- Do I know what I want in a person I date?
- Is this right for me, or do I just want to do what my friends are doing?
- Am I doing this because I like someone, or because I like the idea of having someone?
- Can I handle tough feelings such as jealousy?
- Do I know what I'm ready for in terms of physical intimacy?
- Do I know how I'd say no to sex?

Talk to your parents or guardians about starting to date. They may have rules about things such as when you can be alone with a date. If you don't like the rules, ask calmly about changing them. Staying calm shows that you're getting more mature. Read about talking with parents or guardians.

What Is a Healthy Dating Relationship?

Healthy dating relationships start with the same things that all healthy relationships start with. You can take a quick quiz to help see if your relationship is one to love or one to lose.

You can read some top tips for a healthy dating relationship.

Dating relationships also are different from other relationships. You may have strong feelings of attraction and other intense feelings.

You may even want to spend all of your time together. Try to spend some time apart, though. That way you can connect with other people who care about you, too. And you'll have time for goals and activities that matter to you.

What about Dating and Sexual Feelings?

Sexual feelings can be strong, and you may feel confused. Keep in mind that the sex in movies, music, and TV shows often doesn't reflect real or healthy relationships. So how do you know what's right? Trust your instincts and treat yourself with respect—and make sure your crush does, too.

Talk with the other person ahead of time about what you will and will not do physically. Waiting until the heat of the moment to try to cool things down doesn't work as well.

The person you're with should always respect your right to say no. If you think someone is not treating you with respect, learn more about safety in relationships.

What about hooking up? Different people mean different things when they say "hooking up." Usually, though, it means doing something sexual with somebody you're not dating. Have you heard that hooking up could be fun? Well, hooking up can have some serious downsides. These include feeling embarrassed or upset afterward, getting pregnant, and getting a sexually transmitted disease (also known as an STI).

Should I Date Someone Close to My Age?

It's best to date someone close to your own age. Here are some reasons why:

- Someone older may be more mature and ready for a different kind of relationship.

- Dating someone older increases the odds that your partner will want to have sex before you're ready.

- Younger girls who date older guys are more likely to face an unwanted pregnancy.

- A guy who is legally an adult could get sent to prison if he has sex with you and you're underage. That could happen even if you are 17 and he is 18, depending on the law in your state.

How Can I Stay Safe When Dating?

Dating can be a great way to get to know someone—and to get to know what you want from a relationship. Plus, it can be a lot of fun! But it's not fun to feel scared.

You can take steps to stay safe whenever you go out with someone. For example, try getting to know a person by talking at school or on the phone first. You also can go out with a group of friends to a public place. If the two of you go out alone, tell your parents or guardians who you are going with and where. And follow your parents' rules for things such as curfew, since those rules often are set for your safety.

Section 25.2

What Healthy Dating and Romantic Relationships Look Like

This section includes text excerpted from "What Healthy Dating and Romantic Relationships Look Like," Office of Adolescent Health (OAH), May 31, 2018.

Adolescents may have questions about what is "normal" or "healthy" when it comes to dating. Learning and communicating the facts is important. For example, adolescents often think their peers engage in more sexual activities than they do, including more casual "hooking up." Nearly 85 percent of teens prefer other types of relationship-related activities, such as friendships and sex within serious relationships. The overestimation of a hook-up culture can be harmful to teens, causing embarrassment, shame, and pressure to engage in sexual activity or unhealthy relationship behaviors that they are not prepared for or do not want. Every relationship is different, but healthy romantic relationships are built on a core set of characteristics.

Partners Treat Each Other with Respect and Provide Space

- Partners should treat each other with respect, value each other, and understand the other partner's boundaries or limits in what they do and do not want to do.

- Partners should encourage self-confidence in each other.

- Partners should maintain their own individuality and keep their own friends and hobbies. It also is important for both partners to support each other in making new friends or pursuing hobbies.

- Partners should be role models to their partner, friends, and others and be an example of what respect means.

Partners Communicate

- Partners should practice effective communication. This means speaking honestly and waiting until the other partner is ready to talk.

- Partners should try to understand each other's feelings.

- Partners should be honest with each other and build trust in their relationship.

- Partners should value consent, and not pressure each other to go outside of their comfort zone, including for sexual activity.

- Partners should respect each other's boundaries.

- Partners should feel comfortable and able to say "no" to activities, and those wishes should be respected.

Partners Practice Effective Problem Solving

- Partners can practice good problem solving by breaking problems into manageable parts, coming up with solutions, and talking things through.

- Partners should be willing to compromise and acknowledge the other person's point of view.

- Partners should manage anger in healthy ways, such as using breathing techniques or discussing why they are angry.

- Partners sometimes argue, but when they do, they should try to stay on topic, stay away from insulting their partner, and take some space if the discussion gets too heated.

Although all healthy relationships should contain these core characteristics, relationships may look different as adolescents get older. For middle-school youth, the focus of relationships tends to be on peer relationships and on developing social skills, with less focus on romantic relationships. Also, younger teens are more likely than older teens to hang out with someone of romantic interest in group settings with other friends around. Establishing positive social skills during early adolescence may help youth develop healthy relationships at later ages.

Romantic relationships become more serious among older teens in high school (ages 15–17). At this time, romantic relationships become more exclusive, last longer, and can be more emotionally and sexually intimate.

Section 25.3

Tips for Being a Nurturing Parent

This section includes text excerpted from "Talking with Teens about Relationships," Office of Adolescent Health (OAH), September 20, 2016.

What Teens Want to Hear from Parent

1: Tell me why teen pregnancy isn't a good idea and help me think about positive opportunities for my future.

Don't assume teens only see the bad things about teen pregnancy. Be sure to ask what they think about early pregnancy and parenthood and how it would change their goals for the future. Ask teens about their ideas for the future and provide them with specific ways they can make their dreams a reality. Encourage teens to explore their interests and passions and support them in their pursuit of their goals. Don't be afraid to talk to them about how getting pregnant or causing a pregnancy will get in the way of their goals and don't assume they've thought about this themselves.

2: Just telling me not to have sex or to "be safe" isn't enough. Tell me why you feel the way you do.

Make sure teens understand why you're asking them to do certain things. They want to know what your values and attitudes are about these topics. Remember to talk to them about relationships and some of the emotional aspects of sex, not just the health and safety messages.

Some things you might say:

- It's okay to think about sex and to feel sexual desire. Everybody does. But if you get pregnant/get somebody pregnant, it will be harder for you to graduate from high school and go on to college. It also will be harder for you to reach your goals for the future.

- You shouldn't feel pressure to have sex without using contraception in order to have or keep a relationship with someone. If sex without using contraception is the price of your relationship, you deserve to find someone else.

- I'd really like you to wait to have sex until you're in a serious, committed, adult relationship.

3: Don't assume that just because I ask you a question about sex or contraception it means I'm having sex.

Teens may ask about sex or contraception because they are curious or heard something that they want explained. If you freak out the first time they ask you a question about sex or contraception, they'll probably be shy about asking you again. Also remember that giving young people information about these topics doesn't encourage them to have sex, but it can go a long way toward making sure they have accurate information. It can help begin a series of conversations with them about these topics. When they do ask questions about these topics, make sure you recognize the question, understand the question, and understand what it is they're trying to learn. If you don't know the answer to a question your teen asks, don't be afraid to admit it and suggest looking up the answer together.

Chapter 26

Talk with Your Teen about Healthy Relationships

Basics of Healthy Relationships

Parents can play a big role in teaching kids about healthy relationships. Unfortunately, many teens have relationships that are unhealthy. About one in ten teens who have been on a date have also been:

- Physically abused (hit, pushed, or slapped) by someone they've gone out with

- Sexually abused (kissed, touched, or forced to have sex without wanting to) by someone they've dated

The good news is that you can help your teen develop strong, respectful relationships. Start by talking with your child about how to:

- Set expectations for how they want to be treated

- Recognize when a relationship is unhealthy

- Support friends dealing with unhealthy relationships

This chapter includes text excerpted from "Talk with Your Teen about Healthy Relationships," Office of Disease Prevention and Health Promotion (ODPHP), U.S. Department of Health and Human Services (HHS), January 29, 2018.

Talking about healthy relationships is a great way to show that you are available to listen and answer questions. Together, you can agree on clear rules about dating to help keep your teen safe.

How Do Kids Learn about Relationships?

Kids learn about relationships from the adults around them. When you taught your child to say "please" and "thank you" as a toddler, you were teaching respect and kindness.

Your own relationships also teach your kids how to treat others. When you treat your kids, partner, and friends in healthy and supportive ways, your kids learn from your choices.

Children learn from unhealthy experiences, too. If they experience violence at home or in the community, they are more likely to be in unhealthy relationships later on.

When Should You Start Talking about Dating?

It's best to start talking about healthy relationships before your child starts dating. Start conversations about what to look for in a romantic partner. For example, you could ask your child:

- How do you want to be treated?

- How do you want to feel about yourself when you are with that person?

What Makes a Relationship Healthy?

In a healthy relationship:

- Both people feel respected, supported, and valued

- Both people make decisions together

- Both people have friends and interests outside of the relationship

- Both people settle disagreements with open and honest communication

- Both people respect each other's privacy and space

What Makes a Relationship Unhealthy?

In an unhealthy relationship:

- One or both people try to change the other

- One person makes most or all of the decisions
- One or both people drop friends and interests outside of the relationship
- One or both people yell, threaten, hit, or throw things during arguments
- One or both people make fun of the other's opinions or interests
- One or both people keep track of the other all the time by calling, texting, or checking in with friends

Teens may think it's okay to act in these ways, but these behaviors can develop into violence. If you see any of these signs, talk to your teen.

What Is Dating Violence?

Dating violence is when one person in a romantic relationship is physically or emotionally harmful to the other person. It can happen in any relationship, whether it's an opposite-sex (straight, or heterosexual) or same-sex (gay, or homosexual) relationship.

Dating violence can include:

- **Stalking**, including watching or following a partner, or sending repeated, unwanted phone calls or texts
- **Controlling behavior**, including telling a partner how to dress or who to spend time with
- **Emotional abuse**, including embarrassing a partner or keeping that person away from family and friends
- **Physical abuse**, including pushing, hitting, or throwing things
- **Sexual abuse**, including forcing or trying to force someone to have sex

Dating violence can happen in person, online, or with other technology (such as cell phones). It can also continue to happen after the relationship has ended.

All teens can experience unhealthy or unsafe relationships. Sometimes both partners act in unhealthy or unsafe ways, but using violence is never okay. It's important to talk to all kids about how to have respectful, healthy relationships.

Who Is at Risk for Dating Violence?

Dating violence can happen to anyone. Teens may be more at risk of being in unhealthy relationships if they:

- Use alcohol or drugs

- Are depressed

- Have friends who are violent

- Have trouble controlling their anger

- Struggle with learning in school

- Have sex with multiple partners

- Have experienced or witnessed violence at home or in the community

What Are the Warning Signs of Dating Violence?

It's common for teens to have mood swings, but sudden changes in your teen's attitude or behavior could mean that something more serious is going on. If you are worried, talk to your teen to find out more.

Watch for Signs That Your Teen's Partner May Be Violent

If your teen is in a relationship with someone who is violent, your teen may:

- Avoid friends, family, and school activities

- Make excuses for a partner's behavior

- Look uncomfortable or fearful around a partner

- Lose interest in favorite activities

- Get lower grades in school

- Have unexplained injuries, such as bruises or scratches

Watch for Signs That Your Teen May Be Violent

Teens who use physical, emotional, or sexual violence to control their partners need help to stop. Start a conversation if your teen:

- Is jealous and possessive

- Blames other people for anything that goes wrong

- Damages or ruins a partner's things

- Wants to control a partner's decisions

- Constantly texts or calls a partner

- Posts embarrassing information about a partner on websites such as Facebook (including sexual information or pictures)

Help Your Teen Stay Healthy

Dating violence can have long-term effects for both partners— even after the relationship ends. The good news is that teaching your teen about healthy relationships can help prevent these negative effects.

Someone who has experienced dating violence may struggle with:

- Depression

- Low self-confidence

- Eating disorders

- Drug or alcohol abuse

- Other violent relationships

A partner who has been violent may experience:

- Loss of respect from others

- Suspension or expulsion from school

- Loneliness

- Trouble with the law

You can help prevent these long-term effects of dating violence by helping your teen develop the skills for healthy relationships. Watch for signs of dating violence and help your teen stay healthy now and in the future.

Actions You Can Take for Building Healthy Relationships

Talk with your kids to help them develop realistic and healthy expectations for relationships.

Help Your Teen Develop Problem-Solving Skills

Help your teen think about healthy relationships by asking how they would handle different situations. For example, you might ask, "What would you do if:

- you think your friend's partner isn't treating him right?"

- your partner calls you to come over whenever you try to hang out with your friends?"

- your friend yells at her partner in front of everyone at a party?"

It may help to use examples from television (TV) shows, movies, or songs to start the conversation. Listen respectfully to your teen's answer, even if you don't agree. Then you can offer your opinion and explore other options together. Use these tips to start a conversation with your teen.

Help Your Teen Support a Friend

It's also a good idea to talk with your teen about what she or he can do if a friend is in an unhealthy relationship. Suggest that your teen talk to you or another adult, such as a school counselor, if she or he notices signs of dating violence.

Set Rules for Dating

As kids get older, they gain more independence. But teens still need parents to set boundaries and expectations for their behavior.

Here are some example of rules to talk about with your teen:

- Are friends allowed to come over when you aren't home?

- Can your teen go on a date with someone you haven't met?

- How can your teen reach you if she or he needs a ride home?

Be a Role Model

Treat your kids and others with respect. As you talk with your teen about healthy relationships, think about your own behavior. Does it match the values you are talking about?

Treating your kids with respect also helps you build stronger relationships with them. This can make it easier to communicate with your teen about important issues such as healthy relationships.

Teens who have sex with more than one person are at higher risk of being in an unhealthy relationship. Talk with your teen about your values and expectations.

Talk to Your Kids about Preventing STDs

About half of all sexually transmitted disease (STD) cases in the United States occur in teens and young adults ages 15–24. Learn how to talk with your teen about STD prevention.

Talk with Your Kids about Alcohol and Other Drugs

Alcohol and drugs don't cause violence or unhealthy relationships, but they can make it harder to make healthy choices. Talk to your kids about the dangers of alcohol and drugs.

If You Are Worried, Talk to Your Teen

If you think your teen's relationship might be violent, take these steps:

- Write down the reasons you are worried.
- Tell your teen why you are concerned. Point out specific things that concern you.
- Listen to your teen calmly, and thank them for opening up.

Chapter 27

Preventing and Intervening in Child Abuse

Chapter Contents

Section 27.1

When You Suspect Child Abuse or Neglect

This section includes text excerpted from "When You
Suspect Child Abuse or Neglect," Federal Bureau of
Investigation (FBI), February 23, 2015. Reviewed October 2018.

The Federal Bureau of Investigation (FBI) wants to ensure that
all employees act responsibly when they have cause to believe that
a child's physical or mental health or welfare has been or may be
adversely affected by child abuse or neglect. It should not matter if the
suspected abuse involves a family member, fellow employee, neighbor,
friend, acquaintance, or stranger. As individuals and employees of an
agency charged with protecting the safety of the public, including its
most vulnerable members, we each have the moral responsibility, and
at times the legal duty, to take the necessary actions in protecting children. The impact of abuse and neglect on children is often severe and
long lasting and may include depression, poor school performance and
dropping out, substance abuse, running away, exploitation, self-mu-
tilation, suicide, delinquency, and adult criminality. Over 1,500 children die every year from abuse and neglect and most are under four
years of age. In almost every case, the child's situation was known to
family members, neighbors, or others. The intervention of one caring
individual can literally save the life of a child.

Your Legal Obligation

All states and the District of Columbia (DC) have laws about reporting child abuse and neglect to state or local officials. Reports are generally made to the local or state child protective services agency by
calling a child abuse reporting hotline. It is important that Federal
Bureau of Investigation (FBI) employees know the reporting requirements in their state and local jurisdiction. Most federal and state
child-protection laws address harm to a child caused by parents or
other caregivers. These laws generally do not include harm caused
by other people, such as acquaintances or strangers that should be
reported to law enforcement. The Chief Division Counsel (CDC) and
the Victim Specialist in each field office are familiar with the applicable
requirements and can provide information and guidance.

Children are defined in federal and state laws as being under the
age of 18. The law does not require an individual to be certain that

a child has been abused or neglected before reporting, only to have a good faith reason for suspecting and reporting it.

State and federal laws include a list of professionals who are considered "mandatory reporters" who must report suspected child abuse and neglect within a particular time frame. Some states require all adult citizens to report suspected child abuse and neglect. Mandatory reporters usually include all teachers, daycare workers, school bus drivers, doctors and nurses, mental-health providers, social workers, victim-services providers, law-enforcement officers, and prosecutors. Failure to report suspected child abuse or neglect may be, depending on the circumstances, either a misdemeanor or felony criminal offense. If you're considered a mandatory reporter in your state, reporting suspected child abuse to your employer will not satisfy the obligation under the law. You must report suspected child abuse to the statutorily designated, appropriate authorities such as a law-enforcement agency or child-protection agency. Agency and company policies cannot conflict with or supersede the law requiring you to report child abuse to a law-enforcement agency or child-protection agency. Professionals whose personal communications may otherwise be privileged or confidential are required without exception to report child abuse.

If you encounter or have reason to suspect child abuse in the course of your work on an FBI investigation, there are special procedures for handling the reports. These procedures, and general information about reporting suspected abuse, can be found in Appendix K of the Domestic Investigations and Operations Guide (DIOG), or the Office for Victim Assistance (OVA) Intranet webpage. Consult your Chief Division Counsel (CDC), the Office of the General Counsel (OGC) attorney, or the Office for Victim Assistance for guidance on the law and FBI policy.

Your Legal Protection

Your report of suspected or known child abuse or neglect is confidential and immune from civil or criminal liability as long as the report is made in good faith. "Good Faith" generally means that the person making the report has reason to believe a child was being abused or neglected, took reasonable steps to learn facts that were readily available, and did not intend to injure or violate the rights of another person. An individual who reports in good faith will also be immune from liability if asked to participate in any judicial proceedings that might result from his or her report.

If You Have Reason to Believe That a Child Is Being, or Has Been, Abused

Do not confront the abuser. Do report your reasonable suspicions. However, if you are witnessing a child being abused, do what you can to safely stop the abuse (e.g., call 911) and safeguard the child until authorities arrive.

Even if your report does not bring decisive action, it may help establish a pattern that will eventually be enough to help the child.

The signs of abuse described below do not by themselves necessarily indicate abuse. You might talk to the child a little to see if there is a simple or innocent explanation for what you have observed, but do not overwhelm the child with questions. It is not up to you to determine whether your suspicions are true or not. A trained investigator will evaluate the child's situation.

You Should Suspect Physical Abuse

When you see...

- Frequent injuries such as bruises, cuts, black eyes, or burns, especially when the child cannot adequately explain their causes

- Burns or bruises in an unusual pattern that may indicate the use of an instrument or a human bite; ligature marks on the wrists/ankles or gag marks on the side of the mouth

- Cigarette burns on any part of a child's body; unusual patterns of scalding (glove or sock patterns on hands or feet)

- Injuries that are unusual for the child's age (fractures in a child under the age of four)

- Defensive injuries on backs of arms and hands

- Frequent complaints of pain without obvious injury, which may indicate internal injuries or injuries covered by clothing

- Aggressive, disruptive, and destructive behavior

- Lack of reaction to pain

- Passive, withdrawn, emotionless behavior

- Fear of going home or seeing parents, family members, or others who know the child

- Injuries that appear after the child has not been seen for several days

- Unseasonable clothes hiding injuries to arms or legs

Physical discipline, such as spanking or paddling, is not considered abuse as long as it is reasonable and does not cause harm or injury and does not expose the child to substantial harm or injury. Punching, beating, kicking, biting, shaking, throwing, stabbing, choking, hitting, and burning are considered to be abuse, not reasonable discipline.

You Should Suspect Neglect

When you see...

- Obvious malnourishment
- A child who is consistently dirty or has torn and/or dirty clothes and has severe body odor
- Obvious fatigue and listlessness
- A child unattended for long periods of time
- Need for glasses, dental care, or other medical attention
- Stealing or begging for food
- Frequent absences or tardiness at school
- Lack of sufficient clothing for the weather

You Should Suspect Sexual Abuse

When you see...

- Difficulty in sitting or walking
- Sudden changes in behavior or school performance
- Sudden change in appetite
- Refusal to change for gym or to participate in physical activities
- Extreme fear of being alone with adults, especially of a particular gender
- Sexually suggestive, age inappropriate, or promiscuous behavior
- Sudden reporting of nightmares or bedwetting
- Knowledge about sexual relations beyond what is appropriate for the child's age

- Sexual victimization of other children

- Complaints of painful urination

- Pregnancy or venereal disease, particularly if under the age of 14

Sexual abuse may involve fondling, lewd and lascivious behavior, intercourse, sodomy, oral copulation, penetration of a genital or anal opening, child pornography, child prostitution, or any other sexual conduct that is harmful to a child's mental, emotional, and physical welfare. These acts may be forced upon the child, or the child may be coaxed, seduced, and persuaded to cooperate. A child, however, cannot legally consent to such acts. The absence of force or other discernible coercion does not diminish the abusive nature of the conduct, but it may cause the child to feel responsible for what occurred.

When a Child Discloses

If you are the first person the child tells about sexual abuse, your testimony as an "outcry witness" may be especially important in future legal proceedings. What you say the child told you is not considered hearsay evidence in most states, but is admissible evidence in a trial involving sexual offense against a child. This exception generally applies only to the first person the child approaches.

Emotional Injury

The law recognizes both physical and emotional injury. An angry parent who physically assaults their child is likely to assault them verbally, too. Emotional injury is a common result of all types of abuse and neglect. Emotional injury can be subtle and harder to prove, yet it can be just as devastating and lead to some of the most costly and long-term effects on children: substance abuse, crime, suicide, and perpetuation of violence within families. Emotional abuse can involve constant blaming, berating, and belittling of a child, extremely unpredictable responses and unreasonable demands, and emotional deprivation when a parent withholds or withdraws affection, attention, and approval. Emotionally injured children may withdraw and become depressed or apathetic, attempt suicide, become overly compliant and fearful about not exactly following instructions, or act out in negative ways to get attention. A child's behavior problems may be a fulfillment of the negative labels ("worthless" or "no good") the abuser has applied to the child.

Section 27.2

Keep Your Child Safe from Abusers

This section includes text excerpted from "Child Sexual Abuse,"
National Center for Posttraumatic Stress Disorder (NCPTSD), U.S.
Department of Veterans Affairs (VA), September 2, 2015.
Reviewed October 2018.

What Can Caregivers Do to Help Keep Children Safe?

Although caregivers cannot protect their children 100 percent of the time, it is important to get to know the people who come around you child. You can find out whether someone has been charged with sexual abuse and find out where sexual abusers live in your area by going to the website FamilyWatchdog (www.familywatchdog.com).

Most importantly, provide a safe, caring setting so children feel able to talk to you about sexual abuse.

Other tips to keep your children safe include:

- Talk to others who know the people with whom your child comes in contact.

- Talk to your children about the difference between safe touching and unsafe touching.

- Tell the child that if someone tries to touch his or her body in their private areas or do things that make the child feel unsafe, she or he should say "No" to the person. The child also needs to tell you or a trusted adult about it right away.

- Let children know that their bodies are private and that they have the right not to allow others to touch their bodies in an unsafe way.

- Let them know that they do not have to do everything the babysitter, family member, or group leader tells them to do.

- Alert your children that abusers may use the Internet. Watch over your child on the Internet.

What Should You Do If You Think Your Child Has Been Sexually Abused?

If a child says she or he has been abused, try to stay calm. Reassure the child that what happened is not their fault, that you believe them, that you are proud of them for telling you (or another person), and that you are there to keep them safe. Take your child to a mental-health and medical professional right away. Many cities have child advocacy centers where a child and family can get help. These centers interview children and family members in a sensitive, warm place. They can help you report the abuse to legal authorities. They can help you find a medical examiner and therapist skilled in child sexual abuse. The National Children's Alliance (NCA) (www.nationalchildrensalliance. org) website has more information and a listing of such centers.

Children can recover from sexual abuse and go on to live good lives. The best predictor of recovery is support and love from their main caregiver. As a caregiver, you might also consider getting help for yourself. It is often very hard to accept that a child has been sexually abused. You will not be supporting your child, though, if you respond in certain unhelpful ways. For example, you will not be able to provide support if you are overwhelmed with your own emotions. Don't downplay the abuse ("it wasn't that bad"), but also try not to have extreme fears related to the abuse ("my child will never be safe again"). It will not help children if you force them to talk, or if you blame the child. Getting therapy for yourself can help you deal with your own feelings about the abuse. Then you might be better able to provide support to your child.

Section 27.3

How to Report Suspected Child Maltreatment

This section contains text excerpted from the following sources:
Text in this section begins with excerpts from "Child Sexual Abuse,"
Child Welfare Information Gateway, U.S. Department of Health
and Human Services (HHS), December 13, 2014. Reviewed October
2018; Text under the heading "Penalties for Failure to Report and
False Reporting of Child Abuse and Neglect" is excerpted from
"Penalties for Failure to Report and False Reporting of Child Abuse
and Neglect," Child Welfare Information Gateway (CWIG), U.S.
Department of Health and Human Services (HHS), August 2015.
Reviewed October 2018.

If you suspect a child is being abused or neglected, or if you are a child who is being maltreated, contact your local child protective services office or law-enforcement agency so professionals can assess the situation. Many states have a toll-free number to call to report suspected child abuse or neglect. To find out where to call, consult the Information Gateway publication *State Child Abuse and Neglect Reporting Numbers* (Contact information is provided below.)

Anyone can report suspected child abuse or neglect. Reporting abuse or neglect can protect a child and get help for a family—and it may even save a child's life. In some states, any person who suspects child abuse or neglect is required to report.

Child Welfare Information Gateway (CWIG) is not a hotline for reporting suspected child abuse or neglect, and it is not equipped to accept reports of this nature. Information Gateway is not equipped to offer crisis counseling. As a service of the Children's Bureau in the U.S. Department of Health and Human Services (HHS), Information Gateway does not have the authority to intervene or advise in personal situations.

Childhelp® is a national organization that provides crisis assistance and other counseling and referral services. The Childhelp National Child Abuse Hotline (www.childhelp.org/hotline) is staffed 24 hours a day, 7 days a week, with professional crisis counselors who have access to a database of 55,000 emergency, social service, and support resources. All calls are anonymous. Contact them at 800-4-A-CHILD (800-422-4453).

Penalties for Failure to Report and False Reporting of Child Abuse and Neglect

Many cases of child abuse and neglect are not reported, even when mandated by law. Therefore, nearly every state and U.S. territory imposes penalties, often in the form of a fine or imprisonment, on mandatory reporters who fail to report suspected child abuse or neglect as required by law. In addition, to prevent malicious or intentional reporting of cases that are not founded, many state and the U.S. Virgin Islands impose penalties against any person who files a report known to be false.

Penalties for Failure to Report

Approximately 48 states, the District of Columbia, American Samoa, Guam, the Northern Mariana Islands, and the Virgin Islands impose penalties on mandatory reporters who knowingly or willfully fail to make a report when they suspect that a child is being abused or neglected. In Florida, a mandatory reporter who fails to report as required by law can be charged with a felony. Failure to report is classified as a misdemeanor or a similar charge in 40 states and American Samoa, Guam, and the Virgin Islands. In Arizona and Minnesota, misdemeanors are upgraded to felonies for failure to report more serious situations; while in Connecticut, Illinois, Kentucky, and Guam, second or subsequent violations are classified as felonies. Twenty states and the District of Columbia, Guam, the Northern Mariana Islands, and the Virgin Islands specify in the reporting laws the penalties for a failure to report. Upon conviction, a mandated reporter who fails to report can face jail terms ranging from 30 days to 5 years, fines ranging from $300 to $10,000, or both jail terms and fines. In seven states, harsher penalties may be imposed under certain circumstances. In seven states and American Samoa, in addition to any criminal penalties, the reporter may be civilly liable for any damages caused by the failure to report. Florida imposes a fine of up to $1 million on any institution of higher learning, including any state university and nonpublic college, who fails to report or prevents any person from reporting an instance of abuse committed on the property of the institution or at an event sponsored by the institution.

Obstructing Reports of Abuse or Neglect

Approximately 10 states impose penalties against any employer who discharges, suspends, disciplines, or engages in any action to prevent or prohibit an employee or volunteer from making a report of suspected child maltreatment as required by the reporting laws. In six states, an action to prevent a report is classified as a misdemeanor. In Connecticut, an employer who interferes with making a report will be charged with a felony. Three states specify the penalties for that action, and in four states the employer is civilly liable for damages for any harm caused to the mandatory reporter. In Pennsylvania, a person commits a felony if she or he uses force, violence, or threat; or offers a bribe to prevent a report; or has a prior conviction for the same or a similar offense. In the Northern Mariana Islands, any person who is convicted of interfering with the good-faith efforts of any person making or attempting to make a report shall be subject to imprisonment for up to 1 year, or a fine of $1,000, or both.

Penalties for False Reporting

Approximately 29 states carry penalties in their civil child-protection laws for any person who willfully or intentionally makes a report of child abuse or neglect that the reporter knows to be false. In New York, Ohio, Pennsylvania, and the Virgin Islands, making false reports of child maltreatment is made illegal in criminal sections of State code. Nineteen States and the Virgin Islands classify false reporting as a misdemeanor or similar charge.

In Florida, Illinois, Tennessee, and Texas, false reporting is a felony; while in Arkansas, Indiana, Missouri, and Virginia, second or subsequent offenses are upgraded to felonies. In Michigan, false reporting can be either a misdemeanor or a felony, depending on the seriousness of the alleged abuse in the report. No criminal penalties are imposed in California, Maine, Minnesota, Montana, and Nebraska; however, the immunity from civil or criminal action that is provided to reporters of abuse or neglect is not extended to those who make a false report. In South Carolina, in addition to any criminal penalties, the Department of Social Services may bring civil action against the person to recover the costs of investigation and any proceedings related to the investigation.

Eleven States and the Virgin Islands specify the penalties for making a false report. Upon conviction, the reporter can face jail terms ranging from 90 days to 5 years or fines ranging from $500 to $5,000. Florida imposes the most severe penalties: In addition to a court sentence of 5 years and $5,000, the Department of Children and Family Services may fine the reporter up to $10,000. In six States, the reporter may be civilly liable for any damages caused by the report.

Chapter 28

How the Legal
System Can Help

Chapter Contents

Section 28.1

Laws on Violence against Women

This section includes text excerpted from "Laws on Violence against Women," Office on Women's Health (OWH), U.S. Department of Health and Human Services (HHS), September 13, 2018.

Any type of violence is illegal. Laws addressing violence against women give additional support to women and families affected by violence. The most significant laws related to violence against women are the Violence Against Women Act (VAWA) and the Family Violence Prevention and Services Act (FVPSA).

Violence against Women Reauthorization Act of 2013

The main federal law against violence against women is the Violence Against Women Reauthorization Act of 2013. Domestic violence and abuse are already against the law. This law provides services and support for victims of domestic violence and sexual assault.

The direct services provided for individual women by this law include:

- Free rape exams

- No charge for prosecution or civil protection orders in domestic violence

- Programs to meet the needs of immigrant women and women of different races and ethnicities

- Programs and services for women with disabilities

- Legal aid for survivors of violence

- Services for children and teens

- Protections for victims who are evicted from their homes because of events related to domestic violence or stalking

The Family Violence Prevention and Services Act (FVPSA)

The Family Violence Prevention and Services Act (FVPSA) helps victims of domestic violence and their children by providing shelters and resources.

Under the FVPSA, the Administration for Children and Families, (ACYF) part of the U.S. Department of Health and Human Services (HHS), funds national, state, and community programs, such as state domestic violence coalitions and the Domestic Violence Resource Network (DVRN). The DVRN includes national resource centers on domestic violence and the National Domestic Violence Hotline (NDVH) (800-799-7233).

Local Laws about Violence against Women

Each community has slightly different laws about violence. But no one ever has the right to hurt you physically. In all communities, you should call 911 if you are in immediate danger. Violence is a criminal act. You must contact the local police to report violence and be protected by the law.

Some communities have outdated or limited local laws about sexual assault. The legal definition of rape in your local community may be slightly different than what you expect. The U.S. Department of Justice (DOJ) (a federal agency) defines rape as "the penetration, no matter how slight, of the vagina or anus with any body part or object, or oral penetration by a sex organ of another person, without the consent of the victim." The federal government uses this legal definition to collect information about rape from local police.

Even though local laws can be slightly different from community to community, do not be afraid to report violence to the police. The police will file a report, which is the start of a legal process to get help and protection under the law.

Section 28.2

Mandatory Reporters of Child Abuse and Neglect

This section includes text excerpted from "Mandatory Reporters of Child Abuse and Neglect," Child Welfare Information Gateway, U.S. Department of Health and Human Services (HHS), August 2015. Reviewed October 2018.

Professionals Required to Report

Approximately 48 states, the District of Columbia (DC), American Samoa, Guam, the Northern Mariana Islands, Puerto Rico, and the Virgin Islands designate professions whose members are mandated by law to report child maltreatment. Individuals designated as mandatory reporters typically have frequent contact with children. Such individuals may include:

- Social workers

- Teachers, principals, and other school personnel

- Physicians, nurses, and other healthcare workers

- Counselors, therapists, and other mental-health professionals

- Child-care providers

- Medical examiners or coroners

- Law-enforcement officers

Some other professions frequently mandated across the states include commercial film or photograph processors (in 12 states, Guam, and Puerto Rico) and computer technicians (in six states). Substance-abuse counselors are required to report in 14 states, and probation or parole officers are mandatory reporters in 17 states.

Directors, employees, and volunteers at entities that provide organized activities for children, such as camps, day camps, youth centers, and recreation centers, are required to report in 13 states. Six states and the DC include domestic-violence workers on the list of mandated reporters, while six other states and the DC include animal control or humane officers. Illinois includes both domestic-violence workers and animal control or humane officers as mandatory reporters. Court-appointed special advocates are mandatory reporters in 11 states. Members of the clergy now are required to report in 27 states and Guam.

Eleven states now have faculty, administrators, athletics staff, and other employees and volunteers at institutions of higher learning, including public and private colleges and universities and vocational and technical schools, designated as mandatory reporters.

Reporting by Other Persons

In approximately 18 states and Puerto Rico, any person who suspects child abuse or neglect is required to report. Of these 18 states, 16 states and Puerto Rico specify certain professionals who must report, but also require all persons to report suspected abuse or neglect, regardless of profession. New Jersey and Wyoming require all persons to report without specifying any professions. In all other states, territories, and the DC, any person is permitted to report. These voluntary reporters of abuse are often referred to as "permissive reporters."

Institutional Responsibility to Report

The term "institutional reporting" refers to those situations in which the mandated reporter is working (or volunteering) as a staff member of an institution, such as a school or hospital, at the time she or he gains the knowledge that leads him or her to suspect that abuse or neglect has occurred. Many institutions have internal policies and procedures for handling reports of abuse, and these usually require the person who suspects abuse to notify the head of the institution that abuse has been discovered or is suspected and needs to be reported to child protective services or other appropriate authorities. Statutes in 33 states, the DC, and the Virgin Islands provide procedures that must be followed in those cases. In 18 states, the DC, and the Virgin Islands, any staff member who suspects abuse must notify the head of the institution when the staff member feels that abuse or possible abuse should be reported to an appropriate authority. In nine states, the DC, and the Virgin Islands, the staff member who suspects abuse notifies the head of the institution first, and then the head or his or her designee is required to make the report. In nine states, the individual reporter must make the report to the appropriate authority first and then notify the institution that a report has been made. Laws in 15 states make clear that, regardless of any policies within the organization, the mandatory reporter is not relieved of his or her responsibility to report. In 17 states, an employer is expressly prohibited from taking any action to prevent or discourage an employee from making a report.

Standards for Making a Report

The circumstances under which a mandatory reporter must make a report vary from state to state. Typically, a report must be made when the reporter, in his or her official capacity, suspects or has reason to believe that a child has been abused or neglected. Another standard frequently used is in situations in which the reporter has knowledge of, or observes a child being subjected to, conditions that would reasonably result in harm to the child. In Maine, a mandatory reporter must report when she or he has reasonable cause to suspect that a child is not living with the child's family. Mandatory reporters are required to report the facts and circumstances that led them to suspect that a child has been abused or neglected. They do not have the burden of providing proof that abuse or neglect has occurred. Permissive reporters follow the same standards when electing to make a report.

Privileged Communications

Mandatory reporting statutes also may specify when a communication is privileged. "Privileged communications" is the statutory recognition of the right to maintain confidential communications between professionals and their clients, patients, or congregants. To enable states to provide protection to maltreated children, the reporting laws in most states and territories restrict this privilege for mandated reporters. All but three states and Puerto Rico now address the issue of privileged communications within their reporting laws, either affirming the privilege or denying it (i.e., not allowing the privilege to be grounds for failing to report). For instance:

- The physician–patient and husband–wife privileges are the most common to be denied by states.

- The attorney–client privilege is most commonly affirmed.

- The clergy–penitent privilege is also widely affirmed, although that privilege usually is limited to confessional communications and, in some states, denied altogether. In Louisiana, a mental-health or social-services practitioner is not required to report if the practitioner is engaged by an attorney to assist in the provision of legal services to a child.

Disclosure of the Reporter's Identity

All jurisdictions have provisions in the statute to maintain the confidentiality of abuse and neglect records. The identity of the reporter is specifically protected from disclosure to the alleged perpetrator in 41 states, the DC, American Samoa, Guam, the Northern Mariana Islands, and Puerto Rico. This protection is maintained even when other information from the report may be disclosed. Release of the reporter's identity is allowed in some jurisdictions under specific circumstances or to specific departments or officials, for example, when information is needed for conducting an investigation or family assessment or upon a finding that the reporter knowingly made a false report (in Alabama, Arkansas, Connecticut, Kentucky, Louisiana, Minnesota, Nevada, South Dakota, Vermont, and Virginia). In some jurisdictions (California, Florida, Minnesota, Tennessee, Texas, Vermont, the DC, and Guam), the reporter can waive confidentiality and give consent to the release of his or her name.

Chapter 29

How You Can Help Someone Who Is in an Abusive Situation

Whether you suspect that a friend or family member is being abused or you witnessed someone being abused, you can take steps to help.

What Are Signs That Someone May Be Abused?

According to the National Domestic Violence Hotline (NDVH), some warning signs include the following:

- Their partner insults them in front of other people.

- They are constantly worried about making their partner angry.

- They make excuses for their partner's behavior.

- Their partner is extremely jealous or possessive.

- They have unexplained marks or injuries.

- They've stopped spending time with friends and family.

This chapter includes text excerpted from "How to Help a Friend Who Is Being Abused," Office on Women's Health (OWH), U.S. Department of Health and Human Services (HHS), September 13, 2018.

- They are depressed or anxious, or you notice changes in their personality.

If you think your friend or family member is being abused, be supportive by listening to them and asking questions about how they're doing. The person being abused may not be ready or able to leave the relationship right now.

How Can You Help Someone Who Is Being Abused?

Knowing or thinking that someone you care about is in a violent relationship can be very hard. You may fear for her safety—and maybe for good reason. You may want to rescue her or insist she leaves, but every adult must make her own decisions.

Each situation is different, and the people involved are all different, too. Here are some ways to help a loved one who is being abused:

- **Set up a time to talk.** Try to make sure you have privacy and won't be distracted or interrupted. Visit your loved one in person if possible.

- **Let her know you're concerned about her safety.** Be honest. Tell her about times when you were worried about her. Help her see that abuse is wrong. She may not respond right away, or she may even get defensive or deny the abuse. Let her know you want to help and will be there to support her in whatever decision she makes.

- **Be supportive.** Listen to your loved one. Keep in mind that it may be very hard for her to talk about the abuse. Tell her that she is not alone and that people want to help. If she wants help, ask her what you can do.

- **Offer specific help.** You might say you are willing to just listen, to help her with child care, or to provide transportation, for example.

- **Don't place shame, blame, or guilt on her.** Don't say, "You just need to leave." Instead, say something like, "I get scared thinking about what might happen to you." Tell her you understand that her situation is very difficult.

- **Help her make a safety plan.** Safety planning might include packing important items and helping her find a "safe" word. This is a code word she can use to let you know she is in danger without an abuser knowing. It might also include agreeing on a place to meet if she has to leave in a hurry.

- **Encourage her to talk to someone who can help.** Offer to help her find a local domestic violence agency (DVA). Offer to go with her to the agency, the police, or court. The NDVH, 800-799-SAFE (800-799-7233); the National Sexual Assault Hotline (NSAH), 800-656-HOPE (800-656-4673); and the National Teen Dating Abuse Helpline (NTDAH), 866-331-9474, are all available 24 hours a day, seven days a week. They can offer advice based on experience and can help find local support and services.

- **If she decides to stay, continue to be supportive.** She may decide to stay in the relationship, or she may leave and then go back many times. It may be hard for you to understand, but people stay in abusive relationships for many reasons. Be supportive, no matter what she decides to do.

- **Encourage her to do things outside of the relationship.** It's important for her to see friends and family.

- **If she decides to leave, continue to offer help.** Even though the relationship was abusive, she may feel sad and lonely once it is over. She may also need help getting services from agencies or community groups.

- **Let her know that you will always be there no matter what.** It can be very frustrating to see a friend or loved one stay in an abusive relationship. But if you end your relationship, she has one less safe place to go in the future. You cannot force a person to leave a relationship, but you can let them know you'll help, whatever they decide to do.

How Do You Report Domestic Violence or Abuse?

If you see or hear domestic violence or child abuse in your neighborhood or in a public place, call 911. Don't worry about whether the couple or person will be angry with you for calling. It could be a matter of life and death, and it's better to be safe than sorry. You don't have to give your name if you are afraid for your own safety.

If you want to report abuse but there is no immediate danger, ask local police or child/adult protective services to make a welfare check. This surprise check-in by local authorities may help the person being abused.

Chapter 30

Working with Men and Boys to End Violence against Women and Girls

It is now widely accepted that strategies to end violence against women and girls (VAWG) must include work with men and boys. Much of the evidence relating to such strategies comes from the health sector. Ending VAWG, however, requires coordinated work across many sectors. The need for a multisectoral response to the challenge of ending VAWG has focused attention on the opportunities for and challenges of male engagement strategies outside of the health sector. This chapter reviews documentation of efforts, outside the health sector, to work with men and boys on VAWG to identify promising approaches to, and emerging lessons from, these efforts.

Such approaches are grounded in an understanding of the links between social constructions of masculinity and men's use of violence. Social constructions of gender in patriarchal cultures almost always confer a higher social value on men than women, and privilege the masculine over the feminine. Male violence against women and girls is born of this privilege. The term "positive masculinities," which is

This chapter includes text excerpted from "Working with Men and Boys to End Violence against Women and Girls," U.S. Agency for International Development (USAID), February 2015. Reviewed October 2018.

used in this chapter as a way to characterize the values, norms, and practices that gender-based work with men and boys seeks to promote in order to end VAWG.

This chapter reviews the published and grey literature on male engagement strategies for ending VAG in five sectors from across the Global South. Sectors reviewed include economic growth, trade, and agriculture; education; governance, law enforcement, and justice systems; conflict, postconflict, and humanitarian assistance; and social development.

Ending Violence against Women and Girls Requires Work with Men and Boys

It is now widely accepted that strategies to end violence against women and girls must include work with men and boys. The proliferation of interventions involving men and boys has been motivated by a desire to address men's role in violence perpetration and recognition that patriarchal norms of masculinity are implicated in violence. In its 2008 report to the United States Congress on Response and Policy Issues with respect to International Violence Against Women (I-VAWA), the Congressional Research Service (CRS) identified "The Role of Men and Boys" as the first of its emerging areas in violence against women research, prevention, and treatment, observing that

> Research on VAWG has evolved to include not only treatment and prevalence but also root causes. As a result, many experts and policymakers have increasingly focused on the role of men and boys in preventing violence against women.

This recognition of the importance of male engagement strategies to end VAWG is part of a broader acknowledgment of the roles that men and boys can and must play in work to establish and maintain gender equality. Such roles have gained significant attention from the international community over the past decade, including the 1995 Beijing Platform for Action, the 2000 review of the Programme of Action of the World Summit on Social Development, and the 48th Session of the United Nations Commission on the Status of Women (UNCSW) in 2004.

Not only has the importance of work with men and boys for ending VAWG been established, but there is a growing body of evidence from male engagement interventions about the best ways to work with men and boys on changing gender inequitable attitudes, practices,

314

norms, and policies. Much of this evidence comes from the health sector, as it is within the fields of sexual and reproductive health (SRH) and human immunodeficiency virus (HIV) and acquired immunodeficiency syndrome (AIDS) that much of the early work with men on gender equality was established and where it has been best documented.

Ending VAWG, however, requires coordinated work across many sectors, as an analyses of gender-based violence (GBV) prevention have emphasized. The need for a multisectoral response to the challenge of ending VAWG has focused attention on the opportunities for and challenges of male engagement strategies outside of the health sector.

Men, Masculinities, and Violence against Women and Girls

Violence against women and girls is the most widespread form of abuse worldwide, affecting one third of all women in their lifetime. Such violence takes many forms (physical, sexual, emotional, and economic) and is rooted in women's political, economic, and social subordination. Rape and intimate partner violence (IPV) are found in all societies, with varying prevalence, and culturally specific forms of VAWG may be locally common, such as honor killings or female genital mutilation. However, women's experience of such violence is far from uniform as it is shaped not only by patriarchal norms and institutions, but also by other forms of inequality and discrimination linked to factors such as class, ethnicity, age, sexuality, and disability. Women's and girls' exposure to different forms of violence, their experience of that violence, and their access to justice, health services, and social support in response to that violence are all affected by these multiple and linked forms of inequality that they face. The frequency and severity of VAWG may also increase during periods of conflict and humanitarian emergencies, as well as in the aftermath of such crises.

While it is true that not all men are violent and that some men have been active for many years in work to end VAWG and to promote gender equality, it remains the case that the vast majority of violence experienced by women and girls is perpetrated by men and boys, whether as individuals or as part of male-dominated institutions. Research also suggests that men's use of violence against girls and women is closely related to their use of violence against other men. Studies indicate that men who have themselves experienced violence are more likely

315

to perpetrate intimate partner violence or rape, although the majority of male survivors of violence do not subsequently go on to perpetrate violence.

The biology of the Y chromosome is not an adequate explanation for male violence against women and girls, for there are great global differences in prevalence and patterns, and individual differences between men in any one setting. But a growing body of empirical research and program expertise is addressing the connections between social constructions of masculinity and men's use of violence. Although differing in degree across different societies, social constructions of gender almost always confer a higher social value on men than women and privilege the masculine over the feminine. Male violence against women and girls is born of this privilege, whether because men feel entitled to use violence against those whom they consider "less" than them, or because they fear the loss of such privilege or feel unable to live up to the expectations associated with being the dominant gender. In many societies, boys are raised to believe that violence is a way to demonstrate their masculinity and prove themselves to be "real men"—often at great cost not only to the women and girls in their lives, but also to themselves.

These links between social constructions of masculinity and male violence have been starkly illustrated by several large-scale research projects. Over 10,000 men participated in the United Nations (UN) study in Asia and the Pacific, providing valuable insights into factors associated with men's perpetration of VAWG, and complementing research conducted through the International Men and Gender Equality Survey (IMAGES). Key factors strongly associated with perpetration of IPV and nonpartner rape included controlling behaviors toward women and inequitable gender attitudes, behaviors that emphasized (hetero) sexual prowess (transactional sex and having multiple sexual partners), and involvement in violence with other men. Men struggling to live up to the ideals of manhood because of social exclusion and poverty, and men who had been traumatized through harsh childhoods and violence in adulthood, were also at increased risk of perpetration.

The concept of "hegemonic masculinity," originally developed by Australian sociologist Raewyn Connell, is now widely used to characterize those ideas about and expressions of masculinity associated with male domination and male violence against women and girls. In this sense, the practices and norms of hegemonic masculinity help to keep patriarchy in place. This phenomenon has been emphasized with reference to the male behaviors associated with IPV and nonpartner rape identified by the research findings above.

Many of these behaviors are rooted in expected practices or entitlements that flow from hegemonic ideals of men who are strong, tough, in control over women and their bodies, heterosexual, and sexually dominant.

The concept of hegemonic masculinity has proved particularly useful in work with men on ending VAWG, both because it emphasizes that men's gender identities and practices are learned—and thus can be changed—and because there are other masculinities available to men (i.e., other ways of being a man) that do not conform to these hegemonic ideals, but instead focus on more equitable, respectful, and harmonious gender relations. This emphasis on masculinities as both multiple and changeable has been used in working with men to critically reflect on their socialization, power, privilege, and the costs to themselves as well as to women and girls of conforming to the norms of hegemonic masculinity. It suggests that there are alternative, more 'positive' ways of being a man that do not involve VAWG that can be linked to culturally significant values of trust, respect, and equality that exist in a given community. Importantly, it also highlights the gravity of working with women, as women often take for granted men's power over them. As a result, there is a need to empower women—not just economically, but socially and individually—and to raise their consciousness, so that women understand their role in male gender socialization and demand more equitable relationships.

The term "positive masculinities" has emerged as a way to characterize the values, norms, and practices that gender-based work with men and boys seeks to promote in order to end VAWG. Often, this is taken to refer simply to more equitable, nonviolent relations between men and women. However, as the widespread violence against lesbian, gay, bisexual, transgender, and intersex (LGBTI) people—whether perpetrated by individuals or institutions—makes clear, hegemonic masculinity is not simply about male domination of women, but also the subordination of those whose gender identities and sexual orientations do not conform to the heterosexual hegemonic ideal. The emphasis on different, nonviolent ways of being a man that is central to work on positive masculinities must also seek to support the diversity and multiplicity of gender identities and sexual orientations, in culturally meaningful ways, in order to foster societies in which any violence rooted in hegemonic norms of gender and sexuality is no longer tolerated.

Recommendations

There is now widespread agreement among practitioners, policy advocates, and researchers that action to prevent and respond to violence against women and girls must work across the social ecology of individual, community, institutional, and societal levels to effect change. Thus, the following synthesis of a set of recommendations across the different sectors included in this wide-ranging review uses a modified social ecological framework to discuss key findings from this review at each of the following four levels of change:

- Individual-level attitudes and behaviors

- Community-level norms and practices

- Institutional-level policies and cultures

- Societal-level laws and government policy

Presenting the recommendations in this way is also intended to highlight the importance of linking work across different sectors in order to effect change at these different levels of the social ecology.

Working with Men and Boys for Change at the Individual Level

Start young. The male-engagement interventions reviewed here make clear the value of working with younger adolescents at a time when both their gender identities and their attitudes toward and skills in gender relations are being formed. This is clearly an important emphasis of male-engagement programming on violence within the education sector, but it also suggests a need to extend male-engagement programming in other sectors to younger men and boys where possible.

Adapt effective group-work methodologies. Well-tested, evidence-based, group-work methodologies focused on positive masculinities have been successfully adapted for use in many different sectoral contexts. Successful adaptation relies on adequate investments in situational assessments and engaging the participation of targeted communities and stakeholders in the adaptation process. Skilled facilitation is crucial to the effectiveness of such group-work, emphasizing the need for investments in capacity building and mentoring for facilitators. Although most of the male-targeted group-work reviewed here was led by male facilitators, there are indications that mixed-gender facilitation teams can prove beneficial in helping to model more equitable gender relations.

318

Highlight men's roles in care work. Focusing work with men on the roles they can play as caregivers within their own families and in the broader community as a whole is a promising practice for promoting more positive, nonviolent masculinities. Not only is this approach validated by research on the associations between men's caregiving involvement and more gender-equitable attitudes, but focusing on men's involvement with their families has been found to be an important component of supporting their social reintegration in postconflict situations.

Address men's multiple interests in change. Much of the work with men and boys on VAWG focuses on their gender interests in change with respect to the benefits of more positive masculinities for both themselves and women and girls. Yet, much of this work is targeted at poor and socially marginalized communities, within which many women and men share similar interests (based on class and/or ethnicity and/or other aspects of social marginalization) in struggling for a better life for themselves and their families. Addressing GBV as that which fractures families and communities and jeopardizes their shared struggle for a better life and more social justice is one way to engage women and men in working together to end such violence. Furthermore, while this review has focused specifically on efforts to prevent and respond to VAWG, many different programs found that work with men and boys on such violence is more effective when it acknowledges and addresses men's and boy's own experiences with male violence.

Working with Men and Boys for Change at the Community Level

Nurture supportive male peer groups. Fostering alternative male peer groups is an important way to sustain men's adoption of more equitable masculinities, by creating networks of both support and accountability for men to help them in dealing with peer pressures to conform to dominant and harmful norms of masculinity.

Engage men in collective action. Organizing men to undertake action for change at the community level is a way to both sustain and broaden the impact of a program. While much of the positive-masculinities work discussed in this chapter focuses exclusively on changing men's own attitudes and individual behaviors, there are indications that this individual-level change can be better sustained when men are organized to take specific actions to change aspects of community

319

life that increase women's and girls' vulnerability to violence or inhibit them from accessing needed services.

Increase the focus on men's roles in responding to VAW. The overall sense from the programs reviewed for this report is that much of the male-engagement work concerned with VAWG has focused on prevention, and less attention has been given to men's multiple roles in improving the support given to women and girl survivors. Whether this is as active bystanders intervening to address situations of vulnerability or as referral agents to available health, legal, and social-welfare services, male-engagement programming can better equip men to play an active role in response.

Work with male community leadership, but stay connected to goals for women's empowerment. As work with male community and religious leaders to address harmful traditional practices or reform aspects of alternative justice mechanisms indicates, it is both necessary and possible to engage male leaders in changing aspects of community life without challenging the patriarchal basis of their authority. In seeking to change a practice that is based on inequitable gender norms, and in using but not seeking to change the patriarchal power that men in positions of community leadership have to make this change, this work is both gender transformative and gender aware. Nevertheless, in order to contribute to the broader gender transformative goals of women's empowerment work, it is important that this male-engagement work with male leaders is connected to ongoing efforts to strengthen women's leadership and power within such communities.

Working with Men and Boys for Change at the Institutional Level

Strengthen program capacity to work for institutional-level change. A common finding across the different sectors reviewed for this report is that individual- and community-level strategies for change must be complemented by initiatives directed at reforming the institutions that shape people's lives and affect women's and girls' vulnerability to violence and their ability to access needed services. From workplaces to schools to law-enforcement and justice systems, these institutions not only tend to be led by men, but are often infused with the very patriarchal norms and cultures that underpin VAWG. Reforming the policies and cultures of male-dominated institutions is an important priority for male-engagement programming to end VAWG.

Use institutional hierarchies to facilitate institutional reform. Institutional reform requires internal champions. Male-engagement programming must identify and nurture internal male champions who can provide the necessary leadership to initiate and sustain institutional reform. The need to move beyond externally led pilot initiatives and mainstream gender training as part of institutional reform processes is also widely recognized. Programs reviewed for this report undertook different strategies to accomplish this mainstreaming. Yet there was a common concern that mainstreaming risked dilution of training impact, especially when the training was focused on more participatory and experiential methodologies. This suggests a need to invest sufficient time and resources to train and then mentor the internal-training capacity that is required to fully mainstream such gender training.

Work with the whole person and not only their professional responsibility. Workshops on women's rights, gender equality, and institutional responsibilities with respect to VAW are one of the most common approaches to institutional reform. A common finding across several such initiatives is that such training is more effective when it focuses not only on the professional responsibilities of men within a given institution, but also on men's own experiences with gender socialization, harmful norms of masculinity, and their own experiences of male violence in terms of the women and girls in their lives. Working with the whole person is important in motivating and sustaining men's commitment to changing institutional culture and practice concerning VAWG.

Strengthen oversight and accountability mechanisms. While much of the emphasis in reform processes to improve institutional responses to VAW focused on training, a consistent finding reported from differing sectoral contexts was that such training would have limited impact unless it was complemented by oversight and accountability mechanisms. It is clear that more work is needed to develop such mechanisms. Linked to the above, men's organizations have a role to play in keeping up the pressure to hold institutions accountable to their reform agenda. Fortunately, there are promising examples of organizations that work with men on gender equality taking action collaboratively with women's rights organizations to ensure such accountability (e.g., demanding women's access to justice from law-enforcement and justice systems). Supporting men's organizations to collaborate with women's rights organizations in this way is an important priority.

Working with Men and Boys for Change at the Societal Level

Use a masculinities lens for policy advocacy on VAWG. The promising results of MenEngage Africa (MEA) policy audits and associated advocacy efforts highlight the value of focusing a masculinities lens at the policy level as a contribution to the ongoing advocacy of women's rights groups to improve policy and its implementation on GBV and women's empowerment more broadly. While much of the investment in capacity building for male engagement work has focused on skills needed for individual- and community-level work, this suggests a need also to build the advocacy and campaigning skills of organizations working with men on gender equality.

Hold male authority figures accountable for their public discourse. Another promising and relatively neglected area of work with men on ending VAW is to address the role that men, and the organizations that support men in working for gender equality, can play to create a more conducive public environment for efforts to end VAW. The principle of men holding other men accountable for their patriarchal behavior should be extended to holding male authority figures accountable for their public discourse.

Link male-engagement programming with broader movements for gender equality and social justice. Sustained action to challenge inequitable norms and practices of masculinity requires a movement-building perspective to designing and developing interventions. The challenge of sustaining impact was identified by many of the programs reviewed for this report. One response has been to look at how male-engagement programming can contribute to a broader and ongoing movement for change in a given community or society. This requires attention to fostering links between organizations and investing in movement-building opportunities, not least in terms of building closer relationships between initiatives focused exclusively on working with men on positive masculinities and those working on women's empowerment. The challenge of ending VAWG is the challenge of changing unequal relations of political, economic, and social power. Supporting the efforts of social movements, which are campaigning for gender justice as part of their social-justice work, and targeting male-engagement work at men within such social movements to enlist their support as allies in this work, is an important direction for male-engagement programming to take.

Chapter 31

Interventions and Help for Abusers

Chapter Contents

Section 31.1

Batterer Interventions

"Batterer Interventions,"
© 2016 Omnigraphics. Reviewed October 2018.

Whether or not a person who behaves abusively toward an intimate partner can change is a question that has long interested researchers — as well as couples and families. Some studies have suggested that most perpetrators of verbal, emotional, physical, or sexual abuse cannot effectively change the deep-seated feelings, attitudes, and behaviors that contribute to domestic violence. Other studies have indicated that meaningful change is possible for some abusers, but that achieving healthy relationships is a long and difficult process. One type of program that is intended to stop domestic abuse and rehabilitate abusers is known as a batterer intervention program (BIP). As is the case with other efforts to reform domestic-violence offenders, the results of BIP have been mixed.

Identifying Abusers

The first step toward ending domestic abuse is recognizing that certain types or patterns of behavior are abusive. Both perpetrators and victims of domestic violence need to be aware of the common traits of domestic abusers, including:

- Extreme jealousy, possessiveness, or controlling behavior

- Demanding commitment very quickly

- Isolating victims from family and friends, limiting their social interaction, and insisting that the intimate relationship should fulfill all of their needs

- Being easily insulted or overly sensitive to criticism

- Harboring unrealistic expectations of perfection in relationships

- Believing in rigid, stereotypical gender roles or holding negative attitudes toward the opposite sex

- Making cruel, hurtful, degrading remarks to partners or belittling their accomplishments

- Shifting blame and refusing to take responsibility for problems

- Threatening violence, breaking objects, or using force of any kind during an argument
- Having a past history of violence in relationships
- Being cruel or neglectful toward animals or children
- Abusing alcohol or drugs
- Showing extreme, Jekyll-and-Hyde shifts in personality or behavior

People who are wondering whether their behavior constitutes abuse should consider whether they treat others—such as friends, neighbors, or coworkers—in the same way they treat their intimate partners. They should also try to view their behavior from the perspective of someone outside of the relationship, and consider how they would feel if they saw another person treating a loved one in that manner. Finally, if an intimate partner has ever described certain behaviors as abusive or threatened to leave the relationship, then it seems likely that some interactions may have crossed the line into domestic abuse.

Changing Abusive Behavior

In order to end abusive behavior, the abuser must have a deep desire to change as well as a full commitment to what can be a long and challenging process. Abusive behavior is often rooted in attitudes and feelings that originated in childhood and developed over the course of many years. As a result, it can be extremely difficult to dislodge these long-standing issues and affect true change.

The first step for abusers is admitting that their behavior is wrong and harmful. Abusers often deflect blame onto others, so taking direct personal responsibility for their actions is a vital part of the change process. Some tips for people who are committed to ending abusive behavior include:

- View violence as a choice. Remember that there is no excuse for abuse. Admit the abuse, take full responsibility for it, and avoid blaming others.

- Realize that physical violence is not the only form of domestic abuse. Verbal and emotional abuse also have no place in a healthy, respectful relationship.

- Recognize that abusive behavior hurts others. Respect an intimate partner's right to a safe and healthy relationship.

327

- Accept the consequences of abusive actions, including legal consequences.

- Work to identify underlying attitudes and patterns of behavior involved in abuse.

- Develop new methods of dealing with conflicts and responding to an intimate partner's grievances, criticisms, and anger.

- Make amends for past abuse and develop kind, supportive, respectful, and loving behaviors.

- Avoid seeking recognition or credit for any improvements in behavior.

- Seek help and support from friends, family members, and intervention programs.

- Recognize that achieving change is very difficult, and overcoming abusiveness is a long-term process. Do not expect immediate results and do not give up trying to change.

Batterer Intervention Programs

Professional help is essential in learning to avoid abusive behaviors and treat intimate partners with respect. Batterer Intervention Programs (BIP) are tools that were developed to aid in this process. BIP originated in the 1980s, when increased enforcement of domestic-violence laws led to rising numbers of accused batterers in the criminal-justice system. The courts discovered that some victims of domestic violence did not want their abusive partners put in jail. Instead, they only wanted the abuse to stop. BIP were developed to meet the demand for programs to help abusers reform and potentially return to their families. Many courts began requiring offenders to attend BIP as a condition of probation.

There are several types of BIP based on different theoretical approaches to domestic violence. The most common type of BIP is the Duluth model, a psychoeducational program based on the idea that domestic violence stems from patriarchal ideas that equate masculinity with strength, power, and dominance. This theory claims that cultural norms of masculinity encourage men to exert control over their intimate partners, which sometimes results in abuse. The Duluth model helps abusers confront such attitudes and develop new, more respectful methods of relating to their partners.

Individual and group psychotherapy are also used to treat domestic abusers. These approaches explain domestic violence as stemming from an underlying emotional problem or traumatic childhood experience. They focus on helping abusers uncover the unconscious sources of their behavior and resolve them consciously in order to stop battering. Cognitive-behavioral intervention is another type of BIP. It focuses on training abusers in anger management and other skills to help them change their ways of thinking about relationships and dealing with problems. Other types of BIP tailor their approaches to specific attributes or typologies of batterers, such as ethnicity or socioeconomic status.

Couples or family therapy is also employed in BIP. This approach treats domestic violence as part of a larger pattern of relationship dysfunction and involves all parties in the effort to end the abuse. It has aroused controversy because it appears to assign a share of the blame to victims of abuse. Although some studies have found that BIP can be effective in helping end abusive behavior, other studies have suggested that a very low percentage of abusers succeed in making permanent changes.

References

1. "Can I Stop Being Abusive?" *Love Is Respect*, 2013.

2. "I Think I'm Abusive," *Hidden Hurt*, 2015.

3. Jackson, Shelly. "Batterer Intervention Programs," U.S. Department of Justice (DOJ), June 2003.

4. Robinson, Kathryn. "Is Change Possible in an Abuser?" National Domestic Violence Hotline (NDVH), September 5, 2013.

Section 31.2

Effectiveness of Batterer Intervention Programs

This section includes text excerpted from "Practical
Implications of Current Intimate Partner Violence
Research for Victim Advocates and Service Providers,"
National Criminal Justice Reference Service (NCJRS),
January 9, 2013. Reviewed October 2018.

Do Batterer Intervention Programs Prevent Reabuse?

Commonly, whether diverted, placed on probation, or jailed, many domestic violence offenders are required to attend batterer intervention programs (BIP). These programs have increased dramatically over the past several decades. There have been more than 35 evaluations of BIP, but they have yielded inconsistent results. The largest multi-state study of four batterer programs concluded that approximately a quarter of batterers appeared unresponsive and resistant to batterer intervention regardless of BIP. In this long-term study, based on victim and/or abuser interviews and/or police arrests, approximately half of the batterers assaulted their initial or new partners sometime during the study's 30-month follow-up. Most of the assaults occurred within the first six months of program intake. Nearly a quarter of the batterers repeatedly assaulted their partners during the follow-up, and these offenders accounted for nearly all of the severe assaults and injuries.

The leading researcher suggests that "the system matters." BIP that incorporate enhanced "support and notification to partners, program orientation sessions, open-ended enrollments, curricula that are designed for open-ended enrollments, 'voluntary' postprogram sessions, and on-going risk management that identifies and responds to problematic cases and dropout" may achieve better outcomes. Several meta-analyses of the more rigorous batterer program studies find the programs have, at best, a "modest" treatment effect, producing a minimal reduction in rearrests for domestic violence. In one of the meta-analyses, the treatment effect translated to a five-percent improvement rate in cessation of reassaults due to the treatment. In the other, it ranged from none to 0.26, roughly representing a reduction in recidivism from 13–20 percent. A randomized,

330

experimental evaluation of an "early intervention" BIP with male intimate partner violence (IPV) suspects who had minimal domestic violence criminal history and were detained in a county jail pending trial found that a one-week intervention appeared to reduce controlling behavior and alcohol and drug use in the six months after the program. However, the BIP did not have an effect on physical, sexual, and psychological abuse, threats, and injuries inflicted on victims. Victim partners reported that the intervention did not create problems for them. Participant and victim follow-up data were collected six months after the BIP, and police reports were tracked from 6 to 12 months thereafter.

The "system" in which the BIP program was delivered included a daily, three-hour, Duluth Model-based educational workshop for five days, mandatory detention in a special DV jail unit, supervision by correction officers who had specialized domestic violence training, daily 12-Step Drug/Alcohol addiction support groups, and strict regulations on television (TV) watching, with special, nonviolent education programs as the only available programs. The rate of recidivism eight years following the last class of the Domestic Abuse Intervention Programs (DAIP) Men's program attended by 353 men in Duluth revealed that men enrolling in the DAIP Men's program recidivate at a rate of 28 percent, with noncompleters reoffending at 31 percent and completers at 25 percent. There is a significant difference in the number of reoffenses; noncompleters commit 63 percent more reoffenses than men who complete the program.

Recidivism was measured by arrests, citations for DV, and protection orders issued against program participants by intimate partners or former partners. The DAIP is embedded in the Duluth Coordinated Community Response (CCR) program such that the deterrence must be viewed as a result of the entire criminal-justice process rather than just of the DAIP Men's program. On the other hand, a few studies have found that BIP are associated with higher rates of reabuse or have found no reduction in abuse at all. A meta-analysis of four randomized trials involving more than 2,300 batterers comparing those who received cognitive behavioral therapy (CBT) and those who had no intervention found the positive difference obtained by the CBT participants in terms of reabuse to be so slight that researchers could not conclude there was any clear evidence for an effect. Another single study compared CBT with process-psychodynamic group treatment and found equivocal differences, although the process-psychodynamic treatment proved marginally better.

Do the Type or Length of Batterer Intervention Programs Make a Difference?

Several studies have found that the type of batterer intervention program—whether feminist, psycho-educational, or cognitive-behavioral—does not affect reabuse. One study also found that a "culturally focused" program specifically designed for black male abusers did no better than the program offered to all abusers. In fact, those assigned to a conventional, racially mixed group were half as likely to be arrested for re-assaults compared to those assigned to a black culturally-focused counseling group or a conventional group of all blacks. As to duration of the BIP, in the four-state, multisite study, similar reassault rates were found for the participants in the shorter BIP (13 sessions over three months) as for those in longer ones (nine-month), except that the reported re-assaults were less severe in the nine-month program that included some alcohol treatments.

The shorter BIP outcomes appeared to be related to the swift and certain actions of the court (judicial reviews) and the higher completion rates. However, a rigorous study based in New York City found the length of the program (26 weeks compared to 8 weeks) may make a difference, with the longer program proving more effective at deterring reabuse. The researchers suggest that the longer program's increased effectiveness was due to its longer "suppression effect" while abusers were mandated to attend, whether or not they actually attended. In other words, whether or not they actually attended the program, while they were under court supervision, they were more likely to be on their best behavior.

Are Court-Referred Batterers Likely to Complete Batterer Programs?

Multiple studies of disparate programs around the country have found high noncompletion rates ranging from 25 to 89 percent, with most at around 50 percent. Rates vary because different programs have different standards for monitoring attendance as well as different policies regarding re-enrollment, missed meetings, and so on. A study in California found that, of ten counties examined, only one maintained a database to track offender participation in the mandated batterer intervention program; it reported that 89 percent did not complete the program. Unsurprisingly, requiring additional treatment programs increases noncompletion. For example, although 42 percent of the referred batterers in the Bronx court study failed to complete the BIP, that number increased to 67 percent for those also required to complete drug treatment. For those required to complete drug treatment alone, the noncompletion rate was lower, at 60 percent. High rates of technical violations are common for probationers sentenced for IPV, including violations of no-contact orders, drug abstinence, and failure to attend BIP.

Various probation studies have found technical violation (noncrime) rates ranging from 34 percent of those sentenced in the Brooklyn felony domestic violence court, 41 percent in Colorado, to 61 percent in Champaign County, Illinois. Rates of technical violations may vary based on the practices of the probation officers or others charged with monitoring the probationers. For example, technical violations were found to be 25 percent in Rhode Island for those abusers supervised in regularly mixed caseloads, but 44 percent in specialized IPV-only caseloads.

Do Those Who Complete Batterer Programs Do Better Than Those Who Fail?

Abusers who complete batterer programs are less likely to reabuse than those who fail to attend, are noncompliant, or drop out. The differences have been found to be significant. A Chicago study of more than 500 court-referred batterers referred to 30 different programs found that recidivism after an average of 2.4 years was 14.3 percent for those who completed the program, whereas recidivism for those who did not complete the programs was more than twice that (34.6 percent). Those who did not complete their program mandate in the Bronx court study were four times more likely to recidivate than those who completed their program. A multistate study of four programs found that abusers who completed the programs reduced their risk of reassault in a range of 46 to 66 percent. A Florida study found that the odds that abusers who completed the program would be rearrested were half those of a control group not assigned to the program, whereas the odds of rearrest for those who failed to attend were two and one-half times higher than the control group.

A Massachusetts study found that, over a six-year period, those who completed a certified BIP were significantly less likely to be rearrested for any type of offense, a violent offense, or a protection-order violation. The rate differences for these offenses between those who completed a program and those who did not was as follows: 47.7 versus 83.6 percent for any crime, 33.7 versus 64.2 percent for a violent crime, and 17.4 versus 41.8 percent for violation of a protective order. A Dallas study found that twice as many program dropouts as program completers were rearrested within 13 months: 39.7 versus 17.9 percent for any charge, and 8.1 versus 2.8 percent for assault arrests. A study of almost 2,000 domestic-violence defendants in Alexandria, Virginia, found that noncompliance with court-ordered treatment was associated significantly with being a repeat offender. A few studies have found less dramatic reductions. For example, in Broward County, Florida, the difference was only four percent versus five percent, and in Brooklyn, New York, it was 16 percent versus 26 percent for completers compared to noncompleters.

Which Batterers Are Likely to Fail to Attend Mandated Batterer Intervention Treatment?

Researchers generally agree that there are a number of variables associated with failure to complete programs. They include being younger, having less education, having greater criminal histories and violence in their family of origin, being less often employed and less motivated to change, having substance-abuse problems, having children, and lacking court sanctions for noncompliance. A number of studies emphasize the positive correlation between program completion and "stakes in conformity," including the variables of age (being older), marital status (being married), and employment (being employed). Studies also find that many of the same variables that predict noncompletion also predict reabuse or general recidivism.

In the Florida probation study, an examination of court-referred batterers found that the same characteristics that predicted rearrest (including prior criminal history and stakes in conformity) also predicted missing at least one court-mandated program session. Other studies, including a study of two Brooklyn BIP, also found that employment correlated both positively with completion and negatively with rearrest. However, prior criminal history remains the strongest and most consistent predictor of both noncompletion and new arrests. In the Brooklyn study, defendants with a prior arrest history were found to be four times more likely to fail to complete programs than defendants without prior arrests. The Bronx court study similarly found that prior arrests as well as a history of drug abuse predicted both noncompletion and recidivism and found background demographics to be less important.

When Are Noncompliant Abusers Likely to Drop out of Batterer Programs?

Several studies have found that batterers who do not complete BIP are likely to be noncompliant from the start. Furthermore, these studies found that noncompliance at the first court monitoring predicted both program failure and recidivism. In the Brooklyn study, the strongest predictor of program failure was early noncompliance. Defendants who had not enrolled in a program by the time of their first compliance hearing were significantly less likely to complete the program than those enrolled by the first hearing. These findings are similar to those found in the Bronx study. Defendants who were not in compliance at their first monitoring appearance were six times more likely to fail to complete the program than those in compliance at that time. Attrition may even occur before enrollment in a BIP. In a study of the use of polygraphs in BIP, researchers reported that 46 percent of the "high-risk" abusers did not report to probation or enroll in the BIP. These findings are consistent with extensive research indicating that the largest proportion of court-identified abusers who reabuse are likely to reabuse sooner rather than later.

What Should the Court's Response Be If Court-Referred Abusers Are Noncompliant with Programs?

The Rhode Island probation study that compared probationers in specialized probation supervision caseloads with those in less stringent general caseloads found that the former committed significantly less reabuse over a one-year period. The difference, however, applied only to what researchers called "lower risk" probationers, those without prior arrest histories. Although there were several differences in how the two caseloads were supervised, enforcement of BIP attendance was one of the major differences. The specialized group's program was more rigidly enforced, as measured by significantly more probation sanctions for nonattendance. As a result of the court violation hearings, most of the noncompliant probationers were required to attend weekly compliance court sessions until they completed the program.

An evaluation of two offices on violence against women (OVW) demonstration domestic violence courts found that abusers who participated in the specialized DV court with considerably more probation revocations for noncompliance (12% versus only 1% in the other court) were significantly less likely to reabuse than those in the comparison court. In the court with more revocations, victims reported a lower frequency of physical assaults for up to 11 months after the study incident. The offenders in the court with the higher revocation rates had a significantly higher number of prior arrests than the defendants in the comparison court (8.3% versus 3.7%). Researchers posited that lower rates of recidivism were obtained primarily through early detection and incarceration of probationers who either continued to reabuse or failed to comply with conditions. Broward County probation-study researchers concluded that if abusers are not afraid of violating their court orders, they are also not afraid of the consequences of committing new offenses.

Are Victims Satisfied with Batterer Intervention Program Referrals?

Studies find that most victims are satisfied with their abuser's referral to a BIP. In the Bronx study, 77 percent of victims were satisfied with the sentence imposed by the court if the abuser was ordered to attend a BIP, compared to only 55 percent of victims who were satisfied when the abuser was not required to attend a program. A survey of victims of men attending BIP throughout Rhode Island found most female victims enthusiastic about the batterer programs. Some victims were enthusiastic and felt that the program improved their situation even though they were reassaulted. Victims may be more likely to remain with their abusers if their abusers are in treatment programs and are hopeful that the abusers will "get better." For some victims, the failure of abusers to attend and complete mandated BIP is a key component in their decisions to terminate relationships with violent partners. Many IPV victims want help for their intimate partners. Victims consider BIP participation by abusers an important opportunity to learn and to choose to stop abuse. Listening sessions with African American and Latina women revealed that participants strongly support programming that will assist their abusive partners in stopping IPV. Participants added that services should be offered in community settings apart from traditional DV services and that community engagement should address the economic fragility of the environments in which they live to build safeguards against IPV.

Chapter 32

Workplace Intervention

Chapter Contents

Section 32.1

Workplace Violence

This section includes text excerpted from "Workplace Violence Handbook," U.S. Geological Survey (USGS), January 24, 2017.

Threatening behavior is an individual's threat, either overt or implied, to commit an act of physical aggression or harm at the workplace. Examples include, but are not limited to:

- Threats to cause bodily harm or death to another person (including stalking, bullying, or other abusive or aggressive behavior);

- Threats to commit sabotage or destroy, damage, or deface government or personal property located at the workplace;

- Making harassing or threatening phone calls; and

- Unusual, bizarre, or menacing behavior or statements that a reasonable person would interpret as carrying the potential for violent acts.

Workplace violence is any act or attempted act of physical aggression or harm by an individual that occurs at the workplace. Examples include, but are not limited to:

- Causing or attempting to cause bodily harm or death to another person;

- Acting or attempting to sabotage, destroy, damage, or deface government or personal property in the workplace; and

- Possession of unlawful and unauthorized weapons in the workplace.

Threats and Violence in the Workplace
Warning Signs

No one can always predict when a human being will become violent. There is no absolute specific profile of a potentially dangerous individual; however, indicators of increased risk of violent behavior are available. Some of these indicators may include, but are not limited to:

- Direct or veiled threats of harm;

- Intimidating, belligerent, harassing, bullying, or other inappropriate and aggressive behavior;

- Numerous conflicts with supervisors and other employees;

- Bringing a weapon to the workplace, brandishing a weapon in the workplace, making inappropriate references to guns, or a fascination with weapons;

- Statements showing a fascination with incidents of workplace violence, statements indicating approval of the use of violence to resolve a problem, or statements indicating identification with perpetrators of workplace violence;

- Statements indicating desperation (over family, financial, or other personal problems) to the point of committing suicide;

- Drug/alcohol abuse; and

- Extreme changes in behavior.

Each of these behaviors indicates the potential for escalation of violent behavior. None should be ignored. By identifying the problem and dealing with it appropriately, we may be able to prevent violence from happening. Employees who recognize these behaviors in themselves are encouraged to seek assistance from the Employee Assistance Program (EAP) or their family physician. Any employees who notice the above indicators in coworkers should notify their supervisors. Supervisors who have seen the above indicators in an employee, or have received a report from one employee regarding it in another employee, should immediately contact their Human Resources (HR) office for advice and assistance in determining the appropriate course of action.

Section 32.2

Workplace Violence: Statistics

This section includes text excerpted from "Occupational Violence,"
Centers for Disease Control and Prevention (CDC), March 28, 2018.

Workplace violence is the act or threat of violence, ranging from verbal abuse to physical assaults directed toward persons at work or on duty. The impact of workplace violence can range from psychological issues to physical injury, or even death. Violence can occur in any work-place and among any type of worker, but the risk for fatal violence is greater for workers in sales, protective services, and transportation, while the risk for nonfatal violence resulting in days away from work is greatest for healthcare and social-assistance workers.

Injury Data

According to the U.S. Bureau of Labor Statistics (BLS), 16,890 workers in private industry experienced trauma from nonfatal work-place violence in 2016. These incidents required days away from work.
Of those victims who experienced trauma from workplace violence:

- 70 percent were female

- 67 percent were aged 25–54

- 70 percent worked in the healthcare and social-assistance industries

- 21 percent required 31 or more days away from work to recover, and 19 percent involved 3–5 days away from work

Fatality Data

According to the BLS, 500 U.S. workers were workplace homicide victims in 2016.
Of those victims who died from workplace violence:

- 82 percent were male

- 48 percent were white

- 69 percent were aged 25–54

- 31 percent were working in a retail establishment, 23 percent were performing protective service activities

Section 32.3

What to Do When a Colleague Discloses Abuse

Sometimes people who are experiencing domestic abuse need to tell an outsider about their situation. If they do not trust family members or friends to listen in an unbiased, nonjudgmental way, they may instead choose to confide in someone at work. Likewise, coworkers who see each other every day may be among the first to notice signs of domestic abuse, such as unexplained injuries, repeated absences, sudden declines in productivity, or unusual anxiety or isolation. Either way, a coworker may be the first to learn that a fellow employee is experiencing domestic violence.

If a colleague is being abused, they may not have told anyone about it before. They may have conflicting emotions about their abusive partner that they are struggling to understand. Although the situation may be affecting their work performance, they may not feel comfortable discussing their home life with supervisors or human resources representatives. Finding the courage to confide in a coworker is a big step, and how the coworker reacts can have a major impact on their ability to trust others and seek additional support. Thus, it is important to know how to respond in a sensitive manner if a colleague shows signs of domestic violence or discloses abuse.

Supportive Responses

If you suspect that a coworker may be experiencing domestic violence, it is better to express concern rather than make accusations. Gently mention specific things you may have noticed. If the person denies that there is a problem or offers a different explanation for their injuries, do not push for a confession. Instead, make it clear that no one deserves to be hurt, and offer to listen or provide the phone number of a confidential domestic-violence hotline if they ever want to talk about it.

If a colleague discloses abuse, one of the best ways to help is by listening. Although you may be tempted to ask questions and offer advice, you should not push them to take action or try to fix the problem for them. Instead, experts suggest providing a supportive, sympathetic ear and offering to help them find resources or access support services when they feel ready.

As you talk with your coworker, it is important to remember that people become trapped in abusive relationships through their partners' use of violence and coercion. The victim of abuse is in no way responsible for what is happening to them. Experts suggest responding in a nonjudgmental way, reassuring your colleague that it is not their fault and that you are there to support them. Some possible things to say include:

- I know it was difficult to tell me, but I'm glad you did.
- I believe you.
- I care about your health and safety.
- I'm sorry you are in this situation.
- No one has the right to hurt you.
- It's not your fault.
- No one deserves to be treated this way.
- What's happening to you is against the law.
- I understand that it may take some time to figure out what to do.
- There are people who can help you.
- I will keep this information confidential.
- I will support you no matter what you decide to do.

If your colleague is having problems at work due to ongoing abuse—such as absenteeism or a loss of productivity—they may need reassurance about their job security. They may also need to take some time off from work for doctor appointments, legal consultations, or counseling sessions. Confiding in a supportive colleague at work can help give them the time and resources they need to get out of an abusive situation.

References

1. "Domestic Abuse: How to Respond," Stanford Medicine, 2016.

2. "An Employee/Co-Worker Has Just Disclosed They Experienced Historic Abuse, What Should I Do?" Live Fear Free, n.d.

3. "If You Suspect Abuse," University of Michigan, 2009.

Section 32.4

Managerial Guide for Workplace Sexual Harassment Prevention

This section includes text excerpted from "Manager Workplace Sexual Harassment Prevention Toolkit," Office of Equity, Diversity, and Inclusion (EDI), National Institutes of Health (NIH), September 25, 2014. Reviewed October 2018.

What Is Sexual Harassment?

Unwelcome sexual advances, requests for sexual favors, and other verbal or physical conduct of a sexual nature constitute sexual harassment when:

- Submission to such conduct is made either explicitly or implicitly a term or condition of an individual's employment;

- Submission to or rejection of such conduct by an individual is used as the basis for employment decisions affecting the individual; or

- Such conduct has the purpose or effect of unreasonably interfering with an individual's work performance or creating an intimidating, hostile, or offensive working environment.

What Are Unwelcome Sexual Advances?

Unwelcome sexual advances constitute sexual harassment when submission to such conduct is made either explicitly or implicitly as a term or condition of an individual's employment.

What Law(s) Are Violated by Sexual Harassment?

Sexual harassment is a form of sex discrimination that violates Title VII of the Civil Rights Act of 1964. Title VII applies to employers with 15 or more employees, including state and local governments. It also applies to employment agencies and to labor organizations, as well as to the federal government.

What Course of Action Should a Manager Take If a Sexual Harassment Claim Is Brought to Him or Her?

As a manager you must initiate an immediate administrative inquiry process by contacting your employee-relations specialist, who will assist you in conducting an investigation intended to gather information to determine what action, if any, should be taken. This information is not intended for legal or criminal prosecution.

What Course of Action Should a Manager Take If a Sexual Harassment Claim Is Brought against Him or Her?

If a sexual harassment claim has been brought against you, your behavior will be under increased scrutiny. To avoid exacerbating the situation you should not engage in the behavior cited in the complaint. Reprisal for participation in the equal employment opportunity (EEO) process is prohibited. Therefore, any retaliation against the complainant is barred. It is strongly advised that any behavior that could be perceived as retaliatory be strictly avoided. It is imperative that you be supportive and cooperative of the resolution process and maintain a record of relevant communications and events.

What Course of Action Should a Manager Take If the Victim Elects to Not Pursue the Complaint?

The employing company is legally obligated to investigate any potential allegations of sexual harassment once it is notified of its existence. Once management is made aware of potentially unlawful behavior, it is duty-bound to investigate, regardless of the victim's wishes.

What Course of Action Should a Manager Take If She or He Witnesses Sexual Harassment?

Any manager who witnesses an act of potential sexual harassment is required to initiate an immediate administrative inquiry process. Contact your employee-relations specialist, who can assist you in conducting an investigation.

What Course of Action Should a Manager Take If She or He Learned of the Sexual Harassment via Informal Channels Such as Gossip or Rumors?

To prevent sexual harassment in the workplace, management must take a proactive, not reactive, stance to sexual harassment. Being proactive means adopting a zero-tolerance harassment policy. Managers should investigate all allegations of sexual harassment regardless of how she or he was made aware of the allegations.

Chapter 33

Preventing Workplace Violence

Workplace violence is a frustrating problem facing federal agencies today. While more and more information on the causes of violence and how to handle it is becoming known, there is often no reasonable rationale for this type of conduct and, despite everything we know or do, violent situations happen. No employer is immune from workplace violence and no employer can totally prevent it.

The cost to organizations is staggering. It is impossible to overstate the costs of workplace violence, because a single incident can have sweeping repercussions. There can be the immediate and profound loss of life or physical or psychological repercussions felt by the victim as well as the victim's family, friends, and coworkers; the loss of productivity and morale that sweeps through an organization after a violent incident; and the public-relations impact on an employer when news of violence reaches the media.

Workplace violence affects other areas as well. The adverse impact on organizations and individuals is wide-ranging and can include:

- Temporary/Permanent Absence of Skilled Employees

- Psychological Damage

- Property Damage, Theft, and Sabotage

This chapter includes text excerpted from "DOL Workplace Violence Program," U.S. Department of Labor (DOL), November 19, 2014. Reviewed October 2018.

- Productivity Impediments

- Diversion of Management Resource

- Increased Security Costs

- Increased Workers' Compensation Costs

- Increased Personnel Costs

- Temporary/Permanent Absence of Skilled Employees

There are many theories about the causes of workplace violence. However, caution should be taken when profiling or stereotyping individuals or organizations, since the presence of any of the factors related to these theories does not necessarily indicate a violent act will be carried out. Nevertheless, an incident can be the result of any one or a combination of these factors

Domestic Violence at Workplace

Except when those involved in domestic violence are coworkers, most incidents are perpetrated by individuals outside the agency. It is, therefore, unlikely that the levels of violence described above will be evident. There will, however, be early-warning signs that this type of violence is escalating outside the workplace. The victim may show symptoms such as increased fear, emotional episodes, and/or signs of physical injury. Victims, as well as perpetrators, also show signs of work performance deterioration. By intervening when the early warning signs occur, even though violence may not yet have been committed at work, a serious incident may be prevented.

Response Involving Domestic Violence

In the event the perpetrator shows up at work with the intent of harming the employee and any others who happen to be in the way or involved, follow the procedures described in Level Three in responding to the immediate crisis.

If it is known that an employee is being affected by domestic violence, whether or not the perpetrator has shown up at work, it is important to provide support and assistance. Not only is the person at risk for more and usually escalated violence, but it has an impact on the safety and productivity of the entire workforce. Below are some tips for supervisors when helping an employee affected by domestic violence.

- Talk with the employee about your concern of the possibility of the violence extending into the workplace and recommend that the employee contact the Employee Assistance Program or related resource and referral service, for assistance in dealing with the problem.

- **Recommend** that the employee call the National Domestic Violence Hotline for more information about domestic violence or to help find local resources.

- **Contact** the Employee Assistance Program for more information and/or assistance, if needed.

- **Recommend** that a workplace safety plan be developed in case an incident occurs at the workplace. Think about the safety of the individual as well as everyone around her or him. Don't be a hero if the perpetrator shows up at work. Follow the safety plan and go for help.

Chapter 34

Intervention by Faith Communities

It is well understood that spirituality plays a role in helping many people cope with life problems, including mental illness, death of a loved one, deadly illnesses, racial discrimination, and substance abuse. Spiritual expression can play a similar role for domestic-violence victims. Social support from religious institutions has been found to be a key factor for many women rebuilding their lives after suffering abuse. Other researchers have found that abuse, especially from a loved one, can cause spiritual distress. Spiritual healing can restore life's meaning and empower some victims. The role of spirituality may be of particular importance among African American women, as religion plays a larger role in their lives than among Caucasians. A comparison study of victims of intimate partner violence (IPV) in both African American and Caucasian populations, for example, found that the former found prayer to be more helpful than White victims. African American victims relied on prayer as a coping strategy, while White victims were more likely to rely on mental-health counseling.

A study of 151 physically abused women recruited from courts, local domestic-violence service agencies, and legal services looked at the

This chapter includes text excerpted from "Practical Implications of Current Intimate Partner Violence Research for Victim Advocates and Service Providers," National Criminal Justice Reference Service (NCJRS), December 2013. Reviewed October 2018.

abuse and its impact on victim depression, quality of life (QOL), social support, and self-esteem. It also measured spirituality, the degree to which victims of domestic violence viewed spirituality or God as a source of strength, and the victims' involvement in organized religion. The study found that almost all of the women noted that spirituality or God was a source of strength or comfort to them, even though 31 percent said they had not attended a religious service during the prior year. The research found that the more women attended religious institutions and viewed them as a source of strength or comfort, the less depressed they were and the higher their quality of life. Greater religious involvement significantly increased social support for women of color, but not Whites, although religious involvement did not predict self-esteem. Further, religious involvement appeared to promote greater well-being for victims, decrease depression, and increase quality of life.

The same research found that having children was also associated with increased well-being, greater self-esteem, and decreased depression.

According to the researchers, spirituality and religious involvement are significant aspects of many survivors' identities.

Another study of 65 African American women who experienced IPV in the past year similarly found that women who evinced higher levels of spirituality and greater religious involvement reported fewer depression symptoms. Religious involvement was also found to be negatively associated with posttraumatic stress symptoms. The women who reported higher levels of religious involvement reported higher levels of social support. On the other hand, a study of African American women utilizing a large urban public hospital in the American South found that both those who attempted suicide and those that did not both coped with their victimization through their religious beliefs.

A national survey found religious involvement was protective against IPV. Among 4,662 Catholics and Protestants surveyed, higher levels of church attendance were predictive of lower levels of reported cases of domestic violence. The exception to this pattern was fundamentalist Protestants, who held strong beliefs about the inerrancy of the Bible and patriarchal religious authority.

A Georgia study of IPV homicide victims found that, while only 17 percent had ever accessed IPV services, 30 percent had been actively involved in a religious community. Another survey found that 40 percent of battered women reported they had been involved in religious/spiritual counseling for their IPV.

Chapter 35

Intervention by Healthcare Providers

Many victims regularly come into contact with medical and health-care providers, although the providers may not identify their patients as victims of intimate partner violence (IPV). In fact, early help-seeking by battered women is often with healthcare providers. Healthcare providers are in the position to assess victim health needs (related to abuser violence and victim isolation, depression, or suicidality), to assist in safety planning, to provide preventive healthcare, follow-up consultations, and information-sharing about legal options and supportive community resources.

Research suggests, however, that women victims of IPV may not seek healthcare when they encounter providers who appear "uninterested, uncaring, or uncomfortable" about domestic violence. In addition, screening and risk assessment by healthcare providers makes little sense if they have no idea what to do once IPV is assessed.

Recognizing the importance of effective screening, risk assessment, continuing healthcare, and informed referrals to community agencies, researchers undertook a quasi-experimental study of emergency departments, primary-care facilities, and pediatric clinics in a

This chapter includes text excerpted from "Practical Implications of Current Intimate Partner Violence Research for Victim Advocates and Service Providers," National Criminal Justice Reference Service (NCJRS), December 2013. Reviewed October 2018.

Midwestern university city to determine if explicit changes in health-care practice (i.e., screening, improvements in confidential care, internal advocacy by nursing staff, enhanced capacity of doctors and nurses to discuss sensitive and complex issues related to violence against women, upgraded referral practice, and routine communication with victim-service staff) would improve healthcare delivery to battered women. The study anticipated improved health and safety outcomes for those domestic violence (DV) patients in the "intervention," group rather than those in the "as usual" group.

The design of the study "Healthcare Can Change From Within" (HCCW) was to generate change within the health sector. It was posited that institutionalizing a change model within the healthcare system could better produce change that would be effective, sustained, and modified through ongoing evaluation. The model created an internal network of professionals within each participating health sector who would advocate for essential reforms. The methods of change employed were: saturated training of all staff, adoption of parallel policies and procedures, development of relationships with community victim-services personnel, continuous evaluation of changes, and primary prevention.

Researchers reported that prior efforts at significant change of the healthcare system had generally been initiated by victim advocates and services providers. As a result, adoption of methods of change was uneven. Outcomes for providers and victims were unsatisfactory. Attrition was high. The health of victims appeared compromised over the lifespan, even after the abuse terminated, due to the lack of continuing access to healthcare, among other factors.

As to benefits for victims in the "interventions" as contrasted with the "as usual" group, the results were not as strong as expected. However, the "intervention" and the "as usual" battered women experienced significantly lower rates of violence during the study. The two groups engaged in similar, but modest, increased rates of help-seeking, safety planning, cultivation of relationships and connections within the community, improvement of health, or satisfaction with healthcare services. The researchers suggest that participation in research interviews may have created an unintentional positive intervention related to help-seeking and community connection for the "as usual" group.

Part Five

Emergency Management, Moving Out, and Moving On

Chapter 36

Why Do Victims Stay with Their Abusers?

Factors That Force the Victims to Stay with Abusers

Getting out of an abusive relationship is not always easy. Someone who has never experienced domestic violence (DV) or intimate partner violence (IPV) may wonder why the victims don't just leave. But it's important to understand that there are several untold factors that keep the victims tied to their abusers.

Emotional Factors

Often, the victims of DV or IPV care for and love their partners even though they are being abusive. The victims also fear that they may be alone for the rest of their lives if they leave the relationship. These emotional factors contribute to their remaining in the abusive relationship. In some cases, the victims have children with their abusive partners and feel bound to stay in the relationship in an effort to avoid causing emotional damage to their children.

Fear Factors

Some abusers threaten and terrorize their victims and children when they try to leave. Statistics show that the chances of an abuser harming, injuring, and murdering their victim increases when the victim tries to end the relationship. Victims are usually afraid of what will happen when they leave the relationship. They are also afraid of being judged, shamed, insulted, and hated by others.

Health Factors

Some victims of DV or IPV who are in poor health, for example elderly people, disabled people, or people who are injured by DV or illness, may be physically dependent on their partners even to complete their day-to-day living activities. This can make it especially hard for these victims to leave their abusers until or unless they find another helping hand.

Economic Factors

Lack of money; lack of access to basic needs such as food, shelter, and clothing; lack of jobs; and lack of occupational skills may make victims financially dependent on their abuser. When the abuser has control over their money, the victim also may lack the resources to leave. This situation is made worse when the victim has children whose well-being depends on financial support from the abuser. This kind of economic dependency may create survival fears in the victim's mind, which can heavily influence a decision to move out.

Psychological Factors

When people are constantly abused, shamed, and put down, their self-esteem is greatly affected. Over a period of time, these victims begin to believe that the abuse is their fault and may even justify the actions of the abuser. Eventually, they start living with the false notion that the abuse is normal.

Rural Scenario

Women in rural America face high rates of DV and IPV compared to their urban counterparts. The traditional gender roles and poverty common to many rural communities contribute to an increase in the abuse of women. Rural women also have less chance to become economically independent since the job opportunities for them are very limited. And, if they do find jobs, they often are disadvantaged by the huge male-female wage gap. They are also less likely to receive employer-based benefits such as health insurance, unemployment insurance, etc.

Women in rural America who are victims of DV or IPV also find it difficult to access human services. Lack of amenities, such as telecommunications and transportation, also may prevent them from seeking human services. These factors make it difficult for rural women to leave a violent partner.

References

1. "Leaving an Abusive Relationship," National Women's Health Information Center (NWHIC), Office on Women's Health (OWH), September 13, 2018.

2. "Why Don't They Just Leave?" National Domestic Violence Hotline, June 12, 2015.

3. "Why Do Victims Stay?" Pathways to Safety International, August 21, 2009.

4. Goldsmith, Toby D. "Why Do Abused Victims Stay?" Psych Central, February 1, 2001.

5. "Intimate Partner Violence in Rural America," Health Resources and Services Administration (HRSA), March 2015.

Chapter 37

Staying Safe with an Abuser

In an ideal world, anyone who experienced domestic violence would be able to get out of harm's way by leaving the abusive relationship. In reality, however, some people must remain in abusive relationships—whether due to fear for their safety, manipulation or coercion by their abusive partners; or concerns about housing, finances, or child custody. Until they are able to get out of the violent situation, victims of domestic abuse may benefit from the following strategies designed to help them and their children stay safe.

Safety at Home

- Watch for patterns of abuse in order to recognize signs that your partner may become violent. If the situation appears dangerous, try to leave before any violence occurs.

- Know where any weapons are kept. If possible, lock them away, hide them, or make them difficult to access. In addition to guns and knives, potential weapons may include other heavy or sharp objects, such as a hammer, baseball bat, or ice pick.

- Avoid wearing necklaces or scarves that could be used to choke you.

- Figure out the safest places in the home. Avoid the kitchen and garage, which are likely to contain objects that can be used as weapons, as well as rooms with hardwood or tile floors. Try

"Staying Safe with an Abuser," © 2016 Omnigraphics. Reviewed October 2018.

to get to a room with a lock on the door or a window to escape out of, and stay out of small, enclosed spaces where you can be cornered.

- Keep a phone somewhere that you can reach it quickly. Memorize the numbers for police emergency response (911), the National Domestic Violence Hotline (NDVH) 800-799-SAFE (800-799-7233), and the nearest battered women's shelter.

- If physical violence is imminent, make yourself as small as possible and protect vital areas. Go into a corner, curl up in a ball, and lock your fingers behind your head.

- Tell a trusted friend or neighbor about the abuse. Arrange a signal so they will know when you need help. Make a plan so they will understand what to do in these situations.

- Make copies of important documents—such as birth certificates, passports, bank statements, and medical records—that you would need if you had to leave home in an emergency. Put them in a bag along with money and spare car keys. Keep the bag in a safe place or give it to a friend or neighbor to hold for you.

Keeping Children Safe

- When physical abuse occurs, try to stay away from the part of the house where the children are. Tell them not to get involved or try to help you, as their efforts may result in them getting hurt as well.

- Designate a safe place in the house for the children to go during a violent incident.

- Practice various methods of getting out of the house safely. Create a code word to let the children know that they should leave the house and get help. Teach them to call 911 and give your address to emergency responders.

- Let the children know that violence is always wrong, even when it is done by someone they love, and that it is never their fault.

Leaving an abusive relationship or getting a civil protection order does not guarantee that survivors of domestic violence will remain safe. It is important to take the following precautions to limit the abusive partner's access to you at home, at work, and during court appearances.

Safety at Home and School

- Get an unlisted telephone number. Do not answer the phone unless you recognize the caller; otherwise, let it go to voicemail.

- Change the locks on all doors, put bars on windows, and install a home security system and motion-sensor outdoor lighting.

- Never open the door to someone you do not know.

- Ask your neighbors to call the police if they see the abuser in the neighborhood or at your home.

- Ask the school or daycare provider not to release the children to anyone without checking with you first. Provide them with copies of restraining orders or custody papers, as well as a photograph of the abusive partner.

Safety in the Workplace

- Vary your routines. Avoid leaving for work or doing your grocery shopping at the same time every day.

- Carpool to work with a colleague or have a friend accompany you to the bus stop.

- Give a photograph of your abusive partner to the receptionist or security personnel at work, and ask them to notify you or call the police if they see that person.

- Save any emails or voicemails if the abuser tries to contact you at work.

- When leaving work, have someone walk you to your car. Be wary in the parking lot, and check inside, around, and under the car for danger.

- If your abusive partner follows your car, drive to a police or fire station and honk the horn. Keep a sign in the car that says "CALL POLICE."

Safety in Court

- Ask a friend or relative to accompany you to any court hearings.

- Inquire whether the court has a private waiting area or a separate entrance for victims of domestic violence.

- Sit as far away from your abusive partner as possible and avoid interaction.

- If you fear for your safety in a public place, studies show that yelling "Fire!" is the most effective way to get a quick response.

References

1. "Staying Safe with an Abuser," WomensLaw.org, 2008.

2. "Keeping Safe in Abusive Relationships or While Trying to Leave," Hidden Hurt, 2015.

Chapter 38

Managing a Domestic Violence Emergency

More than one in three women and one in four men across the United States have experienced violence from an intimate partner. If you or someone you know has experienced domestic violence, you are not alone. The Family Violence Prevention and Services Program (FVPSA), is the primary federal funding stream for a national network of domestic violence shelters and programs.

Reaching out for help to stop domestic violence in your relationship, and navigating the complex resources in your community can be difficult. It can be hard to know where to go for the help you want and it may not be clear how these programs can support your efforts to live a life free of violence and abuse—but you are not alone! The resources listed below are great places to start your journey toward safety, hope, and healing. Many of these national organizations can guide you to more in-depth and knowledgeable resources in your community and surrounding areas.

National Hotlines

These hotlines offer support from well-trained, caring advocates 24/7/365 (including holidays). Advocates help victims and survivors of domestic violence and rape or sexual violence find support and

This chapter includes text excerpted from "Getting Help with Domestic Violence," Administration for Children and Families (ACF), U.S. Department of Health and Human Services (HHS), December 19, 2016.

assistance in their communities, even if you only need someone to talk to before making that first step.

- **National Domestic Violence Hotline (NDVH):** 800-799-7233 or TTY 800-787-3224—Secure online chat at www.thehotline. org/what-is-live-chat

- **National Teen Dating Abuse Helpline (NTDAH):** 866-331-9474 or TTY 866-331-8453—Secure online chat at www. loveisrespect.org/get-help/contact-us/chat-with-us or text "loveis" to 22522

- **National Sexual Assault Hotline (RAINN):** 800-656-4673 Choose #1 to talk to a counselor—Secure online private chat at ohl.rainn.org/online.

- **Stalking Resource Center:** Access online resources to learn things you can do if you or someone you know is being stalked.

By calling any of the national hotlines, a trained advocate will be able to connect you to a program in your community. As you make decisions about how to get away from the abuse and ensure your own safety, developing a safety plan becomes more and more important. Caring advocates on the hotline and in your local program can help you think through how to be safe in an emergency, during a domestic violence incident, while getting help from resources in the community, and when you're with your children—this is called a "safety plan."

Tribal Resources

To learn more about tribal domestic violence programs and resources available for Native/Indigenous communities, contact the National Indigenous Women's Resource Center (NIWRC) (www.niwrc.org). The U.S. Department of Justice's (DOJ) Office on Violence Against Women (OVW) funds tribal domestic violence services.

State Domestic Violence and Sexual Assault Coalitions

There is a domestic violence coalition for every state and United States territory. Each coalition represents the domestic violence and sexual violence service providers in their state or territory; they are connected to more than 2,000 local domestic violence programs and shelters. You can find the domestic violence coalition working with programs in your state at the National Network to End Domestic Violence's (NNEDV) website. Select your state from the list and then look for the link to their members or programs for a listing of the resources in your city or county.

Local/Community-Based Domestic Violence and Sexual Assault Programs

In addition to offering safe, emergency shelter, there are many ways that local domestic violence programs and advocates can partner with you to live a life free of violence and abuse. Services may vary from place to place, but most include:

- Safety planning assistance

- Legal assistance and referrals for obtaining protection orders (which may include evicting an abusive partner from a shared home, obtaining emergency child custody, and many such remedies to increase your safety)

- Counseling and support groups for survivors and their children

- Help applying for public assistance and housing subsidies

- Transitional housing

- Referrals to counseling, mental health, and addiction services

National Resource Centers and Culturally Specific Institutes

All of the service providers listed above—the hotlines, shelters, state coalitions, and tribal programs—work together and receive training, assistance, guidance, and support from several national resource center and culturally specific institutes. These organizations make up the Domestic Violence Resource Network (DVRN), which is funded by the U.S. Department of Health and Human Services (HHS) to inform and strengthen domestic violence intervention and prevention efforts at the individual, community, and societal levels.

There are two national resource centers working collaboratively to promote practices and strategies to improve the nation's response to domestic violence:

1. The National Resource Center on Domestic Violence (NRCDV)

2. The National Indigenous Women's Resource Center (NIWRC)

There is a national network of specialized resource centers that work to address domestic violence responses across these specific systems:

1. Criminal and Civil Justice Systems

2. Child Protection System and Child Custody

3. Mental Health Systems

There is also a network of culturally specific resource centers that works to address the impact of domestic violence within and culturally relevant responses for the following ethnic and racially specific communities:

1. African American Communities

2. Asian and Pacific Islander Communities

3 Hispanic and Latinx Communities

Chapter 39

Documenting Domestic Violence

Physicians and other healthcare providers know that often the first thing victims of domestic violence need is medical attention. They also know they may have a legal obligation to inform the police when they suspect the patient they are treating has been abused. What they may not know is that they can help the patient win her case in court against the abuser by carefully documenting her injuries.

In the past decade, a great deal has been done to improve the way the healthcare community responds to domestic violence. One way that effort has paid off is in medical documentation of abuse. Many healthcare protocols and training programs now note the importance of such documentation. But only if medical documentation is accurate and comprehensive can it serve as objective, third-party evidence useful in legal proceedings.

For a number of reasons, documentation is not as strong as it could be in providing evidence, so medical records are not used in legal proceedings to the extent they could be. In addition to being difficult to obtain, the records are often incomplete or inaccurate and the handwriting may be illegible. These flaws can make medical records more harmful than helpful.

Healthcare providers have received little information about how medical records can help victims of domestic violence take legal action

This chapter includes text excerpted from "Documenting Domestic Violence: How Health Care Providers Can Help Victims," U.S. Department of Justice (DOJ), September 2001. Reviewed October 2018.

against their abusers. They often are not aware that admissibility is affected by subtle differences in the way they record the injuries. By making some fairly simple changes in documentation, physicians and other healthcare professionals can dramatically increase the usefulness of the information they record and thereby help their patients obtain the legal remedies they seek.

Why Thorough Documentation Is Essential

The victim's attorney, or the victim acting on her own behalf as a pro se litigant, can submit medical documentation as evidence for obtaining a range of protective relief (such as a restraining order).

Victims can also use medical documentation in less formal legal contexts to support their assertions of abuse. Persuasive, factual information may qualify them for special status or exemptions in obtaining public housing, welfare, health and life insurance, victim compensation, and immigration relief related to domestic violence and in resolving landlord–tenant disputes.

For formal legal proceedings, the documentation needs to be strong enough to be admissible in a court of law. Typically, the only third-party evidence available to victims of domestic violence is police reports, but these can vary in quality and completeness. Medical documentation can corroborate police data. It constitutes unbiased, factual information recorded shortly after the abuse occurs, when recall is easier.

Medical records can contain a variety of information useful in legal proceedings. Photographs taken in the course of the examination record images of injuries that might fade by the time legal proceedings begin, and they capture the moment in a way that no verbal description can convey. Body maps can document the extent and location of injuries. The records may also hold information about the emotional impact of the abuse. However, the way the information is recorded can affect its admissibility. For instance, a statement about the injury in which the patient is clearly identified as the source of information is more likely to be accepted as evidence in legal proceedings. And, as noted earlier, poor handwriting on written records can affect their admissibility.

Overcoming Barriers to Good Documentation

There are several reasons medical recordkeeping is not generally adequate. Healthcare providers are concerned about confidentiality and liability. They are concerned about recording information that might inadvertently harm the victim. Many are confused about whether, how, and why to record information about domestic violence, so in an effort to be "neutral," some use language that may subvert the patient's legal case and even support the abuser's case. Some healthcare providers are afraid to testify in court. They may see the risks to the patient and themselves as possibly outweighing the benefits of documenting abuse. Even healthcare providers who are reluctant to testify can still submit medical evidence. Although the hearsay rule prohibits out-of-court statements, an exception permits testimony about diagnosis and treatment. In addition, some states also allow the diagnosis and treatment elements of a certified medical record to be entered into the evidentiary record without the testimony of a healthcare provider. Thus, in some instances, physicians and other healthcare providers can be spared the burden of appearing in court.

The patient's "excited utterances" or "spontaneous exclamations" about the incident are another exception to the prohibition of hearsay. These are statements made by someone during or soon after an event, while in an agitated state of mind. They have exceptional credibility because of their proximity in time to the event and because they are not likely to be premeditated.

Excited utterances are valuable because they allow the prosecution to proceed even if the victim is unwilling to testify. These statements need to be carefully documented. A patient's report may be admissible if the record demonstrates that the patient made the statement while responding to the event stimulating the utterance (the act or acts of abuse).

Noting the time between the event and the time the statements were made or describing the patient's demeanor as she made the statement can help show she was responding to the stimulating event. Such a showing is necessary to establish that a statement is an excited utterance or spontaneous exclamation, and thus an exception to the hearsay rule.

What the Records Lack

It appears that, at present, many medical records are not sufficiently well-documented to provide adequate legal evidence of domestic violence. A study of 184 visits for medical care in which an injury or other evidence of abuse was noted revealed major shortcomings in the records:

- For the 93 instances of an injury, the records contained only 1 photograph. There was no mention in any records of photographs filed elsewhere.

- A body map documenting the injury was included in only 3 of the 93 instances. Drawings of the injuries appeared in 8 of the 93 instances.

- Doctors' and nurses' handwriting was illegible in key portions of the records in one-third of the patients' visits in which abuse or injury was noted.

- All three criteria for considering a patient's words an excited utterance were met in only 28 of the more than 800 statements evaluated (3.4%). Most frequently missing was a description of the patient's demeanor, and often the patient was not clearly identified as the source of the information.

On the plus side, although photographs and body maps documenting injuries were rare, injuries were otherwise described in detail. And in fewer than one percent of the visits were negative comments made about the patient's appearance, manner, or motive for stating that abuse had occurred.

What Healthcare Providers Can Do

Medical records could be much more useful to victims of domestic violence in legal proceedings if some minor changes were made in documentation. Clinicians can do the following:

- Take photographs of injuries known or suspected to have resulted from domestic violence.

- Write legibly. Computers can also help overcome the common problem of illegible handwriting.

- Set off the patient's own words in quotation marks or use such phrases as "patient states" or "patient reports" to indicate that the information recorded reflects the patient's words. To write "patient was kicked in abdomen" obscures the identity of the speaker.

- Avoid such phrases as "patient claims" or "patient alleges," which imply doubt about the patient's reliability. If the clinician's observations conflict with the patient's statements, the clinician should record the reason for the difference.

- Use medical terms and avoid legal terms such as "alleged perpetrator," "assailant," and "assault."

- Describe the person who hurt the patient by using quotation marks to set off the statement. The clinician would write, for example: The patient stated, "My boyfriend kicked and punched me."

- Avoid summarizing a patient's report of abuse in conclusive terms. If such language as "patient is a battered woman," "assault and battery," or "rape" lacks sufficient accompanying factual information, it is inadmissible.

- Do not place the term "domestic violence" or abbreviations such as "DV" in the diagnosis section of the medical record. Such terms do not convey factual information and are not medical terminology. Whether domestic violence has occurred is determined by the court.

- Describe the patient's demeanor, indicating, for example, whether she is crying or shaking or seems angry, agitated, upset, calm, or happy.

- Even if the patient's demeanor belies the evidence of abuse, the clinician's observations of that demeanor should be recorded. Record the time of day the patient is examined and, if possible, indicate how much time has elapsed since the abuse occurred.

Model Protocol under Development

Increasing the number of medical charts that contain information useful in legal settings is the goal of a follow-up study now underway. Professor V. Pualani Enos is developing a protocol that seeks to improve the way domestic violence is documented.

Developing training for practitioners is a major part of this NIJ-sponsored study. Design of the training will draw on input from practitioners, researchers, and survivors of domestic violence. An evaluation will document the new protocol and compare medical records before and after the protocol is adopted.

Chapter 40

Leaving an Abusive Relationship

No one should feel unsafe. If you are in an unsafe, violent relationship, you might be thinking of leaving. You do not have to leave immediately or do it all at once. But a safety plan can help you know what to do when you are ready to leave. Having a plan in place can help you get out safely later if you do decide to leave.

What Are Some Things to Consider as You Decide Whether to Leave?

Leaving an abusive relationship can seem overwhelming. Women often leave several times before finally deciding to end the relationship. There are many complicated reasons why it is difficult to leave an abusive partner.

You may have doubts or fears or just feel overwhelmed at the thought of leaving. That's normal. But consider the following as you make your decision:

- **Domestic violence often starts as emotional abuse and becomes physical later.** It's important to ask for help as soon as possible.

- **Your partner may try to make you think the violence is your fault.** It's not. You cannot make someone hurt or mistreat

This chapter includes text excerpted from "Leaving an Abusive Relationship," Office on Women's Health (OWH), U.S. Department of Health and Human Services (HHS), September 13, 2018.

you. Your partner is responsible for his or her own behavior. Violence and abuse are never the victim's fault.

- **Abuse is not normal or okay.** You may think that abuse is a sign that your partner loves you. It's not. Your partner may love you, but abuse is not a sign of that love. You may think that romantic love is passionate and that physical abuse is a sign of passion. It's not. A healthy relationship is one in which you feel safe and which has no physical, sexual, emotional, or verbal abuse.

- **Abuse can happen to anyone.** Some women and men believe that abuse is not something that could happen to them. Abuse can happen to anyone, regardless of whether you have a college education, which neighborhood you live in, your age, your gender, your sexual orientation, or whether you're married, dating, or single.

- **Your partner may be very good to you at times.** Most abusers have a pattern of abuse followed by making it up to you or making you feel special and loved. It's most likely that the abuse will happen again. Abuse usually gets worse over time, not better.

- **You cannot help or fix an abusive partner.** It's not your responsibility to convince a violent or abusive partner to get help. Your responsibility is to your own safety and the safety of any children in the household. Some abusive partners say they will get help as a way to "make it up to you" after violence. But getting help does not always mean the violence will stop.

- **Intimate partner violence is linked to serious physical and emotional problems.** The longer it continues, the more damage it can cause.

Also, if you have children, consider their safety. Consider whether you are willing to allow your partner to visit them if you decide to leave the relationship. Many abusers get even more violent after their victims leave. That's why a safety plan, agreed on with others in your life, can help keep you safe after you leave.

Who Can I Talk to about Leaving an Abusive Relationship?

Many people can help you think about your options to leave an abusive relationship safely. It might be unsafe if an abusive partner finds out you're thinking about leaving. Try to talk only to people who will not tell the abuser about your plans:

- **Your doctor or nurse.** Most people visit the doctor at least once a year for a checkup, so try to visit the doctor or nurse without your partner. If your partner insists on going with you, try to write a note to the office staff saying that you want to see the doctor or nurse alone. Or, tell your partner that you need privacy to speak about a woman's health issue that you're too embarrassed to talk about. Or, tell your partner, where others can hear you, that the doctor's policy is patients only in the exam room.

- **A teacher, counselor, or principal at your child's school.** An adult at your child's school can help connect you to shelters and other safe places in your community. Teachers and others at your child's school want to help the families of the children they teach.

- **Human resources**. If you work outside the home, the human resources (HR) department at your workplace may be able to connect you to an Employee Assistance Program (EAP) or other resources in your community.

- **Family or friends.** Family or friends who knew you before you met an abusive partner might be able to help you. If more than one family member or friend can help you, it might be good for a few people to work together to help.

- **A free 1-800 telephone hotline.** You can talk to trained advocates at the National Domestic Violence Hotline (www. thehotline.org), for free 24 hours a day, 7 days a week without giving your name or address. The counselors can help you talk through the steps of leaving an abusive relationship. You can call a hotline as many times as you need to.

How Can You Plan to Leave and Keep Yourself Safe?

Even if you don't leave right away, creating a safety plan can help you know what to do if your partner abuses you again. It can help you be more independent when you leave.

Your safety plan will help you be prepared:

- **Identify a safe friend or friends and safe places to go.** Create a code word to use with friends, family, or neighbors to let them know you are in danger without the abuser finding out. If possible, agree on a secret location where they can pick you up.

- **Keep an alternate cell phone nearby.** Try not to call for help on your home phone or on a shared cell phone. Your partner might be able to trace the numbers. If you don't have a cell phone, you can get a prepaid cell phone. Some domestic violence shelters offer free cell phones.

- **Memorize the phone numbers of friends, family, or shelters.** If your partner takes your phone, you will still be able to contact loved ones or shelters for a safe place to stay.

- **Make a list of things to take if you have to leave quickly.** Important identity documents and money are probably the top priority. See the Safety Packing List for a detailed list of items to pack. Get these items together, and keep them in a safe place where your partner will not find them. If you are in immediate danger, leave without them.

- **If you can, hide an extra set of car keys** so you can leave if your partner takes away your usual keys.

- **Ask your doctor** how to get extra medicine or glasses, hearing aids, or other medically necessary items for you or your children.

- **Contact your local family court** (or domestic violence court, if your state has one) for information about getting a restraining order. If you need legal help but don't have much money, your local domestic violence agency may be able to help you find a lawyer who will work for free or on a sliding scale based on what you can pay.

- **Protect your online security** as you collect information and prepare. Use a computer at a public library to download information, or use a friend's computer or cellphone. Your partner might be able to track your planning otherwise.

- **Try to take with you any evidence of abuse or violence if you leave your partner.** This might include threatening notes from your partner. It might be copies of police and medical reports. It might include pictures of your injuries or damage to your property.

- **Keep copies** of all paper and electronic documents on an external thumb drive.

Advocates at the National Domestic Violence Hotline (www.thehotline.org), 800-799-SAFE (800-799-7233), can help you develop your safety plan. The National Center on Domestic and Sexual Violence (NCDSV) provides a form for developing your own safety plan. You can also find more tips on developing your safety plan. Every person deserves to be safe.

What Do You Need to Include in Your Safety Packing List?

When you leave an abuser, the most important thing is your life and safety as well as your children's. If you are able to plan ahead, it will help you to have important information with you, in addition to money, clothing, medicine, and other basic items.

Even if you are not sure you want to or are ready to leave, go ahead and make copies of as many of the following documents as you can, or secure them in a safe place outside of the home:

- Birth certificates, Social Security cards, and passports or immigration papers for you and your children

- Health insurance cards for you and your children

- Financial records, including recent bank statements and stocks or mutual fund records

- Housing documents, such as rental agreements, mortgage statements, or the title or deed

- Your most recent credit report

- The title or lease paperwork for your car

- Statements for any retirement plans

- The past two years' tax returns

- A written copy of phone numbers or important addresses in case you cannot get to your cellphone or address book

Many of these records are available online, so try to keep access to these accounts if you do not have paper copies.

You may also want to take photos of any valuable assets in the home (anything you think may be worth some money). Also, if you have any family heirlooms (such as jewelry), take them with you or put them in a safe place before you leave. You can get a safe deposit box at the bank to store copies of the paperwork listed, as well as small valuable items. If you have a joint checking account, consider opening your own checking account and storing money there. Any adult has the right to open their own bank account, even if they are married or dependent on another person.

What If I'm Too Scared to Leave?

Leaving a relationship is not easy. You may still care about your partner or have hope that things will get better. It may also be difficult or frightening to leave because:

- Your partner may be a coparent to your children

- Your partner may have isolated you from your friends and family so you feel you have no place to go

- Your partner may control the money so you feel you have no resources to leave

- Your partner may have threatened you or your children

- You don't want to disrupt your children's lives

- You may have an elderly relative or disabled child needing care

- Your health may be poor because you were injured in the domestic violence or because of illness

- You may still have feelings for your partner or worry that you'll be alone for the rest of your life

You can get help dealing with all of these issues. Talk to a friend, a loved one, or a counselor at the National Domestic Violence Hotline (www.thehotline.org), 800-799-SAFE (800-799-7233). People want to help you.

Even if it seems like the only way you can be safe is to leave, you may still be feeling confused and frightened about leaving. That is normal. You don't have to decide to leave immediately. But if you are in an abusive relationship, you need to get help.

How Can You Leave If You Don't Have Any Money?

In abusive or controlling relationships, it is common for the abusive partner to maintain control of all of the money. Often, an abusive partner will not allow a woman to work outside of the home or talk to family and friends.

Even if you do not have any money, you can find the closest women's shelter by calling the 24-hour National Domestic Violence Hotline (www.thehotline.org) at 800-799-SAFE (800-799-7233) for free. You do not have to pay money to stay at a domestic violence shelter.

Many domestic violence shelters can help you pay for a ride to the shelter. If you are already in a temporary but safe place, call the shelter to ask about help with transportation.

Where Can You Go If You Decide to Leave?

Even if you don't have a friend or family member to go to, you still have a safe option. A domestic violence shelter, also sometimes called a women's shelter, is a safe place for a woman who has a violent partner. Its location is usually not public, making it harder for an abusive partner to find. These shelters have rooms for women and children.

Find a women's shelter near you (www.domesticshelters.org). If your safety and well-being depend on leaving your violent partner, help is available. Go online or call the National Domestic Violence Hotline (NDVH), 800-799-SAFE (800-799-7233); or the National Sexual Assault Hotline, 800-656-HOPE (800-656-4673), 24 hours a day, 7 days a week.

What Happens after You Arrive at a Domestic Violence or Women's Shelter?

Domestic violence shelters provide basic items for women who have to leave in a hurry and arrive with nothing. They may also provide food and child care. These services are usually free.

Domestic violence shelters often provide:

- Individual and family counseling and support groups

- Help enrolling children in school

- Job training and help finding work

- Legal help

- Help getting financial aid

- Help finding permanent housing

Housing in a domestic violence shelter is usually short term and limited. The shelter can help you with the next step in housing.

What Happens after Your Time in a Shelter Is Up?

The next step can be transitional housing. This type of housing is usually independent, separate apartments for each family. It allows a family to find safety and time to recover from domestic violence. The shelter can help you find transitional housing.

Services offered by these facilities may include:

- Counseling
- Support groups
- Job training
- Legal help
- Child care
- Help finding permanent and affordable housing

Chapter 41

Planning for Safety: Personal Safety and Safety of Children and Pets

People who experience domestic violence may be able to increase their safety through advance planning. Experts suggest creating an emergency escape plan for personal safety, along with safety plans to protect children and pets. Safety plans may include a variety of actions designed to help victims of domestic violence stay safe during a crisis, as well as preparations to help them leave an abusive situation.

Emergency Escape Plan

If you need to get away from an abuser quickly, it may be helpful to make the following preparations in advance:

- Plan and practice your escape, including what doors or windows you will use, where you will go, and how you will get there.

- Make copies of important documents, such as your birth certificate, passport, driver's license, car registration, mortgage or rental agreement, insurance policies, bank account numbers, medical records, custody agreements, restraining orders, and divorce papers. Put them in a safe place, such as a friend's house, your lawyer's office, or a safe deposit box.

"Planning for Safety: Personal Safety and Safety of Children and Pets," © 2016 Omnigraphics. Reviewed October 2018.

- Pack an emergency suitcase with extra clothing, spare keys, money, and medications. Keep it somewhere you can get to quickly.

- Open a savings account in your own name at a different bank than the one you usually use. Make sure statements are sent to a friend's address, your workplace, or a post office box rather than to your home.

- Keep a record of physical abuse, including dates, circumstances, witnesses, and photographs of injuries. If you get medical attention, ask the doctor or hospital to document your visit.

- Tell a trusted friend or neighbor about the abuse. Arrange a signal or code word so they will know when you need them to call the police.

- To facilitate a quick getaway, make a habit of backing the car into the driveway. Always keep the car keys handy and the gas tank full.

- Consider asking a friend or family member to accompany you when you leave, or request a police escort.

- Do not tell your partner where you are going. Clear your phone of recently dialed numbers. Have a backup plan in place in case your partner learns of your destination.

- File for a restraining order to prevent your partner from contacting you. Consult with an attorney about other legal means of protection.

Safety Plan for Children

Domestic violence can be very traumatic for children who experience or witness it in their homes. Developing a safety plan can help limit the damage to their physical and emotional health. It is important to emphasize to children that violence is always wrong, even when it is done by someone they love, and that it is never their fault. The following strategies may also help protect children from the effects of domestic violence:

- Tell them not to get involved or try to help you when physical abuse occurs, as their efforts may result in them getting hurt as well. Instead, they should leave the room and implement the safety plan.

- Identify a safe place in the home for the children to go. An ideal place would be a locked room with a telephone in it.

- Tell the children to avoid hiding in closets or other small spaces where they could become trapped, and to stay out of the kitchen, garage, and other rooms that contain objects that could be used as weapons.

- Practice various methods of getting out of the house safely. Create a code word to let the children know that they should leave the house and get help.

- Designate a safe place for the children to go in an emergency, such as the home of a friend, relative, or neighbor.

- Teach children to call 911 and give your address to emergency responders. Rehearse exactly what they should say on the phone, such as "Someone is hurting my mom."

Safety Plan for Pets

Domestic violence can also endanger pets in the household. Pets may be abused or neglected, or the abusive partner may use threats to the pets' well-being as a way to control or manipulate members of the family. Creating a safety plan for pets can help protect them from the effects of domestic violence. Some possible steps to take include:

- Know the location and phone number of the nearest twenty-four-hour veterinary clinic.

- Establish ownership of pets by putting adoption or purchase papers, licenses, and veterinary records in your name.

- Pack a bag with emergency pet supplies, such as food, medicine, toys, leash, license, and copies of ownership papers and health records. Keep it somewhere safe and accessible, such as a friend's house.

- Identify a safe emergency shelter for your pets where your abusive partner will not be able to find them.

- After you have left an abusive situation, be careful to keep pets indoors whenever possible, avoid leaving them outdoors alone, pick a safe time and place to exercise them, and switch to a new veterinarian.

References

1. "Develop a Safety Plan," Center for Relationship Abuse Awareness, 2015.

2. "Safety for My Children," The Healing Journey, 2006.

3. "Safety Planning for Pets of Domestic Violence Victims," Animal Welfare Institute (AWI), 2016.

Chapter 42

Internet Safety for Victims of Domestic Violence

Chapter Contents

Section 42.1

Technology Tips for Domestic Violence and Stalking Victims

This section contains text excerpted from the following sources:
Text in this chapter begins with excerpts from "Technology Tips for
Domestic Violence and Stalking Victims," Federal Trade Commission
(FTC), February 5, 2015. Reviewed October 2018; Text under the
heading "Choosing and Protecting Passwords" is excerpted from
"Choosing and Protecting Passwords," U.S. Department of
Homeland Security (DHS), September 28, 2018.

We love technology. So it's disturbing when it's used to threaten or harass people—especially domestic violence and stalking victims.

With computers and mobile phones, abusers have more tools for stalking. They can install spyware to hack into your email, use Bluetooth or GPS to track your every move, even secretly turn on your device's camera or microphone to watch and listen to you.

Online safety is important for everyone but for domestic violence victims, these tips may be particularly useful:

- Use strong passwords and change them frequently. Make sure you have passwords on your phone, computer, and all online accounts. Keep your passwords private.

- If you think someone may be monitoring you, then try to use a safer computer—one that the abuser does not have access to. It's especially important to use a safer computer if you are researching an escape plan, new jobs, or a place to live.

- Change usernames and passwords of your online accounts on the safer computer. Then, don't log into those accounts on any computer that you think is monitored.

Abusers may not stop at your computer. If you're using a mobile phone, here are a few more things to consider:

- Know where your phone is at all times. Malware, spyware, and tracking apps can be installed in just a few minutes.

- Check your phone's settings. Bluetooth and GPS can be used to track you. A victim advocate can help strategize a specific tech safety plan for your situation.

- If you think your phone is being monitored, get a new one. The safest thing is to get a new phone with an account that the abuser does not have access to. Remember to put a password on your new phone, then disable Bluetooth and GPS.

Choosing and Protecting Passwords
Why You Need Strong Passwords

You probably use a number of personal identification numbers (PINs), passwords, and passphrases every day: from getting money from the ATM or using your debit card in a store to logging into your email or into an online retailer. Keeping track of all of the number, letter, and word combinations may be frustrating at times, but you've seen enough news coverage to know that hackers represent a real threat to your information. Often, an attack is not specifically about your account, but about using the access to your information to launch a larger attack.

One of the best ways to protect information or physical property is to ensure that only authorized people have access to it. Verifying that those requesting access are the people they claim to be is the next step. This authentication process is more important and more difficult in the cyber world. Passwords are the most common means of authentication, but only work if they are complex and confidential. Many systems and services have been successfully breached because of insecure and inadequate passwords. Once a system is compromised, it's open to exploitation by other unwanted sources.

How to Choose Good Passwords
Avoid Common Mistakes

Most people use passwords that are based on personal information and are easy to remember. However, that also makes it easier for an attacker to crack them. Consider a four-digit PIN. Is yours a combination of the month, day, or year of your birthday? Does it contain your address or phone number? Think about how easy it is to find someone's birthday or similar information. What about your email password—is it a word that can be found in the dictionary? If so, it may be susceptible to dictionary attacks, which attempt to guess passwords based on common words or phrases.

Although intentionally misspelling a word ("daytt" instead of "date") may offer some protection against dictionary attacks, an even better method is to rely on a series of words and use memory techniques, or mnemonics, to help you remember how to decode it. For example, instead of the password "hoops," use "IlTpbb" for "[I] [l]ike [T]o [p]lay [b]asket[b]all." Using both lowercase and capital letters adds another layer of obscurity. Changing the same example used above to "Il!2pBb." creates a password very different from any dictionary word.

Length and Complexity

The National Institute of Standards and Technology (NIST) has developed specific guidelines for strong passwords. According to NIST guidance, you should consider using the longest password or passphrase permissible (8–64 characters) when you can. For example, "Pattern2baseball#4mYmiemale!" would be a strong password because it has 28 characters. It also includes the upper- and lowercase letters, numbers, and special characters. You may need to try different variations of a passphrase—since some applications limit the length of passwords, and some do not accept spaces or certain special characters. Avoid common phrases, famous quotations, and song lyrics.

Dos and Don'ts

Once you've come up with a strong, memorable password, it's tempting to reuse it—don't! Reusing a password, even a strong one, endangers your accounts just as much as using a weak password. If attackers guess your password, they would have access to all of your accounts. Use the following techniques to develop unique passwords for each of your accounts:

- Do use different passwords on different systems and accounts.

- Don't use passwords that are based on personal information that can be easily accessed or guessed.

- Do use the longest password or passphrase permissible by each password system.

- Don't use words that can be found in any dictionary of any language.

- Do develop mnemonics to remember complex passwords.

- Do consider using a password manager program to keep track of your passwords.

How to Protect Your Passwords

Now that you've chosen a password that's easy for you to remember, but difficult for others to guess, you have to make sure not to leave it someplace for people to find. Writing it down and leaving it in your desk, next to your computer—or, worse, taped to your computer—is just making it easy for someone who has physical access to your office. Don't tell anyone your passwords, and watch for attackers trying to trick you through phone calls or email messages requesting that you reveal your passwords.

Programs called "password managers" offer the option to create randomly generated passwords for all of your accounts. You then access those strong passwords with a master password. If you use a password manager, remember to use a strong master password.

Password problems can stem from your web browsers' ability to save passwords and your online sessions in memory. Depending on your web browsers' settings, anyone with access to your computer may be able to discover all of your passwords and gain access to your information. Always remember to log out when you are using a public computer (at the library, an Internet cafe, or even a shared computer at your office). Avoid using public computers and public Wi-Fi to access sensitive accounts such as banking and email.

There's no guarantee that these techniques will prevent an attacker from learning your password, but they will make it more difficult.

Don't forget security basics:

- Keep your operating system, browser, and other software up-to-date.

- Use and maintain anti-virus software and a firewall.

- Regularly scan your computer for spyware. (Some anti-virus programs incorporate spyware detection.)

- Use caution with email attachments and untrusted links.

- Watch for suspicious activity on your accounts.

Section 42.2

Keeping Children Safe Online

This section includes text excerpted from "Keeping
Children Safe Online," U.S. Department of Homeland
Security (DHS), May 7, 2018.

What Unique Risks Are Associated with Children?

When a child is using your computer, normal safeguards and security
practices may not be sufficient. Children present additional challenges
because of their natural characteristics: innocence, curiosity, desire
for independence, and fear of punishment. You need to consider these
characteristics when determining how to protect your data and the child.

You may think that because the child is only playing a game, or
researching a term paper, or typing a homework assignment, she
or he can't cause any harm. But what if she unintentionally visits a
malicious web page that infects your computer with a virus? This is
just a possible scenario. Mistakes happen, but children may not realize
what they have done or may not tell you what happened because they
are afraid of getting punished.

Online predators present another significant threat, particularly
to children. Because the nature of the Internet is so anonymous, it is
easy for people to misrepresent themselves and manipulate or trick
other users. Adults often fall victim to these ploys, and children, who
are usually much more open and trusting, are even easier targets.
Another growing problem is cyberbullying. These threats are even
greater if a child has access to email or instant messaging programs,
visits chat rooms, and/or uses social networking sites.

What Can You Do?

- **Be involved.** Consider activities you can work on together,
  whether it be playing a game, researching a topic you had been
  talking about (e.g., family vacation spots, a particular hobby, a
  historical figure), or putting together a family newsletter. This
  will allow you to supervise your child's online activities while
  teaching good computer habits.

- **Keep your computer in an open area.** If your computer
  is in a high-traffic area, you will be able to easily monitor the
  computer activity. Not only does this accessibility deter children

from doing something they know they are not allowed to do, it also gives you the opportunity to intervene if you notice a behavior that could have negative consequences.

- **Set rules and warn about dangers.** Make sure your children knows the boundaries of what activities are allowed on the computer. These boundaries should be appropriate for a child's age, knowledge, and maturity, but they may include rules about how long your child is allowed to be on the computer, what sites, what software programs, and what tasks or activities are allowed.

- You should also talk to children about the dangers of the Internet so that they recognize suspicious behavior or activity. Discuss the risks of sharing certain types of information (e.g., that they're home alone) and the benefits to only communicating and sharing information with people they know. The goal isn't to scare them; it's to make them more aware. Make sure to include the topic of cyberbullying in these discussions.

- **Monitor computer activity.** Be aware of what your children are doing on the computer, including which websites they are visiting. If they are is using email, instant messaging, or chat rooms, try to get a sense of who they are corresponding with and whether they actually know them.

- **Keep lines of communication open.** Let your children know that they can approach you with any questions or concerns about behaviors or problems they may have encountered on the computer.

- **Consider partitioning your computer into separate accounts.** Most operating systems give you the option of creating a different user account for each user. If you're worried that your children may accidentally access, modify, and/or delete your files, you can give them a separate account and decrease the amount of access and number of privileges.

- If you don't have separate accounts, you need to be especially careful about your security settings. In addition to limiting functionality within your browser, avoid letting your browser remember passwords and other personal information. Also, it is always important to keep your virus definitions up to date.

- **Consider implementing parental controls.** You may be able to set some parental controls within your browser. For example,

Internet Explorer allows you to restrict or allow certain websites to be viewed on your computer, and you can protect these settings with a password.

• There are other resources you can use to control and/or monitor your children's online activity. Some Internet service providers (ISPs) offer services designed to protect children online. Contact your ISP to see if any of these services are available. There are also special software programs you can install on your computer. Different programs offer different features and capabilities, so you can find one that best suits your needs.

Section 42.3

Staying Safe on Social Networking Sites

This section includes text excerpted from "Staying Safe on Social Networking Sites," U.S. Department of Homeland Security (DHS), June 5, 2015. Reviewed October 2018.

What Are Social Networking Sites?

Social networking sites, sometimes referred to as "friend-of-a-friend" sites, build upon the concept of traditional social networks where you are connected to new people through people you already know. The purpose of some networking sites may be purely social, allowing users to establish friendships or romantic relationships, while others may focus on establishing business connections.

Although the features of social networking sites differ, they all allow you to provide information about yourself and offer some type of communication mechanism (forums, chat rooms, email, instant messenger) that enables you to connect with other users. On some sites, you can browse for people based on certain criteria, while other sites require that you be "introduced" to new people through a connection you share. Many of the sites have communities or subgroups that may be based on a particular interest.

What Security Implications Do These Sites Present?

Social networking sites rely on connections and communication, so they encourage you to provide a certain amount of personal information. When deciding how much information to reveal, people may not exercise the same amount of caution as they would when meeting someone in person because

- The Internet provides a sense of anonymity

- The lack of physical interaction provides a false sense of security

- They tailor the information for their friends to read, forgetting that others may see it

- They want to offer insights to impress potential friends or associates

While the majority of people using these sites do not pose a threat, malicious people may be drawn to them because of the accessibility and amount of personal information that's available. The more information malicious people have about you, the easier it is for them to take advantage of you. Predators may form relationships online and then convince unsuspecting individuals to meet them in person. That could lead to a dangerous situation. The personal information can also be used to conduct a social-engineering attack. Using information that you provide about your location, hobbies, interests, and friends, a malicious person could impersonate a trusted friend or convince you that they have the authority to access other personal or financial data.

Additionally, because of the popularity of these sites, attackers may use them to distribute malicious code. Sites that offer applications developed by third parties are particularly susceptible. Attackers may be able to create customized applications that appear to be innocent while infecting your computer or sharing your information without your knowledge.

How Can You Protect Yourself?

- **Limit the amount of personal information you post.** Do not post information that would make you vulnerable, such as your address or information about your schedule or routine. If your connections post information about you, make sure the combined information is not more than you would be comfortable with strangers knowing. Also be considerate when posting information, including photos, about your connections.

- **Remember that the Internet is a public resource.** Only post information you are comfortable with anyone seeing. This includes information and photos in your profile and in blogs and other forums. Also, once you post information online, you can't retract it. Even if you remove the information from a site, saved or cached versions may still exist on other people's machines.

- **Be wary of strangers.** The Internet makes it easy for people to misrepresent their identities and motives. Consider limiting the people who are allowed to contact you on these sites. If you interact with people you do not know, be cautious about the amount of information you reveal or agreeing to meet them in person.

- **Be skeptical.** Don't believe everything you read online. People may post false or misleading information about various topics, including their own identities. This is not necessarily done with malicious intent; it could be unintentional, an exaggeration, or a joke. Take appropriate precautions, though, and try to verify the authenticity of any information before taking any action.

- **Evaluate your settings.** Take advantage of a site's privacy settings. The default settings for some sites may allow anyone to see your profile, but you can customize your settings to restrict access to only certain people. There is still a risk that private information could be exposed despite these restrictions, so don't post anything that you wouldn't want the public to see. Sites may change their options periodically, so review your security and privacy settings regularly to make sure that your choices are still appropriate.

- **Be wary of third-party applications.** Third-party applications may provide entertainment or functionality, but use caution when deciding which applications to enable. Avoid applications that seem suspicious, and modify your settings to limit the amount of information the applications can access.

- **Use strong passwords.** Protect your account with passwords that cannot easily be guessed. If your password is compromised, someone else may be able to access your account and pretend to be you.

- **Check privacy policies.** Some sites may share information such as email addresses or user preferences with other companies. This may lead to an increase in spam. Also, try to locate the policy for handling referrals to make sure that you do not unintentionally sign your friends up for spam. Some sites will continue to send email messages to anyone you refer until they join.

- **Keep software, particularly your web browser, up to date.** Install software updates so that attackers cannot take advantage of known problems or vulnerabilities. Many operating systems offer automatic updates. If this option is available, you should enable it.

- **Use and maintain anti-virus software.** Anti-virus software helps protect your computer against known viruses, so you may be able to detect and remove the virus before it can do any damage. Because attackers are continually writing new viruses, it is important to keep your definitions up to date.

Children are especially susceptible to the threats that social networking sites present. Although many of these sites have age restrictions, children may misrepresent their ages so that they can join. By teaching children about Internet safety, being aware of their online habits, and guiding them to appropriate sites, parents can make sure that the children become safe and responsible users.

Chapter 43

Navigating the Legal System

Chapter Contents

Section 43.1

Questions to Ask before You Hire an Attorney

"Questions to Ask before You Hire an Attorney," © 2016
Omnigraphics. Reviewed October 2018.

In relationships affected by domestic violence, it often becomes necessary for survivors to hire an attorney to assist them with divorce, child custody, or criminal assault cases. After gathering the names of possible attorneys from personal recommendations, state bar associations, and other sources, the next step is to schedule a meeting with each candidate to learn more about their background, qualifications, skills, experience, approach, strategy, and fees. Although the process of choosing an attorney may seem overwhelming, asking detailed questions during the initial consultation can help people make an informed decision.

Some examples of good questions to ask about a family law attorney's background and experience include:

- Where did you attend law school?

- How long have you been practicing family law?

- Do you only handle divorce and family law cases?

- How many cases do you handle annually?

- Have you handled many cases similar to mine?

- How much experience do you have with courtroom litigation?

To assess whether an attorney's legal philosophy and approach to family law is a good fit with the circumstances of a specific case, some recommended questions to ask include:

- How would you describe your overall philosophy as an attorney?

- Do you offer your clients options and allow them to decide, or do you tell them what to do?

- How would you assess my case?

- What approach would you take?

- What problems might I encounter?

- Do you think my case will go to trial?

- What outcomes can I expect?

- How long do you think it will take to resolve the case?

Since family law practices can range from large firms to sole practitioners, it may also be valuable to ask questions concerning how the case will be managed, such as:

- Will you be managing my case personally, or will another attorney take primary responsibility?
- Who will handle court appearances and negotiations?
- Who else will be involved with my case, and what will their roles be?
- How often will I receive updates on the status of my case?
- How will we communicate about the case?
- How quickly can I expect responses to my questions?

Legal Fees

Hiring a family law attorney can be an expensive proposition. Before signing an agreement for representation, it is important to understand exactly what types of legal fees the attorney will charge. In general, the fees will depend on the attorney's skill and experience in handling family law or domestic violence cases, as well as the complexity of the specific case. Although it may be more expensive to hire a highly experienced attorney, the extra cost may be worthwhile if it increases the likelihood of achieving the desired outcome. In addition, a less-experienced lawyer might require more billable hours to complete the necessary work.

There are many different types of legal fees that may be charged in family law cases. It is important to be aware that some attorneys charge a fee for the initial consultation, even before a potential client decides whether or not to hire them. Although some attorneys charge a flat fee for straightforward cases, such as a summary dissolution of a marriage, most charge an hourly rate for their work on a case. While a flat fee may seem attractive, it is not generally recommended for cases that are contested or may require multiple court appearances.

Before hiring an attorney, experts suggest asking for a written retainer agreement that lays out the hourly rate and any additional fees, as well as the amount of the initial deposit and the schedule for payment. Some other questions to ask an attorney about legal costs include:

- How exactly do you charge for your services?
- What other fees and expenses will I be expected to pay?
- Do you require a retainer payment?

- How often do you send out bills?

- What is your estimate of the total cost of my case?

References

1. Farzad, B. Robert. "What Are Questions to Ask a Divorce Lawyer at the Consultation and before Hiring One?" Farzad Family Law, June 28, 2014.

2. "Questions to Ask before Hiring Child Custody Lawyers," Attorneys.com, 2016.

3. "Watch out for the Cost of a Domestic Violence Suit," Laws. com, 2015.

Section 43.2

Restraining Orders

This section includes text excerpted from "Getting a Restraining Order," Office on Women's Health (OWH), U.S. Department of Health and Human Services (HHS), September 13, 2018.

If you are in an abusive relationship, you can take steps to protect yourself, such as getting a restraining order. There are also laws to protect you. One option is leaving the relationship. Many people can support you in leaving safely, including police, social workers, shelter workers, and friends and family. You can also create a safety plan if you decide to leave in the future.

What Happens If I Call the Police about Abuse?

First, the police will make sure everyone is safe, which might mean arresting someone who has a weapon or is physically hurting or threatening you.

Once you are safe, the police will ask you questions about what happened. The police can also offer information about community resources for temporary housing and other support you might need. If the alleged abuser is present, police will probably take you to separate areas to talk individually about what happened.

It can be difficult to talk to strangers—police, counselors, or health-care professionals. You might feel scared, ashamed, or embarrassed. It can also be difficult to tell your story many times to different people. Take your time. They are there to help. The questions they ask are necessary for the official police report, which will be used to support a court case if there is one.

What Is the Difference between a Police Report and Filing Charges?

When the police investigate a crime, or ask you and other witnesses questions about what happened, they must file a report. A police report is not the same thing as filing charges. This police report is important. It documents the violence, even if the abuser denies the violence, and creates an official record that can be used as evidence in court.

The police may decide to file criminal charges against the abuser after their investigation is completed. Once the police file criminal charges, a lawyer for the state (called a prosecutor) will begin a court case against the abuser.

What Should I Tell the Police If I've Been Abused?

You can choose what to share with the officers who respond. Only you can decide what to say, because you know your situation better than anyone else.

If you want to hold the person criminally accountable:

- Tell the police about anything your partner did or said that would be an example of a crime, such as physical or sexual violence or threats made to you verbally or in writing.

- Show the police any injuries or bruises you have. It may be painful to talk about or show, but the more information you can give the police, the better it is for documenting the abuse.

- Remember: Even if you do not have physical bruises or other signs of abuse, that does not mean your partner has not committed a crime.

- Share whatever you are comfortable with in order to help the officers understand the circumstances and why you're seeking support. If you have any emails, screenshots, or texts that show abuse, show the police. Any written or video evidence you have will also be helpful.

Even if there isn't a criminal charge filed against your partner, you can use the police report to help you if you go to family court or get a protection order.

Will We Go to Court If I Call the Police?

Maybe. If you've been abused and call the police, the police must file a report. A lawyer for the state government, called the prosecutor, may decide to file a criminal charge in court against the person who hurt you. When this happens, the state government brings charges against the person who harmed you. At this point, you can no longer drop the charges, because it is the state government, not you, that has filed the charges. In court, the state will try to prove its case against the person who hurt you.

What Is a Protection Order or Restraining Order?

Protection orders, often called restraining orders, are meant to keep you safe from a person who is harassing or hurting you. The police can arrest a person who violates a restraining order and charge them with a crime. Depending on the laws in your state, restraining orders may also allow you to have sole custody of children, make an abuser move out of a shared home, and make an abuser pay your court and legal fees. Federal law says that you can get a restraining order for free.

You can get more than one type of restraining order at the same time. Laws about restraining orders or other orders of protection are different in each state.

Common types of restraining orders include:

- **Emergency restraining order.** The police may issue this if you are in immediate danger or cannot get to the courthouse right away to file a more permanent restraining order. It usually expires after a few days.

- **Temporary restraining order.** A judge may issue this to help keep you safe in the time before your case goes to court. Temporary restraining orders usually last for about 14 days.

- **No-contact order.** A judge may issue this if the case goes to court and the abuser is charged with a crime. It is a punishment for a crime and it means the abuser may not have any contact with you. A no-contact order can last for a short or long time, depending on the facts of your case.

- **Domestic violence restraining order.** A judge may issue this after a court hearing. A domestic violence restraining order lasts longer than emergency or temporary restraining orders, possibly for several years.

How Does a Restraining Order Help?

A restraining, or protection, order can legally force someone who abuses you or harasses you to:

- Stay away from you physically and have no contact with you by phone, by email, through social media, or otherwise, even through another person
- Pay temporary child support, continue making mortgage payments on a home you own together or rental payments if the person's name is on the lease, and allow you to stay in the home while the other person lives somewhere else
- Turn over any guns to the police
- Have regular drug testing and attend counseling for domestic violence or drug and alcohol use
- Stay away from your children and your children's school, or visit the children only with supervision
- Do other things designed to protect you. Judges have flexibility and will work with you to ensure that the order, if granted, meets your needs.

If you have a restraining order and the person who hurt you does not follow it (tries to contact you or your children), call the police right away. The police can arrest the person for not following the order.

Where Do I Get a Restraining Order?

You can apply for a restraining (or protection) order at courthouses, women's shelters, lawyers' offices, and some police stations. You do not need a lawyer to get a restraining order. Federal law says that you can get a restraining order for free.

Still, you might want to get help from a lawyer to understand your rights. Often, a local domestic violence agency can help you find a

405

lawyer. Some lawyers will help you for free. You can find a list in your state of organizations and lawyers that provide free and low-cost legal services at WomensLaw.org (www.womenslaw.org/find-help/finding-lawyer).

How Do I File for a Restraining Order?

To file most types of restraining, or protection, orders, you will go to a family court located in the county where you live, where the person who hurt or harassed you lives, or where the abuse happened. You will fill out forms and provide specific information about when, where, and how the abuse or harassment happened.

What Is the Difference between a Family Court and a Criminal Court?

A family court is very different from a criminal court. A family court will view you and your partner as equals. It becomes your word against your partner's, unless you have police reports and documents showing criminal charges against your partner. The family court must include those documents when making a judgment about your case.

If you decide to go to family court, work with an experienced attorney to prepare your case. Collect police reports, arrest records, and documents showing charges filed against your partner. If you have pictures of injuries, hospital records, or pictures of property damage, include them. Tell your attorney about any witnesses to the abuse so the witnesses can provide statements about what they saw.

How Can I Find a Lawyer?

You can find a lawyer to help you at WomensLaw.org (www.womenslaw.org/find-help/finding-lawyer). You can also call the National Domestic Violence Hotline (NDVH) (www.thehotline.org), 800-799-SAFE (800-799-7233), or the National Sexual Assault Hotline (www.rainn.org), 800-656-HOPE (800-656-4673), 24 hours a day, 7 days a week. They can answer questions or help you find resources in your area. The Victim Connect Resource Center (victimconnect.org/get-help/connect-directory) also provides referrals to local services.

How Can I Protect My Children?

Your partner may threaten to take your children if you leave. Here are some steps to help protect your children:

- **Keep their identity documents.** Keep important legal documents such as birth certificates and Social Security cards with you or in a safe place. Make sure you have recent pictures of your children and their birth certificates. The police can help you more easily if you have these items showing you are their parent.

- **Get contact information for family.** Make a list of your partner's family and friends, including their addresses and phone numbers. This can help the police find your children if your partner takes them without your permission.

- **Get a restraining order.** Apply for a restraining order that says your partner has to stay away from you and your children.

- **Apply for sole custody.** Apply for a custody order in family court that says your children have to live with you. You can also ask for the order to say that your partner may not take your children out of the United States.

If you have a restraining order or custody order, give a copy to your children's school and child care providers. Ask them not to release the children to the abuser or anyone else not authorized to be with your children.

- Talk to a legal professional before leaving the state to get away from someone who hurt you. State laws vary and can affect whether you or your children are required to return to your original state.

- Notify the U.S. Department of State's (DOS) alert program if you're worried your partner will try to take your children out of the country. This program lets you refuse a passport for children up to age 18. Call 888-407-4747 or visit the alert program website for more information.

Are There Laws to Protect Me from Domestic Violence?

Yes. There are laws against domestic and sexual violence, and they can help protect you. To protect you, a law must be enforced. For it to be enforced, a person must report domestic violence to the police as soon as possible after it happens.

Most domestic violence and sexual assault laws are state laws, which means they might be different in different states. So what is against the law in one state might not be in another. Regardless of the specific laws in your state, domestic or sexual violence is never your fault. It is never okay to hurt or abuse someone else.

How Can I Protect Myself If I Don't Leave?

It can be difficult to think about leaving your home, your partner, and the life you have right now. You may not be ready to leave the relationship right away, but if you are in immediate danger, get to a safe place. You can start thinking about what to do if you need to leave in a hurry, and how you can be safe.

If you can't leave or you decide not to leave right now, consider these tips for protecting yourself:

Create a safety plan. Leaving an abusive relationship can be dangerous, but you can make a plan to make it safer. Start with your safety packing list, which includes a list of the most important documents, medicines, and items to take when you leave.

- **Find a place you can go in a hurry.** It could be a friend's house or a local women's shelter. You may not stay there permanently, but you need a temporary place where you know you will be safe. Try to have more than one place in case you need to escape in a hurry.

- **Find out what resources are in your community.** Contact your local domestic violence or sexual assault program and ask for the help and support you need. There are programs that may help you with finding a place to stay, buying food, and finding healthcare if you need it. If you work or go to school, ask whether there is an employee assistance program or a student counselor. Get involved with people and activities outside your home.

You may think you can stop your partner's abusive behavior. But only your partner is in control of changing his or her behavior. You must take steps to protect yourself and your children.

Section 43.3

Federal Domestic Violence Laws

This section includes text excerpted from "Federal
Domestic Violence Laws," U.S. Department of
Justice (DOJ), December 6, 2017.

In 1994, Congress passed the Violence Against Women Act
("VAWA"). This Act, and the 1996 additions to the Act, recognize
that domestic violence is a national crime and that federal laws
can help an overburdened state and local criminal justice system.
In 1994 and 1996, congress also passed changes to the Gun Control
Act making it a federal crime in certain situations for domestic
violence abusers to possess guns. The majority of domestic violence
cases will continue to be handled by your state and local authorities. In some cases, however, the federal laws and the benefits
gained from applying these laws, may be the most appropriate
course of action.

Who Should I Call to Report a Possible Federal Crime?

Always contact your local authorities in cases of an emergency. Your
local District Attorney's Office will refer appropriate cases for federal
prosecution to the United States Attorney's Office. If you are unsure
of the violation, please contact your local authorities.

What Are the Federal Crimes?

All the federal domestic violence crimes are felonies.

It is a federal crime under the Violence Against Women Act
("VAWA"):

- To cross state lines or enter or leave Indian country and
  physically injure an "intimate partner";

- To cross state lines to stalk or harass or to stalk or harass within
  the maritime or territorial lands of the United States (this
  includes military bases and Indian country); and

- To cross state lines to enter or leave Indian country and violate a
  qualifying Protection Order.

It is a federal crime under the Gun Control Act:

- To possess a firearm and/or ammunition while subject to a qualifying protection Order; and

- To possess a firearm and/or ammunition after conviction of a qualifying misdemeanor crime of domestic violence.

In a VAWA case, the Court must order restitution to pay the victim the full amount of loss. These losses include costs for medical or psychological care, physical therapy, transportation, temporary housing, child care expenses, loss of income, attorney's fees, costs incurred in obtaining a civil protection order, and any other losses suffered by the victim as a result of the offense.

In a Gun Control Act case, the Court may order restitution. Please keep a record of all expenses caused by the domestic violence crime.

Can My Concerns Be Heard in a Federal Court?

A victim in a VAWA case shall have the right to speak to the Judge at a bail hearing to inform the Judge of any danger posed by the release of the defendant. Any victim of a crime of violence shall also have the right to address the Court in person at the time of sentencing.

Victims' Rights

A federal domestic violence victim has the following rights under 42 U.S.C. Section 10606(b):

1. The right to be treated with fairness and with respect for the victim's dignity and privacy

2. The right to be reasonable protected from the accused offender

3. The right to be notified of court proceedings

4. The right to be present at all public court proceedings related to the offense, unless the court determines that testimony by the victim would be materially affected if the victim heard other testimony at the trial

5. The right to confer with the attorney for the Government in the case

6. The right to restitution

7. The right to information about the conviction, sentencing, imprisonment, and release of the offender

Chapter 44

Identity Protection for Abuse Victims

Chapter Contents

Section 44.1

Tips for Protecting Your Identity

"Tips for Protecting Your Identity," © 2016
Omnigraphics. Reviewed October 2018.

Even after leaving an abusive relationship, survivors of domestic violence may still be vulnerable to an abuser's efforts to harass or control them. An increasingly common method abusers may use to continue to exert power in the relationship is identity theft. For instance, an abuser may use a survivor's personal information—such as Social Security number (SSN), credit cards, or bank accounts—without their knowledge to incur debts, commit crimes, and ruin the survivor's credit or reputation. Abusers may also use information posted on social media sites to locate and stalk their former partners. The following tips can help survivors of domestic violence protect their identity and maintain their safety and independence:

- Consider getting a post office box to prevent an abuser from stealing your mail and accessing your personal information. Or arrange to have paperless statements sent to you online.

- Open an account at a new bank and get a new credit card in your own name. Check bank statements and credit card bills as soon as you receive them. If bills do not arrive on time, call the company to inquire whether someone may have changed the contact information for the account. Report any unauthorized withdrawals or charges immediately.

- Shred your mail before throwing it away to prevent an abuser from gaining access to personal information by going through your garbage. Opt out of preapproved credit card offers, which may enable an identity thief to open accounts in your name, by calling 888-5OPTOUT (888-567-8688) or visiting www.optoutprescreen.com.

- Obtain a free credit report once a year by calling 877-322-8228 or visiting www.annualcreditreport.com. Check the reports carefully. If you suspect fraudulent activity, close the account immediately and notify the Federal Trade Commission at 877-ID-THEFT (877-438-4338).

- Contact the major credit bureaus (Equifax, Experian, and TransUnion) to place a fraud alert on your credit report, which makes it more difficult for an identity thief to open new lines of credit in your name.

- Protect your personal information, especially your Social Security number. Do not provide the number to anyone who calls or emails you claiming to be a store, bank, or government agency. Most legitimate businesses will never request the information in this manner.

- Use firewall, antivirus, and spyware protection programs on your computers and smartphones and keep the programs updated. Make strong passwords using a mix of at least eight letters, numbers, and symbols, and use a different password for each account.

- Be careful about sharing personal information on social media sites, such as Facebook and Twitter. Never publish your home address, workplace address, daily schedule, current whereabouts, or vacation plans. All of this information can reveal your location to an abusive partner and enable them to stalk you.

References

1. "How to Protect Your Identity," DomesticShelters.org, July 7, 2014.

2. "Top 10 Tips for Identity Theft Protection," State of California Department of Justice, 2015.

Section 44.2

Address Confidentiality Programs

This section includes text excerpted from "Domestic Violence
Awareness Month: Focus on Resources, Collaboration
and Confidentiality IM-14-03," Administration for
Children and Families (ACF), U.S. Department of
Health and Human Services (HHS), March 30, 2017.

Confidentiality is a key concern for survivors of domestic violence. A
survivor must be able to flee from violence without being located. It is
vitally important that engagement with a child-support program does
not inadvertently endanger a family by disclosing information. Carefully considered data-sharing protocols and safeguarding are essential.

Family violence indicator ("FVI") policies are not a complete
approach to protecting the identity of or information about a victim of
violence nor are they a complete domestic violence policy. The FVI is
just one protection provided victims seeking child support. Under federal law, states are required to have an FVI process (Section 453(b)(2)
and 454(26) of the Social Security Act). The law prohibits the release
of specific information when evidence of domestic violence or child
abuse exists. The FVI prevents any information from being released
from the Federal Parent Locator Service (FPLS).

While states have taken great care in crafting policies and practices
for the placement and removal of an FVI, such efforts do not ensure
total confidentiality. The presence or absence of an FVI is not defini-
tive of whether or not there is a history of domestic violence, particularly as family circumstances (and trust of the child support program)
may change over time. Additionally, policies and practices regarding
placement and removal of the FVI are only one component of a child
support program's domestic violence plan or policies. Apart from the
FVI, a comprehensive domestic violence plan should address disclosure, training, confidentiality, referrals, legal practice, and internal
procedures for responding to domestic violence.

To further assist with the safety issues raised in seeking child
support, child support programs can provide information and assist
victims through address confidentiality programs. PIQ 12-02, expressly
states that child support programs can "use federal financial participation (FFP) to develop alternative address/confidentiality systems
for survivors in the child support program. This may be in partnership with family violence service organizations." Additionally, many

states have existing address confidentiality program visit disclaimer page. Enhanced safeguards and attention to confidentiality are especially necessary in interstate cases and interstate communications. For example, court documents protected in one jurisdiction may be public in another system.

Apart from data sharing where there are safety concerns, child support professionals must be careful not to communicate any information about child support customers unless they are required to by law. Even when child support programs pay careful attention to the safety needs of families, there will always be risks to engaging with the child support system. Therefore, it is important not to promise total safety or confidentiality, particularly given the prevalence of information on the Internet. Office of Child Support Enforcement (OCSE) recommends ongoing review of existing confidentiality policies.

Section 44.3

Applying for a New Social Security Number

This section includes text excerpted from "New Numbers for Domestic Violence Victims," U.S. Social Security Administration (SSA), August 2017.

Anyone can be a victim of domestic violence. If you're a victim of family violence, harassment, abuse, or life-endangering situations, Social Security may be able to help you.

Public awareness campaigns stress how important it is for victims to develop safety plans that include gathering personal papers and choosing a safe place to go. Sometimes, the best way to evade an abuser and reduce the risk of further violence may be to relocate and establish a new identity. Following these changes, getting a new Social Security number (SSN) may also be helpful.

Although Social Security doesn't routinely assign new numbers, you get a new SSN when evidence shows you are being harassed or abused, or your life is endangered.

Applying for a new number is a big decision. Your ability to interact with federal and state agencies, employers, and others may be affected;

your financial, medical, employment, and other records will be under your former SSN and name (if you change your name). If you expect to change your name, please do so before applying for a new number.

How to Apply for a New Number

You must apply in person at any Social Security Office. In addition, you must present

- evidence documenting the harassment, abuse, or life endangerment;
- your current SSN;
- evidence documents establishing your
- U.S. citizenship or work-authorized immigration status
- age
- identity
- evidence of your legal name change if you've changed your name

Also, other documents showing you have custody of any children for whom you're requesting new numbers and documentation proving their U.S. citizenship, ages, and identities will be needed.

All documents must be either originals or copies certified by the issuing agency. Photocopies or notarized copies of documents are not accepted. One document may be used for two purposes. For example, U.S. passport may be used as proof of both citizenship and identity. Or, your U.S. birth certificate may be used as proof of age and citizenship. However, you must provide at least two separate documents.

Citizenship or Immigration Status

U.S. citizen: Only certain documents as proof of U.S. citizenship are accepted. These include a U.S. birth certificate or a U.S. passport.

Noncitizen: To prove your U.S. immigration status, show your current immigration document such as your I-94, Arrival/Departure Record, showing a class of admission permitting work, or your Form I-766, Employment Authorization Document (EAD, work permit). If you're an F-1 or M-1 student, you also must show your I-20, Certificate of Eligibility for Nonimmigrant Student Status. If you're a J-1 or J-2exchange visitor, show your DS-2019, Certificate Of Eligibility for Exchange Visitor Status.

Age

U.S.-born: You must present your birth certificate if you have one. If you don't have a birth certificate, the following documents may be acceptable:

- Religious record made before age five showing the date of birth
- U.S. hospital record or birth
- U.S. passport or passport card

Foreign-born: You must present your foreign birth certificate if you have it or can get a copy within 10 business days. If you can't get it, you may give one of the following documents.

- Foreign passport
- I-551, permanent resident (PR) card
- I-766, employment authorization document (EAD)
- I-94 arrival/departure record

Identity

An acceptable document must be current (not expired) and show your name, identifying information and preferably a recent photograph.

U.S. citizen: Social Security will ask to see a U.S. driver's license, U.S. state-issued nondriver identification card, or U.S. passport as proof of identity. If you don't have the specific documents, you may be asked for other documents, including:

- Certificate of Naturalization
- Certificate of U.S. Citizenship
- Employee identification card
- School identification card
- Health insurance card (not a Medicare card)
- U.S. military identification card

Noncitizen: Social Security will ask to see your current U.S. immigration documents. Acceptable Immigration documents include your

- I-551, permanent resident (PR) card

- I-94, arrival/departure record with your unexpired foreign passport, or

- I-766, employment authorization document (EAD)

Changing Your Name on Your Card

The U.S. Social Security Administration can accept only a court-order-approved legal name change document that supports your requested name change.

Providing the Evidence You Need

The best evidence of abuse comes from third parties, such as police or medical personnel, and describes the nature and extent of harassment, abuse, or life endangerment. Other evidence may include court restraining orders and letters from shelters, family members, friends, counselors, or others who have knowledge of the domestic violence or abuse.

Blocking Access to Your Record

You can choose to block electronic access to your Social Security record. When you do this, no one, including you, will be able to get or change your personal information online or through an automated telephone service. If you block access to your record, and then change your mind, you can contact Social Security and ask to unblock it. Go to www.socialsecurity.gov/blockaccessto block electronic access to your personal record.

Contacting Social Security

The most convenient way to contact Social Security anytime, anywhere is to visit www.socialsecurity.gov. There, you can: apply for benefits; open a Social Security account, which you can use to review your Social Security Statement, verify your earnings, print a benefit verification letter, change your direct deposit information, request a replacement Medicare card, and get a replacement SSA-1099/1042S; obtain valuable information; find publications; get answers to frequently asked questions; and much more.

If you don't have access to the Internet, call toll-free 800-772-1213 or TTY number, 800-325-0778, if you're deaf or hard of hearing.

Chapter 45

Life after Abuse: Looking after Yourself and Moving On

Getting out of an abusive relationship requires a great deal of courage and resiliency. But leaving is often only the first step in what can be a long and difficult recovery process. Domestic violence harms victims emotionally and mentally as well as physically. Many survivors struggle to move on and regain their self-confidence long after their physical injuries have healed.

Struggling to Move On

In an abusive relationship, the abuser controls you through manipulation, coercion, or violence. You are forced to surrender your power and independence. Even after leaving an abusive situation, you may still feel bound to the abuser and struggle to regain control of your own life. You may find yourself on an emotional rollercoaster, as your thoughts, feelings, and emotions seem to fluctuate wildly. You may blame yourself for the abuse and second guess your decision to leave the relationship. You may wonder if you did something wrong, or if you could have tried harder. All of these feelings are normal.

Many survivors of domestic violence experience feelings of loss, depression, or guilt. It is not uncommon for survivors to have symptoms of posttraumatic stress disorder (PTSD), such as anxiety, insomnia, and being easily startled or frightened. Survivors may also feel emotionally numb and have trouble reconnecting with friends and maintaining relationships. Although experiencing domestic violence can cause lasting damage, it is important to remember that anyone who manages to get out of an abusive relationship has tremendous strength. The key to healing and moving on is channeling that strength into rebuilding your self-esteem and forging a happy and healthy future.

Tips for Looking Forward

Moving forward after an abusive relationship is a gradual process. It involves accepting that you were not to blame, forgiving yourself for loving and believing in a person who hurt you, and understanding that you are a worthwhile person who deserves to feel safe and happy. Following the steps below may aid in your recovery:

- **Ensure that you remain safe and beyond the abuser's control.** You may need to cut off all contact with the abuser, obtain a civil protection order, change your phone number, or even move away from the area. If the abuser ever harasses, threatens, or frightens you, keep a detailed written record of each incident and contact the police if necessary.

- **Deal with emotional turmoil in a healthy way.** Feelings of anger, sadness, or grief are normal at the end of any relationship. Expressing those feelings in a healthy manner— such as writing poetry, painting, dancing, singing, or exercising—can increase your sense of power and control over your life.

- **Start by making small choices.** When the abuser was in control, you may not have been allowed to make decisions for yourself. As a result, the many choices you face every day may seem overwhelming. It may be helpful to start by making small decisions, such as what to eat for lunch or what to watch on television, to begin reestablishing control over your life. Then you can move on to bigger decisions as you grow more confident and independent.

- **Acknowledge and celebrate your successes.** Give yourself credit for the tremendous courage and determination it took to end an abusive relationship. Write down even minor achievements on your road to recovery. Look back on them and feel proud of how far you have come.

- **Take care of your health.** Eating a balanced diet, exercising daily, and getting plenty of sleep will help ensure that you have the physical and mental energy you need to rebuild your life. If you relied on drugs or alcohol to cope with the abuse, try to cut back or quit.

- **Establish a support network.** Many abusers isolate their victims from family and friends in order to solidify their control. Getting back in touch with these people can provide a valuable source of support in your recovery and help you reconnect with ordinary life. It may also be helpful to talk to people who have been through similar experiences through online forums or local support groups for victims of domestic violence.

- **Rebuild Relationships with Your Children.** If you have children, work to rebuild your relationship with them. Sometimes going for a walk, tossing a ball, or having a picnic in the park will reduce the pressure on children and make it easier for them to talk about their feelings and experiences.

- **Help other people.** Volunteering in a school, church, or community center is a great way to feel useful and valued, give back to the community, and meet new people in a casual atmosphere. Taking a class, learning a skill, or joining a team can also help rebuild self-esteem.

References

1. "Take Your Power Back: Life after Abuse," CheriSpeak, October 29, 2013.

2. "Tips for Life after Violence and Abuse," Single Parent Action Network, 2016.

3. "Why Am I Struggling to Move On after Abuse?" Love Is Respect, July 31, 2013.

Part Six

Additional Help and Information

Chapter 46

Glossary of Terms Related to Domestic Abuse

abandonment: When a parent leaves a child without adequate care, supervision, support, or parental contact for an excessive period of time.

affidavit: A written statement of facts confirmed by the oath of the party making it. Affidavits must be notarized or administered by an officer of the court with such authority.

affirmed: Judgment by appellate courts where the decree or order is declared valid and will stand as decided in the lower court.

aggravated assault: Unlawful, intentional causing of serious bodily injury with or without a deadly weapon, or unlawful, intentional attempting or threatening of serious bodily injury or death with a deadly or dangerous weapon.

batterer: An individual who uses abusive tactics over his intimate partner in order to exercise power and control over his partner. Other terms used are perpetrator and abuser.

child abuse: Maltreatment or neglect of a child, including nonaccidental physical injuries, sexual abuse/exploitation, severe or general

---

This glossary contains terms excerpted from documents produced by several sources deemed reliable.

neglect, unjustifiable mental suffering/emotional abuse, and willful cruelty or unjustifiable punishment of a child.

contract: An agreement between two or more persons that creates an obligation to do or not to do a particular thing.

cyberbullying: Hurting someone again and again using a computer, a cellphone, or another kind of electronic technology.

dating violence: Physical, sexual, psychological, or emotional violence within a dating relationship, including stalking. It can occur in person or electronically and might occur between a current or former dating partner.

defendant: In a civil suit, the person complained against; in a criminal case, the person accused of the crime.

economic abuse: Making or attempting to make an individual financially dependent by maintaining total control over financial resources, withholding one's access to money, or forbidding one's attendance at school or employment.

elder abuse: Abuse perpetrated by a caretaker on an elderly individual who depends on others for support and assistance.

emotional abuse: Undermining an individual's sense of self-worth and/or self-esteem is abusive.

ex parte: A proceeding brought before a court by one party only, without notice to or challenge by the other side.

felony: A serious crime, usually punishable by at least one year in prison.

gang violence: Criminal acts committed by a group of three or more individuals who regularly engage in criminal activity and identify themselves with a common name or sign.

human traffic: Sex trafficking in which a commercial sex act is induced by force, fraud, or coercion, or in which the person induced to perform such act has not attained 18 years of age; or the recruitment, harboring, transportation, provision, or obtaining of a person for labor or services, through the use of force, fraud, or coercion, for the purpose of subjection to involuntary servitude, peonage, debt bondage, or slavery.

litigation: A case, controversy, or lawsuit. Participants (plaintiffs and defendants) in lawsuits are called litigants.

misdemeanor: An offense punishable by one year of imprisonment or less.

perpetrator: A perpetrator is an individual who commits or threatens to commit an act of domestic violence, sexual assault, and/or stalking.

petitioner: A person who presents a petition to the court; a person who files legal forms to start a court case.

physical abuse: Hitting, slapping, shoving, grabbing, pinching, biting, hair pulling, etc. are types of physical abuse.

probation: A sentencing alternative to imprisonment in which the court releases convicted defendants under supervision as long as certain conditions are observed.

prosecute: To charge someone with a crime. A prosecutor tries a criminal case on behalf of the government.

psychological abuse: Elements of psychological abuse include—but are not limited to—causing fear by intimidation; threatening physical harm to self, partner, children, or partner's family or friends; destruction of pets and property; and forcing isolation from family, friends, or school and/or work.

remand: When an appellate court sends a case back to a lower court for further proceedings.

respondent: If you are the person that answers the original petition, you are the respondent. Even if you later file an action of your own in that case, you are still the respondent for as long as the case is open.

restitution: Giving something back to its owner. Or, giving the owner something with the same value, like paying to fix his or her property.

restraining order: A court order that tells a person to stop doing something for a certain amount of time, usually until a court hearing is held.

safety plan: Guidelines for stalking victims that, if implemented, may reduce the odds of physical or emotional harm from a stalker.

sentence: The punishment ordered by a court for a defendant convicted of a crime.

settlement: Parties to a lawsuit resolve their dispute without having a trial. Settlements often involve the payment of compensation by one party in at least partial satisfaction of the other party's claims, but usually do not include the admission of fault.

sexual abuse: Coercing or attempting to coerce any sexual contact or behavior without consent.

sexual assault: Means a rape, aggravated sexual assault, or sexual assault as defined in the *Peace Corps Consolidated Incident Reporting Guide.*

stalking: Any unwanted contact between two people that directly or indirectly communicates a threat or places the victim in fear.

status quo: A child's usual place of residence, current schedule and daily routine for at least the last three months.

subpoena: A command to a witness to appear and give testimony.

temporary restraining order: Akin to a preliminary injunction, it is a judge's short-term order forbidding certain actions until a full hearing can be conducted. Often referred to as a TRO.

threat: Any oral, written expression, or gesture that could be interpreted by a reasonable person as conveying intent to cause physical harm to persons or property.

verdict: The decision of a trial jury or a judge that determines the guilt or innocence of a criminal defendant, or that determines the final outcome of a civil case.

victim safety: Means a plan developed by Designated Staff and a Volunteer to address the immediate and ongoing personal safety and emotional needs of the Volunteer following a sexual assault, including, when necessary, housing changes.

visitation: The time that third parties, often grandparents or stepparents, will spend with children. When the time with children is for parents, it is called parenting time.

warrant: Court authorization, most often for law enforcement officers, to conduct a search or make an arrest.

witness: A person who has information or evidence concerning a crime and provides information regarding his/her knowledge to a law enforcement agency.

workplace violence: Any act of violent behavior, threats of physical violence, harassment, intimidation, bullying, verbal, or nonverbal threat, or other threatening, disruptive behavior that occurs at the workplace.

youth violence: A serious problem that can have lasting harmful effects on victims and their family, friends, and communities.

Chapter 47

Directory of Domestic Violence Resources

Abused Deaf Women's Advocacy Services (ADWAS)
8623 Roosevelt Way N.E.
Seattle, WA 98115
Phone: 206-922-7088
Fax: 206-726-0017
Website: www.adwas.org
E-mail: adwas@adwas.org

AbuseofPower.info
Website: www.abuseofpower.info

Alabama Coalition Against Domestic Violence (ACADV)
Toll-Free: 800-650-6522
Phone: 334-832-4842
Website: www.acadv.org
E-mail: info@acadv.org

Asian Pacific Institute on Gender-Based Violence (APIGBV)
500 12th St.
Ste. 330
Oakland, CA 94607
Toll-Free: 800-799-7233
Phone: 415-568-3315
Website: www.api-gbv.org
E-mail: info@api-gbv.org

Aurora Center for Advocacy & Education
University of Minnesota
128 Pleasant St. S.E.
Minneapolis, MN 55455
Phone: 612-626-2929
Website: aurora.umn.edu
E-mail: aurora@umn.edu

Resources in this chapter were compiled from several sources deemed reliable; all contact information was verified and updated in October 2018.

Break the Cycle
P.O. Box 811334
Los Angeles, CA 90081
Phone: 424-265-7346
Website: www.breakthecycle.org

Centers for Disease Control and Prevention (CDC)
National Center for Injury Prevention and Control (NCIPC)
1600 Clifton Rd.
Atlanta, GA 30329-4027
Toll-Free: 800-CDC-INFO
(800-232-4636)
Phone: 404-498-1515
Toll-Free TTY: 888-232-6348
Website: www.cdc.gov
E-mail: cdcinfo@cdc.gov

Centre for Research & Education on Violence Against Women & Children (CREVAWC)
Faculty of Education Building,
Western University
1137 Western Rd.
Rm. 1158
London, ON N6G 1G7
Phone: 519-661-4040
Fax: 519-850-2464
Website: www. learningtoendabuse.ca
E-mail: crevawc@uwo.ca

Child Witness to Violence Project (CWVP)
Website: www. childwitnesstoviolence.org

FaithTrust Institute
2414 S.W. Andover St.
Ste. D208
Seattle, WA 98106
Phone: 206-634-1903
Website: www. faithtrustinstitute.org

Florida Council Against Sexual Violence (FCASV)
1820 E. Park Ave.
Ste. 100
Tallahassee, FL 32301
Toll-Free: 888-956-7273
Phone: 850-297-2000
Fax: 850-297-2002
Website: www.fcasv.org
E-mail: information@fcasv.org

Futures Without Violence
100 Montgomery St.
San Francisco, CA 94129
Phone: 415-678-5500
Toll-Free TTY: 866-678-8901
Fax: 415-529-2930
Website: www. futureswithoutviolence.org
E-mail: info@ futureswithoutviolence.org

Gay Men's Domestic Violence Project (GMDVP)
Toll-Free: 800-832-1901
Website: www.gmdvp.org
E-mail: cs@gmdvp.org

Houston Area Women's Center (HAWC)
1010 Waugh Dr.
Houston, TX 77019
Toll-Free: 800-256-0551
(Domestic Violence Hotline);
Toll-Free: 800-256-0661 (Sexual Assault Hotline)
Phone: 713-528-RAPE (713-528-7273) (Sexual Assault Hotline);
Phone: 713-528-2121 (Domestic Violence Hotline)
TDD: 713-528-3625 (Domestic Violence Hotline); TDD: 713-528-3691 (Sexual Assault Hotline)
Website: www.hawc.org
E-mail: info@hawc.org

Loveisrespect.org
Toll-Free: 866-331-9474
Toll-Free TTY: 866-331-8453
Website: www.loveisrespect.org

Minnesota Coalition for Battered Women (MCBW)
60 E. Plato Blvd.
Ste. 130
St. Paul, MN 55107
Toll-Free: 800-289-6177
Phone: 651-646-6177
Fax: 651-646-1527
Website: www.mcbw.org

National Center for Victims of Crime (NCVC)
2000 M St. N.W.
Ste. 480
Washington, DC 20036
Phone: 202-467-8700
Fax: 202-467-8701
Website: www.victimsofcrime.org
E-mail: webmaster@ncvc.org

National Center on Domestic and Sexual Violence (NCDSV)
4612 Shoal Creek Blvd.
Austin, TX 78756
Toll-Free: 800-799-SAFE (800-799-7233)
Phone: 512-407-9020
Toll-Free TTY: 800-787-3224
Fax: 512-407-9020
Website: www.ncdsv.org

National Coalition Against Domestic Violence (NCADV)
One Bdwy.
Ste. B210
Denver, CO 80203
Phone: 303-839-1852
Website: www.ncadv.org
E-mail: mainoffice@ncadv.org

National Council on Child Abuse & Family Violence (NCCAFV)
1025 Connecticut Ave. N.W.
Ste. 1000
Washington, DC 20036
Phone: 202-429-6695
Fax: 202-521-3479
Website: www.nccafv.org
E-mail: info@nccafv.org

National Crime Prevention Council (NCPC)
2614 Chapel Lake Dr.
Ste. B
Gambrills, MD 21054
Phone: 443-292-4565
Website: www.ncpc.org

National Network to End Domestic Violence (NNEDV)
1325 Massachusetts Ave. N.W.
Seventh Fl.
Washington, DC 20005-4188
Phone: 202-543-5566
Fax: 202-543-5626
Website: nnedv.org

National Resource Center on Domestic Violence (NRCDV)
1012 14th St. N.W.
Ste. 209
Washington, DC 20005
Toll-Free: 800-537-2238
Website: www.nrcdv.org
E-mail: nrcdvTA@nrcdv.org

New York City Alliance Against Sexual Assault (NYCAASA)
32 Bdwy.
Ste. 1101
New York, NY 10004
Phone: 212-229-0345
Fax: 212-229-0676
Website: www.svfreenyc.org
E-mail: contact-us@svfreenyc.org

New York State Coalition Against Domestic Violence (NYSCADV)
119 Washington Ave.
Albany, NY 12210
Toll-Free: 800-942-6906
(Hotline)
Phone: 518-482-5465
Fax: 518-482-3807
Website: nyscadv.org

New York State Office for the Prevention of Domestic Violence (OPDV)
Alfred E. Smith Bldg., 80 S. Swan St.
11th Fl., Rm. Number 1157
Albany, NY 12210
Phone: 518-457-5800
Fax: 518-457-5810
Website: www.opdv.ny.gov
E-mail: opdvpublicinfo@opdv.ny.gov

Peaceful Families Project (PFP)
P.O. Box 771
Great Falls, VA 22066
Phone: 703-474-6870
Website: www.peacefulfamilies.org
E-mail: info@peacefulfamilies.org

Rape, Abuse & Incest National Network (RAINN)
2000 L St. N.W.
Ste. 406
Washington, DC 20036
Toll-Free: 800-656-HOPE
(800-656-4673)
Phone: 202-544-1034
Fax: 202-544-3556
Website: www.rainn.org
E-mail: info@rainn.org

South Carolina Coalition Against Domestic Violence and Sexual Assault (SCCADVASA)
P.O. Box 7776
Columbia, SC 29202
Phone: 803-256-2900
Website: www.sccadvasa.org

Stop Abuse For Everyone (SAFE)
3400 Calloway Dr.
Bakersfield, CA 93312
Phone: 661-829-6848
Website: www.stopabuseforeveryone.org

U.S. Department of Health and Human Services (HHS)
Office on Women's Health (OWH)
200 Independence Ave. S.W.
Washington, DC 20201
Toll-Free: 800-994-9662
Phone: 202-690-7650
Fax: 202-205-2631
Website: www.womenshealth.gov

Washington State Coalition Against Domestic Violence (WSCADV)
1511 Third Ave.
Ste. 433
Seattle, WA 98101
Phone: 206-389-2515
Fax: 206-389-2520
Website: www.wscadv.org
E-mail: wscadv@wscadv.org

Women's Justice Center
P.O. Box 7510
Santa Rosa, CA 95407
Phone: 707-575-3150
Website: www.justicewomen.com
E-mail: rdjustice@monitor.net

Child Abuse

Child Welfare Information Gateway
Children's Bureau/ACYF
330 C St. S.W.
Washington, DC 20201
Toll-Free: 800-394-3366
Website: www.childwelfare.gov
E-mail: info@childwelfare.gov

Child Witness to Violence Project (CWVP)
Website: www.childwitnesstoviolence.org

National Children's Advocacy Center (NCAC)
210 Pratt Ave.
Huntsville, AL 35801
Phone: 256-533-KIDS (256-533-5437)
Website: www.nationalcac.org

Elder Abuse

National Center on Elder Abuse (NCEA)
c/o University of Southern California (USC) Keck School of Medicine, Department of Family Medicine and Geriatrics
1000 S. Fremont Ave.
Unit 22 Bldg. A-6
Alhambra, CA 91803
Toll-Free: 855-500-ELDR (855-500-3537)
Fax: 626-457-4090
Website: www.ncea.acl.gov
E-mail: ncea-info@aoa.hhs.gov

National Clearinghouse on Abuse in Later Life (NCALL)
1245 E. Washington Ave.
Ste. 150
Madison, WI 53703
Phone: 608-255-0539
Fax/TTY: 608-255-3560
Website: www.ncall.us
E-mail: ncall@endabusewi.org

U.S. Department of Justice (DOJ)
Elder Justice Initiative
601 D St., N.W.
#1217
Washington, DC 20004
Phone: 202-514-2000
Website: www.justice.gov/elderjustice
E-mail: elder.justice@usdoj.gov

Chapter 48

Domestic Violence Hotlines

National Domestic Abuse Hotlines

National Domestic Violence Hotline
Toll-Free: 800-799-SAFE
(800-799-7233)
Toll-Free TTY: 800-787-3224
Website: www.thehotline.org

Rape, Abuse, and Incest National Network (RAINN) National Hotline
Toll-Free: 800-656-HOPE
(800-656-4673)
Website: www.rainn.org

Safe Horizon Domestic Violence Hotline
Toll-Free: 800-621-HOPE
(800-621-4673)
Website: www.safehorizon.org

Domestic Violence Hotlines by State

If your state is not listed below, call the National Domestic Violence Hotline (listed above).

Alabama Coalition Against Domestic Violence (ACADV)
Toll-Free: 800-650-6522
Website: www.acadv.org

Alaska Network on Domestic Violence and Sexual Assault (ANDVSA)
Phone: 907-586-3650
Website: www.andvsa.org

Resources in this chapter were compiled from several sources deemed reliable; all contact information was verified and updated in October 2018.

Arizona Coalition to End Sexual & Domestic Violence (ACESDV)
Toll-Free: 800-782-6400
TTY: 602-279-7270
Website: www.acesdv.org

Arkansas Coalition Against Domestic Violence (ACADV)
Toll-Free: 800-269-4668
Website: www.domesticpeace.com

Florida Coalition Against Domestic Violence (FCADV)
Toll-Free: 800-500-1119 (Florida callers only)
Toll-Free TTY: 800-621-4202
Website: www.fcadv.org

Hawaii State Coalition Against Domestic Violence (HSCADV)
Toll-Free: 808-832-9316
Website: www.hscadv.org

Iowa Coalition Against Domestic Violence (ICADV)
Toll-Free: 800-942-0333
Website: www.icadv.org

Idaho Coalition Against Sexual and Domestic Violence
Toll-Free: 800-669-3176
Website: www.icdv.idaho.gov

Maine Coalition to End Domestic Violence (MCEDV)
Toll-Free: 866-834-HELP (866-834-4357) (Maine callers only)
Website: www.mcedv.org

Minnesota Day One Domestic Violence Crisis Line
Toll-Free: 866-223-1111
Website: www.dayoneservices.org

Mississippi State Coalition Against Domestic Violence (MCADV)
Toll-Free: 800-898-3234
Website: www.mcadv.org

New Hampshire Coalition Against Domestic and Sexual Violence
Toll-Free: 866-644-3574
Toll-Free: 800-277-5570 (Sexual assault)
Website: www.nhcadsv.org

Ohio Domestic Violence Network (ODVN)
Toll-Free: 800-934-9840
Website: www.odvn.org

Rhode Island Coalition Against Domestic Violence (RICADV)
Toll-Free: 800-494-8100
Website: www.ricadv.org

South Dakota Coalition Against Domestic Violence and Sexual Assault
Toll-Free: 800-572-9196
Website: www.sdcedsv.org

Utah Domestic Violence Coalition
Toll-Free: 800-897-LINK (800-897-5465)
Website: www.udvc.org

Vermont Network Against Domestic and Sexual Violence
Toll-Free: 800-228-7395 (Domestic violence)
Toll-Free: 800-489-7273 (Sexual violence)
Website: www.vtnetwork.org

Virginia Family Violence and Sexual Assault Hotline
Toll-Free: 800-838-8238
Website: www.vsdvalliance.org

Washington State Domestic Violence Hotline
Toll-Free: 800-562-6025
Website: www.dshs.wa.gov

Elder Abuse Resources

Eldercare Locator
Toll-Free: 800-677-1116
Website: www.eldercare.acl.gov

Elder Abuse Resources by State
For state reporting numbers, government agencies, state laws, state-specific data and statistics, and other resources, visit ncea.acl.gov/resources/state. html.

Chapter 49

State Child Abuse Reporting Numbers

Alabama

Alabama Department of Human Resources (DHR)
Phone: 334-242-1310
Fax: 334-353-1115
Website: dhr.alabama.gov/
services/Child_Protective_
Services/Abuse_Neglect_
Reporting.aspx

Alaska

Alaska Office of Children's Services (OCS)
Toll-Free: 800-478-4444
Fax: 907-269-3939
Website: dhss.alaska.gov/ocs/
Pages/default.aspx

Arizona

Arizona Department of Economic Security (DES)
Toll-Free: 800-882-4151
Phone: 602-252-4045
Website: des.az.gov/services/
child-and-family/arizona-child-
support-services-home-page

Arkansas

Arkansas Department of Human Services (DHS)
Phone: 855-372-1084
Toll-Free TTY: 800-285-1131
Website: access.arkansas.gov/
Voter.aspx

Resources in this chapter were compiled from several sources deemed reliable; all contact information was verified and updated in October 2018.

439

California

California Department of Social Services (DSS)
Toll-Free: 800-952-5253
Phone: 916-651-8848
Toll-Free TDD: 800-952-8349
Website: www.cdss.ca.gov

Connecticut

Connecticut Department of Children and Families (DCF)
Toll-Free: 800-842-2288
Website: www.ct.gov/dcf/site/default.asp

Delaware

Department of Services for Children, Youth and their Families (DSCYF)
Toll-Free: 800-292-9582
Website: kids.delaware.gov/services/crisis.shtml

District of Columbia

Child and Family Services Agency (CFSA)
Phone: 202-442-6100
Fax: 202-727-6505
Website: cfsa.dc.gov/service/working-child-welfare

Georgia

Division of Family and Children Services (DFCS)
Toll-Free: 855-GA CHILD (855-422-4453)
Website: dfcs.dhs.georgia.gov/child-abuse-neglect

Hawaii

Hawaii Department of Human Services (DHS)
Phone: 808-832-5300
Website: humanservices.hawaii.gov

Illinois

Illinois Department of Children and Family Services (DCFS)
Toll-Free: 800-25-ABUSE (800-252-2873)
Website: www.illinois.gov/dcfs/Pages/default.aspx

Indiana

Indiana Department of Child Services (DCS)
Toll-Free: 800-800-5556
Website: www.in.gov/dcs/2372.htm

Iowa

Iowa Department of Human Services (DHS)
Toll-Free: 800-362-2178
Website: dhs.iowa.gov

Kansas

Kansas Department of Children and Families (DCF)
Toll-Free: 800-922-5330
Toll-Free TTY: 785-296-1491
Website: www.dcf.ks.gov/Pages/Default.aspx

Kentucky

Cabinet for Health and Family Services (CHFS)
Toll-Free: 877-KYSAFE1
(877-597-2331)
Website: chfs.ky.gov/Pages/
index.aspx

Louisiana

Department of Children and Family Services (DCFS)
Toll-Free: 855-4LA-KIDS
(855-452-5437)
Website: www.dss.state.la.us

Maine

Maine Department of Health and Human Services (DHHS)
Toll-Free: 888-568-1112
Phone: 207-624-7900
Fax: 207-287-5282
Website: www.maine.gov/dhhs

Massachusetts

Massachusetts Bureau of Family Health and Nutrition
Phone: 617-624-6060
Toll-Free TTY: 617-624-5992
Fax: 617-624-6062
Website: www.mass.gov/orgs/
bureau-of-family-health-and-
nutrition

Michigan

Michigan Department of Health & Human Service (DHHS)
Toll-Free: 855-444-3911
Phone: 517-373-3740
Website: www.michigan.
gov/mdhhs/0,5885,7-339-
73971_7119---,00.html

Minnesota

Minnesota Department of Human Services (DHS)
Phone: 651-431-4661
Website: mn.gov/dhs/
general-public/about-dhs/
contact-us/

Missouri

Missouri Department of Social Services (DSS)
Toll-Free: 800-392-3738
Website: dss.mo.gov/cd/can.htm

Montana

Montana Child and Family Services Division (CFSD)
Toll-Free: 866-820-5437
Website: dphhs.mt.gov/cfsd/
index

New Hampshire

New Hampshire Division for Children, Youth and Families (DCYF)
Phone: 603-271-6562
Toll-Free TDD: 800-735-2964
Fax: 603-271-6565 (Report Child Abuse Fax)
Website: www.dhhs.state.nh.us/dcyf/cps/contact.htm

New Jersey

New Jersey Department of Children and Families (DCF)
Toll-Free: 855-INFO-DCF (855-463-6323)
Website: www.state.nj.us/dcf

New Mexico

New Mexico Children, Youth and Families Department (CYFD)
Toll-Free: 855-333-SAFE (855-333-7233)
Website: cyfd.org/child-abuse-neglect

New York

New York Office of Children and Family Services (OCFS)
Toll-Free: 800-342-3720
Toll-Free TDD/TTY: 800-638-5163
Website: ocfs.ny.gov/main/cps/Default.asp

North Carolina

North Carolina Department of Health & Human Services (DHHS)
Toll-Free: 877-362-8471
Website: www.ncdhhs.gov

North Dakota

North Dakota Department of Human Services (DHS)
Toll-Free: 800-472-2622
Phone: 701-328-2310
Toll-Free TTY: 800-366-6888
Fax: 701-328-2359
Website: www.nd.gov/dhs/services/childfamily/cps/#reporting

Ohio

Ohio's Public Children Services Agencies (PCSAs)
Phone: 614-224-5802
Fax: 614-228-5150
Website: www.pcsao.org

Oklahoma

Oklahoma Department of Human Services (DHS)
Phone: 405-521-3931
Website: www.okdhs.org/Pages/default.aspx

Oregon

Oregon Department of Human Services (DHS)
Toll-Free: 800-799-SAFE (800-799-7233)
Website: www.oregon.gov/DHS/pages/index.aspx

Pennsylvania

Pennsylvania Department of Human Services (DHS)
Toll-Free: 800-932-0313
Website: www.dhs.pa.gov

Rhode Island

Rhode Island Department of Children, Youth and Family (DCYF)
Toll-Free: 800-RI-CHILD
(800-742-4453)
Phone: 401-528-3500
Website: www.dcyf.ri.gov/child_care.php

South Carolina

South Carolina Department of Social Services (DSS)
Toll-Free: 800-422-4453
Phone: 803-898-7601
Website: dss.sc.gov

South Dakota

South Dakota Department of Social Services (DSS)
Toll-Free: 800-227-3020
Phone: 605-773-3165
Website: dss.sd.gov/childcare

Tennessee

Department of Children's Services (DCS)
Toll-Free: 877-237-0004 or 877-54ABUSE (877-542-2873)
Website: apps.tn.gov/carat

Utah

Utah Child & Family Services
Toll-Free: 855-323-DCFS
(855-323-3237)
Website: dcfs.utah.gov

Vermont

Vermont Department for Children and Families (DCF)
Toll-Free: 800-649-5285
Website: dcf.vermont.gov/protection

Virginia

Virginia Department of Social Services (VDSS)
Toll-Free: 800-552-7096
Phone: 804-786-8536
Website: www.dss.virginia.gov/family/cps/index.cgi

Washington

Washington Department of Social and Health Services (DSHS)
Toll-Free: 866-ENDHARM (866-363-4276) or 800-562-5624
Toll-Free TTY: 800-624-6186
Website: www.dshs.wa.gov/ca/child-safety-and-protection/how-report-child-abuse-or-neglect?2=

West Virginia

West Virginia Bureau for Children and Families (BCF)
Toll-Free: 800-352-6513
Website: www.dhhr.wv.gov/bcf/Pages/default.aspx

Wisconsin

Wisconsin Department of Children and Families (DCF)
Phone: 608-422-7000
Fax: 608-266-6836
Website: dcf.wisconsin.gov

Wyoming

Wyoming Department of Family Services (DFS)
Toll-Free: 800-457-3659
Website: dfsweb.wyo.gov

Chapter 50

Programs Providing Shelter for Pets of Domestic Violence Victims

Alabama

Mobile County Animal Shelter
7665 Howells Ferry Rd.
Mobile, AL 36618
Phone: 251-574-3647
Fax: 251-574-6441
Website: www.mobilecountyal.
gov/animals/contact.html

Arizona

City of Mesa Animal Control
20 E. Main St.
Ste. 250
Mesa, AZ 85201
Phone: 480-644-2268
Fax: 480-644-4994
Website: www.mesaaz.gov/
residents/animal-control
E-mail: animalcontrol.info@
mesaaz.gov

Resources in this chapter were compiled from several sources deemed reliable; all contact information was verified and updated in October 2018.

California

Assistance Dog Special Allowance (ADSA)
744 P St.
Sacramento, CA 95814
Phone: 916-651-8848
Website: www.cdss.ca.gov
E-mail: piar@dss.ca.gov

Colorado

Centennial Animal Services
13133 E. Arapahoe Rd.
Centennial, CO 80112
Phone: 303-325-8000
Fax: 720-488-0933
Website: www.centennialco.gov/
Animal-Services

Florida

Miami-Dade County Animal Services
3599 N.W. 79th Ave.
Doral, FL 33122
Phone: 305-468-5900
Website: www.miamidade.gov/
animals
E-mail: pets@miamidade.gov

Georgia

Augusta Animal Services
4164 Mack Ln.
Augusta, GA 30906
Phone: 706-790-6836
Fax: 706-798-8978
Website: www.augustaga.
gov/586/Animal-Services

Indiana

Bloomington Animal Shelter
401 N. Morton St.
Bloomington, IN 47404
Phone: 812-349-3492
Fax: 812-349-3440
Website: bloomington.in.gov/
animal-shelter

Kansas

Wichita Animal Shelter
3313 N. Hillside St.
Wichita, KS 67219
Phone: 316-524-9196
Fax: 316-554-0356
Website: www.wichita.gov/
Government/Departments/WPD/
Pages/AnimalControl.aspx

Maryland

Baltimore County Animal Services
13800 Manor Rd.
Baldwin, MD 21013
Phone: 410-887-PAWS
(410-887-7297)
Fax: 410-817-4257
Website: www.
baltimorecountymd.gov/
Agencies/health/animalservices
E-mail: animalservices@
baltimorecountymd.gov

Missouri

City of St. Louis Animal Care and Control
2801 Clark Ave., 1520 Market St.
Ste. 4051
St. Louis, MO 63103
Phone: 314-657-1500
Fax: 314-612-5367
Website: www.stlouis-mo.gov/
government/departments/health/
animal-care-control

Nebraska

City of Lincoln Animal Control
3131 N. St.
Lincoln, NE 68510
Phone: 402-441-7900
Fax: 402-441-8626
Website: lincoln.ne.gov/city/
health/animal
E-mail: animal@lincoln.ne.gov

New Jersey

Gloucester County Animal Shelter
1200 N. Delsea Dr.
Clayton, NJ 08312
Phone: 856-307-7100
Website: www.
gloucestercountynj.gov/depts/a/
shelter
E-mail: dkappler@co.gloucester.
nj.us

New Mexico

City of Albuquerque Animal Welfare
8920 Lomas N.E.
Albuquerque, NM 87112
Phone: 505-768-2000
Website: www.cabq.gov/pets

Ohio

Lake County Dog Shelter
2600 N. Ridge Rd.
Painesville, OH 44077
Phone: 440-350-2640
Website: www.lakecountyohio.
gov/dogs/dogshelterhome.aspx
E-mail: lcdogs@lakecountyohio.
gov

Pennsylvania

City Of Pittsburgh Animal Care and Control
3001 RailRoad St.
Pittsburgh, PA 15201
Phone: 412-255-2631
Website: pittsburghpa.gov/
animalcontrol

Texas

Arlington Animal Services
1000 S.E. Green Oaks Blvd.
Arlington, TX 76018
Phone: 817-459-5898
Fax: 817-459-5698
Website: www.arlington-tx.gov/
animals
E-mail: animalservices@
arlingtontx.gov

Virginia

Fairfax County Animal Shelter
12000 Government Center Pkwy
Fairfax, VA 22035
Phone: 703-324-7329
Website: www.fairfaxcounty.gov/
animalshelter

Washington

Clark County Animal and Pets
1300 Franklin St.
Vancouver, WA 98660
Phone: 360-397-2489
Website: www.clark.wa.gov/
community-development/
animals-and-pets
E-mail: animal@clark.wa.gov

Index

Index